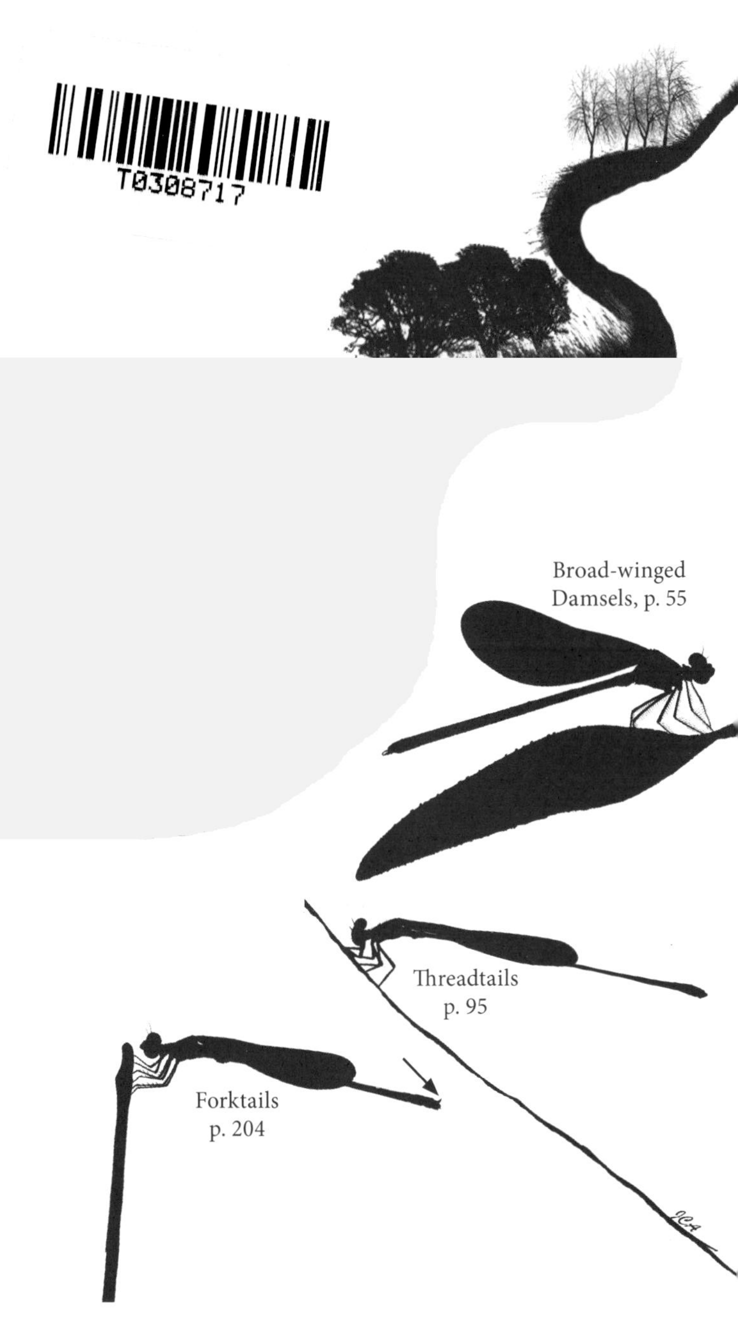
T0308717
Broad-winged
Damsels, p. 55
Threadtails
p. 95
Forktails
p. 204

DAMSELFLIES OF TEXAS

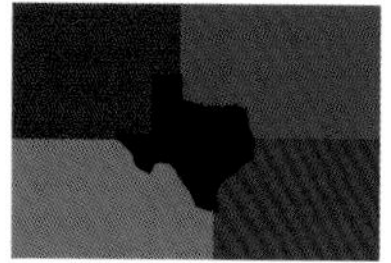

TEXAS NATURAL HISTORY GUIDES™

DAMSELFLIES OF TEXAS

A FIELD GUIDE

JOHN C. ABBOTT
Illustrations by Barrett Anthony Klein

UNIVERSITY OF TEXAS PRESS
Austin

The publication of this book was made possible in part through the generous support of Suzanne and Marc Winkelman and the RGK Foundation.

Printed in China
First edition, 2011

♾ The paper used in this book meets the minimum requirements of ANSI/NISO Z39.48-1992 (R1997) (Permanence of Paper).

LIBRARY OF CONGRESS CATALOGING-IN-PUBLICATION DATA

Abbott, John C., 1972–
Damselflies of Texas : a field guide / John C. Abbott ; illustrated by Barrett Anthony Klein. — 1st ed.
p. cm. — (Texas natural history guides)
ISBN 978-0-292-71449-6 (pbk. : alk. paper)
1. Damselflies—Texas—Identification. I. Klein, Barrett Anthony. II. Title. III. Series: Texas natural history guides.
QL520.2.U6A225 2011
595.7′3309764—dc22

2010028964

I dedicate
this book to Kendra.
Without her continued
encouragement, love,
and support, this book
would never have
been completed.

CONTENTS

PREFACE

The year 2000 was a pivotal one in the world of dragonfly and damselfly field guides in North America. It marked the publication of Sid Dunkle's *Dragonflies through Binoculars*, the first widely distributed field guide to odonates. Before that, there were very few resources available for identification, and nearly all of them were technical in nature, primarily geared toward microscope work. It is amazing for me to think how things have changed in the 20 years I have been studying odonates and specifically since 2000. More than 35 books, mostly field guides, now sit on my shelf, making the field identification of North American odonates a much easier task. This provided a tremendous set of resources (see Appendix D for a complete list of those dealing with damselflies) for me as I began to write and assemble this field guide.

Ed Lam's *Damselflies of the Northeast* provided particular inspiration for me, and I see this Texas field guide as a nice complement to Ed's book. With the addition of 52 species found in the South but not in the Northeast, the 2 books combined cover 102 of the 138 damselfly species currently known in North America. The remaining species are largely found west of the Rocky Mountains.

I have chosen to use relatively few photographs in this field guide and instead to illustrate the species in a uniform and consistent way. I would not have been able to do this if it weren't for the immense talents of Barrett Klein. He is not only a good friend and a great entomologist, but also an exceptional artist, as I think the users of this field guide will quickly determine. I am so pleased with the illustrations that he has produced and recognize that this field guide would suffer without them.

I have tried to point out distinguishing characteristics of Texas damselflies that are reliable and easily seen. In most cases, careful observation through a pair of good, close-focusing binoculars will be enough to determine a species' identity. Sometimes, however, it may be necessary to net an individual and examine it more closely. I have provided microscopic photographs of the male's terminal appendages and the female's mesostigmal plates for the groups for which this will be helpful. It is easiest to see these structures using a microscope, but, with a little practice, most can be seen and differentiated in the field using a hand lens or by inverting a pair of binoculars.

The intent of this book is to facilitate the field identification of those damselflies that occur in Texas. All 77 species currently known from the state are illustrated and described. Because of Texas's large size and geographic positioning, this represents over half of the North American fauna. I wrote my 2005 book, *Dragonflies and Damselflies of Texas and the South-Central United States*, for a more technical audience. Though it contains photographs of all the damselflies species known from Texas at the time, it also included dichotomous keys and technical descriptions of the species. It has not been lost on me that this book did not provide many of the growing number of field observers the resource they wanted. This point was perhaps made most clearly when I ran into a dragonfly watcher at the Santa Ana National Wildlife Refuge. He noticed me photographing odonates and came over to see what I was doing. Upon introducing myself, he said, "Oh, so you are the one responsible for this pain in my ass!" I was taken aback at first, then he pulled out my 2005 book from his fanny pack and started laughing. This was his kind way of saying, something a little less technical and weighty, please! I hope this field guide fills that need. With it and its eventual accompanying volume on dragonflies, Texas will become the first state with both field guides and a technical manual. Since Texas does support more than half the North American fauna, I guess this is entirely appropriate.

The first work specific to damselflies of Texas was Cliff Johnson's 1972 monograph *The Damselflies (Zygoptera) of Texas*. It provided the basis for much of our knowledge on the distributions of species in the state. Since its publication, though, the fauna has increased by 31%, from 53 to 77 species, and I believe there are certainly more to be discovered. I hope this field guide is able to play a key role in facilitating those discoveries.

John C. Abbott, 2010

ACKNOWLEDGMENTS

This book would not have been possible without the help and encouragement of people too numerous to mention. The growth of the Odonata community in Texas has been impressive, and this is in large part thanks to Tony Gallucci for starting the Tex-Odes e-mail list, which facilitates the discussion of a tremendous amount of information on Texas damselflies and dragonflies. By extension, I would like to thank all those odonate enthusiasts in Texas who have played a pivotal role in our understanding of species' ranges, behavior, and natural history in the state. There are too many to list here, but some of those that have been particularly active in contributing information include Jim Bangma, Bob Behrstock, Jan and David Dauphin, Mike Dillon, Victor Fazio, Terry Fuller, Tony Gallucci, Jerry Hatfield, Terry Hibbitts, Troy Hibbitts, Eric Isley, Tom Langschied, Martin Reid, Josh Rose, and Bob Thomas. In particular, I must single out Greg Lasley, whose unrelenting quest to fill in distributional gaps in Texas has resulted in not only a wealth of information, but also the deposition of more than 2,500 specimens to the University of Texas Insect Collection.

I also have to extend my thanks to a number of colleagues who have been valuable mentors over the years, providing not only knowledge but also encouragement. These include Nick Donnelly, Sid Dunkle, Rosser Garrison, George Harp, Mike May, Dennis Paulson, Ken Tennessen, and Natalia von Ellenrieder.

There are now many odonate field guides available for North America. Two of these really set the bar high and provided me with inspiration. Ed Lam's *Damselflies of the Northeast* made damselfly field identification attainable for many. His beautiful illustrations and creative layout set a new standard for the odonate community. Giff Beaton's *Dragonflies and Damselflies of Georgia and the Southeast* is, in my opinion, simply the best regional field guide that has been published to date. I unabashedly took what I considered the best elements of these books and incorporated them in this one, adding my own creative elements. I thank Ed and Giff for the inspiration their guides provided. Elements of two other field guides, Roger Tory Peterson's *Field Guide to the Birds of Texas* and Brian and Shirley Loflin's *Texas Cacti,* also served as inspiration.

Bill Abbott, Ellie Abbott, Kendra Bauer, Giff Beaton, Rosser Garrison, Steve Krotzer, Greg Lasley, and Natalia von Ellenrieder all graciously agreed to review the manuscript and provided valuable editorial comments.

Kendra Bauer provided invaluable help in creating the maps for the introduction and the species accounts, and Dennis Paulson provided helpful comments on the pronunciation of scientific names.

Sincere thanks to my good friend Greg Lasley for his constant encouragement and companionship in the field. I couldn't ask for a better photography buddy or friend. I learn something new from him on every outing.

This book wouldn't have been completed if it weren't for the support and encouragement of my wife, Kendra Bauer, and my parents, Bill and Ellie Abbott. Finally, I would like to thank Kip Keller, who copyedited the book, and Bill Bishel, Lynne Chapman, and the entire team at the University of Texas Press for all their help in seeing this book through its final production stages.

J. C. Abbott

Ed Lam and Steve Buchanan openly and generously shared their illustration techniques with me, and I employed elements of each of their methods. Sara Pratt was invaluable for her assistance with scanning specimens and processing those scans as well as maintaining order among the multitude of digital and actual damselflies. Karen Anne Klein, my mother and great artistic inspiration, aided with cleaning and assembling some of the damselfly scans. Without the superb assistance of these two people, I would likely have been forced to sacrifice my dissertation—the very reason I moved to Texas and was fortunate enough to meet and befriend John Abbott.

B. A. Klein

DAMSELFLIES OF TEXAS

Caribbean Yellowface

Introduction

What Is a Damselfly?

On any warm summer day, you can easily observe damselflies around a vegetated pond or the rocks along the banks of a stream. They are a group of insects in the order Odonata. Like most insects, they possess 2 pairs of wings, 6 legs, a pair of antennae, and a distinct head, thorax, and abdomen. This order contains both damselflies and dragonflies. The derivation of Odonata is from the Greek root *odont* which means "tooth" and refers to the large mandibles these insects have as adults. As a result of this name, the group is often collectively referred to as odonates.

Within this insect order, there are typically 2 suborders recognized: the Anisoptera, or dragonflies, and the Zygoptera, or damselflies. These suborders are easily distinguished by the following characteristics:

Suborder	Wing Shape	Wing Position at Rest	Eyes
Zygoptera (damselflies)	Fore- and hindwings similarly shaped	Wings typically held together over the abdomen	Widely separated and never touching
Anisoptera (dragonflies)	Hindwings broader basally than forewings	Wings spread out away from the body	Large and often touching at least at a single point

In addition to the above characteristics, damselflies are typically less robust, and weaker fliers, than dragonflies. Male damselflies also have 2 pairs of appendages, or claspers, at the tip of the abdomen, which are used in mating. Dragonflies, however, have 1 pair of appendages with a single unpaired structure below them. In Europe and other parts of the world, the term "damselfly" is not used and all members of the order are referred to as dragonflies.

A damselfly, the Comanche Dancer (*Argia barretti*).

A dragonfly, the Common Whitetail (*Plathemis lydia*).

There are several groups of insects that are sometimes confused with adult odonates. In particular, dobsonflies and fishflies and ant lions and owlflies (order Neuroptera). Dobsonflies and fishflies have mandibles projecting forward (rather than down) and hold their wings flat on top of the abdomen. Ant lions and owlflies are perhaps the most similar, but they both have larger, differently shaped antennae than damselflies or dragonflies.

Ant lion (order Neuroptera) has hooked antennae and holds wings roof-like over the abdomen.

Fishfly (order Neuroptera; sometimes considered the order Megaloptera) has long, often serrated antennae, wings held flat over the abdomen, and mandibles that project forward.

Damselfly Anatomy

It is useful to know some of the basic terminology used to describe the anatomy of damselflies. They are visually oriented predators and as a result have large compound eyes that occupy much of the head. Their wings are flexible but tough and allow for tremendous agility in the air. The following pages illustrate the basic terms used throughout this guide. A discussion of these follows, and a full glossary is presented at the end of the book.

HEAD. The large ***compound eyes*** are the most distinctive feature on a damselfly's head. These eyes are composed of many small facets (ommatidia) fused together, and each forms a distinct image. Eye color is often distinctive and therefore useful in identification. In many, the top half of the eye is a different color from the bottom half. Damselflies see a wide spectrum of colors, including not only the visible spectrum but also ultraviolet and polarized light. This explains why some females try to oviposit, or lay eggs, on a shiny asphalt road or car hood. They are presumably mistaking the horizontally polarized reflection of these structures with that of water. In addition to their large compound eyes, damselflies have three ***ocelli***, or simple eyes, that are used for light detection. These are found on top of the head in a triangular pattern. Many damselflies have a pair of colored spots, called ***eyespots*** or ***postocular spots***, just behind the eyes. These differ in color and shape from one species to the next and can be useful in identification. A stripe of color, called the ***occipital bar***, may be present between these eyespots. The antennae are small and do not perform a major sensory role. The largest area between the eyes is the ***forehead,*** or ***frons***. Below that is the ***clypeus*** (divided into the ***postclypeus*** and ***anteclypeus***), followed by the upper lip, or ***labrum***, which lies in front of the ***mandibles***.

THORAX. The thorax comprises three segments; beginning immediately behind the head and moving backward, they are designated as the ***prothorax***, ***mesothorax,*** and ***metathorax***. Each bears a pair of legs, and the last two (meso- and metathorax) bear a pair of wings each, and are collectively referred to as the ***pterothorax***. The first segment, the prothorax, is so reduced as to appear almost neck-like, and articulates with the fused mesothorax and metathorax. In females, there are a pair of structures termed the ***mesostigmal plates***, which are well-developed on the ***pronotum*** (top part of prothorax) and are the location where males grasp them during mating. Stripes are often visible on the pterothorax, and terms have been applied to them. Starting in the top-middle of the pterothorax and working down, there is a ***middorsal carina*** (a ridge), which may be covered by a ***middorsal stripe***; a ***pale shoulder***, or ***antehumeral, stripe***; a ***dark shoulder,*** or ***humeral, stripe***; the ***interpleural suture***; and finally the ***second thoracic,*** or ***metapleural, stripe***. The principal parts of the legs include a ***femur,*** a ***tibia,*** multiple segments called ***tarsi***, and a paired claw. There are often prominent ***spines*** located on the legs.

WINGS. Two pairs of similarly shaped wings attach to the thorax. The name Zygoptera means "yoked wings" and refers to this similarity in the wings. The pair of wings closest to the head are the forewings, and the pair behind those are the hindwings. These wings are made up of numerous ***veins*** enclosing ***cells***. The arrangement of the veins and cells is often useful in identifying damselflies. For that reason, many of these cells and veins have been given specific names. I have generally not used wing venation in my species descriptions, but more advanced damselfly enthusiasts will want to learn these terms and the venational differences among families, genera, and species. The anterior-most vein in each wing is called the ***costa.*** This vein is slightly notched toward the middle of its length at a region termed the ***nodus***. The veins closest to the body and before the nodus along the anterior margin of the wing are termed ***antenodal crossveins***. Likewise, those beyond the nodus are ***postnodal crossveins***. The ***pterostigma*** (sometimes called the ***stigma***) is a colored area at the tip of the wing along the costal margin; it is thought to stabilize the wing in flight.

ABDOMEN. The abdomen, elongated in all damselflies, comprises 10 segments, the first (S1) and last (S10) of which are reduced and often hard to see. The color pattern on these segments is often useful in making field identifications. Females typically have slightly broader abdomens than males and always have an ***ovipositor*** (a bladelike egg-laying structure) on S9. This structure can be useful in identifying female spreadwings. A series of structures originate off S10. There are a pair of ***superior appendages*** (or ***cerci***) and below them a pair of ***inferior appendages*** (or ***paraprocts***). Together, these are known as the ***terminal appendages,*** or ***claspers***. In males, these structures are well developed and used for grasping females during mating. In females, they are reduced, but the cerci are usually still visible. In closely related species, the shape of these appendages in males can be the only truly reliable way of determining a species' identity.

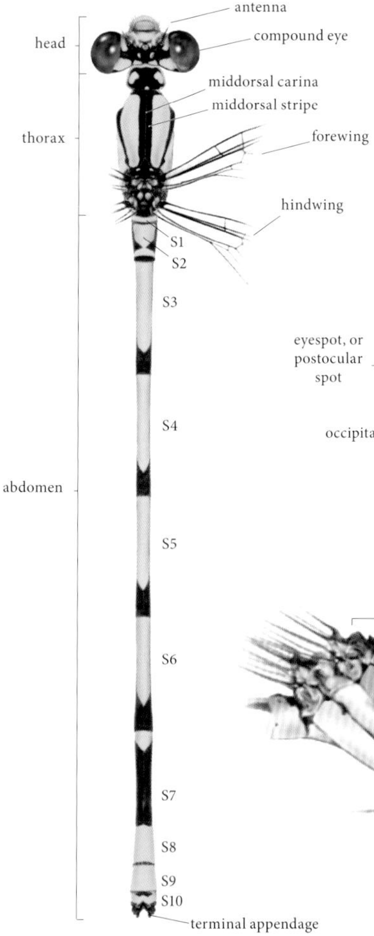

antenna
compound eye
head
middorsal carina
middorsal stripe
thorax
forewing
hindwing
S1
S2
S3
S4
abdomen
S5
S6
S7
S8
S9
S10
terminal appendage

labrum
clypeus
frons
eyespot, or
postocular
spot
ocellus
pronotum
occipital bar

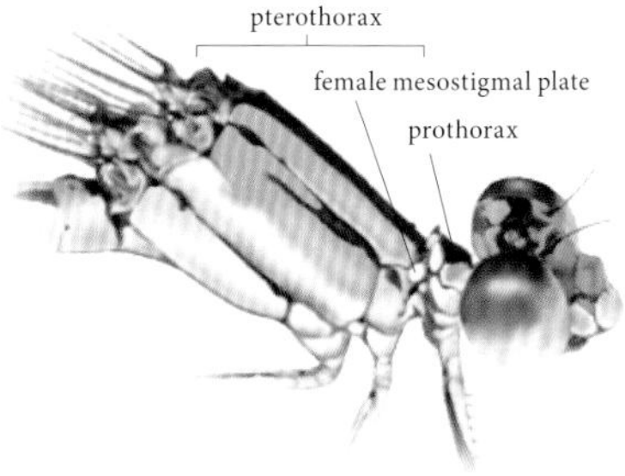

pterothorax
female mesostigmal plate
prothorax

S7
S8
S9
S10
cercus
stylus
basal plate
ovipositor

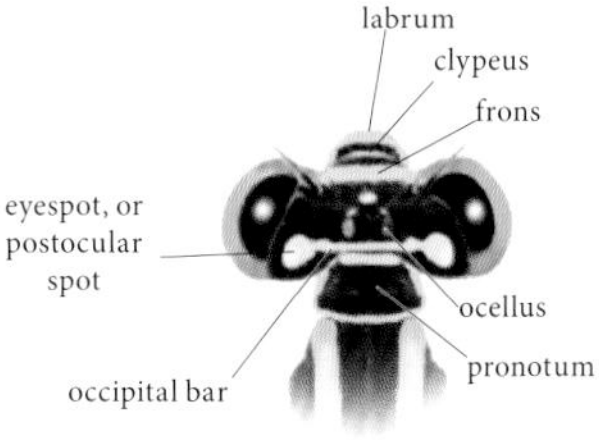

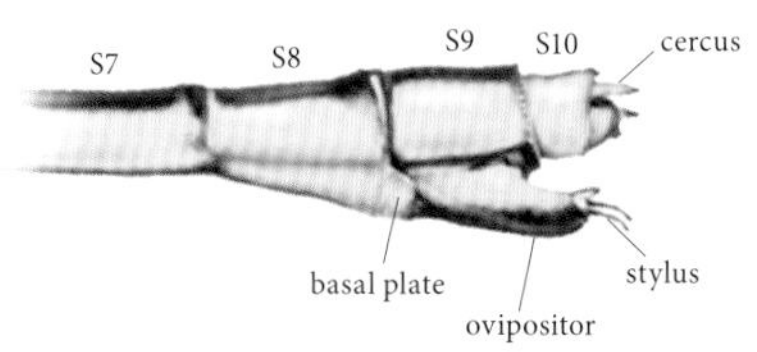

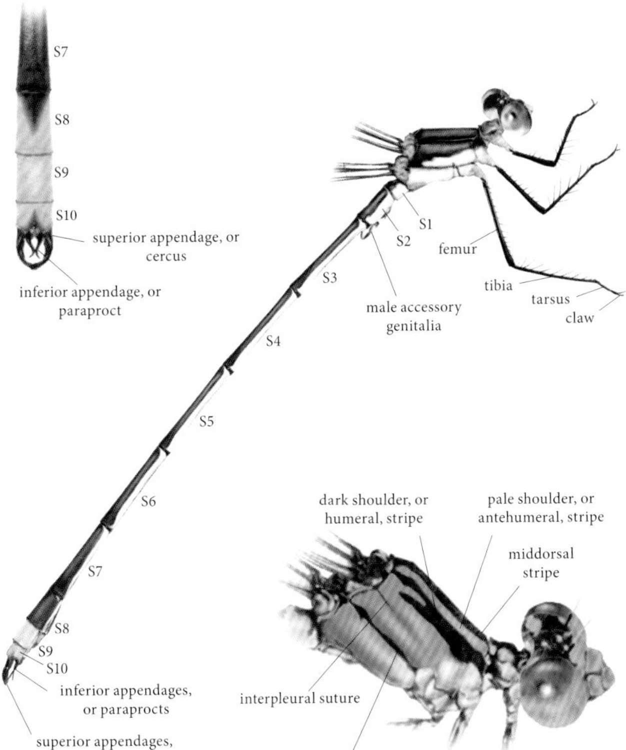

S7
S8
S9
S10
superior appendage, or cercus
inferior appendage, or paraproct
S1
S2
femur
S3
male accessory genitalia
tibia
tarsus
claw
S4
S5
S6
S7
S8
S9
S10
inferior appendages, or paraprocts
superior appendages, or cerci
dark shoulder, or humeral, stripe
pale shoulder, or antehumeral, stripe
middorsal stripe
interpleural suture
second thoracic, or metapleural, stripe

antenodal crossveins
postnodal crossveins
costa
nodus
pterostigma
M1
arculus
M4
Rs
M2
Cu1
M3
quadrangle
Cu2

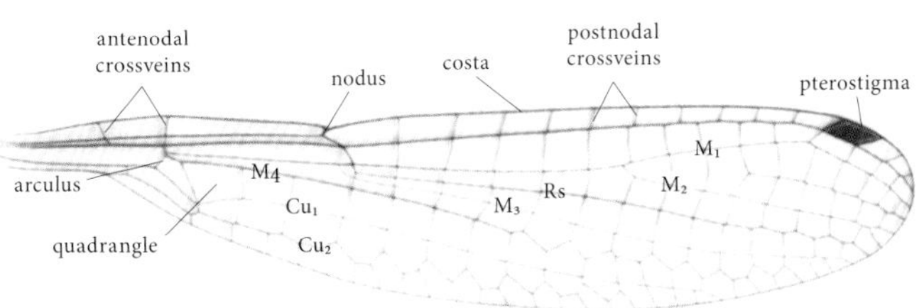

SEXES. It is important to determine the sex of a damselfly because males and females, even of the same species, can look quite different. Male odonates are unique in that they have ***accessory***, or ***secondary, genitalia*** below S2, including an intromittent organ, which conveys sperm to the female. For a description of how this process occurs, refer to the life history section. Because of this structure, males' basal abdominal segments are often slightly expanded on an otherwise thin abdomen. The abdomen in females is generally thicker throughout and lacks the basal swelling. Males also have the previously described terminal appendages used to grasp females during mating. Females lack these well-developed appendages, but do have an ovipositor originating below S8 and S9. As with birds, males are generally more brightly colored than females. In many species, females are found around water only when they are mating, whereas males are always present. As a result, males are more often encountered.

COLORATION. The beautiful and varied coloration of odonates is a significant factor in their appeal. In damselflies, pigments produce most of the blacks, browns, reds, and yellows. Blue, however, one of the most common colors in damselflies, is generally structural and the result of blue light being reflected by microscopic differences in the surface of the cuticle. A few species of damselflies also produce metallic colors as a result of cuticle structure. In many cases, coloration is an important and useful tool for making field identification, but it is important to recognize some of the difficulties of using color. Damselflies of many species are sexually dimorphic in this respect; the males and females differ in coloration. Moreover, many species, especially bluets and dancers, are known to change colors with temperature. Individuals will often become darker when exposed to cooler temperatures, and brighter when heated up. This is important to remember when observing damselflies on a cool early morning. Several species, such as the Springwater Dancer and the Blue-fronted Dancer, also become darker while mating. In a number of species, especially the forktails, females occur in more than one form, which is known as polymorphism or polychromatism. Typically there is a form colored similar to the male (the male-like, or andromorphic, form) and one or more forms that are differently colored (non-male-like, or gynomorphic, forms). Individuals also change in color with maturity. A bloom of pruinescence, or blue-white waxy covering, will develop in older individuals and can envelop the head, thorax, and/or abdomen. These color differences or forms can be likened to plumage differences in birds.

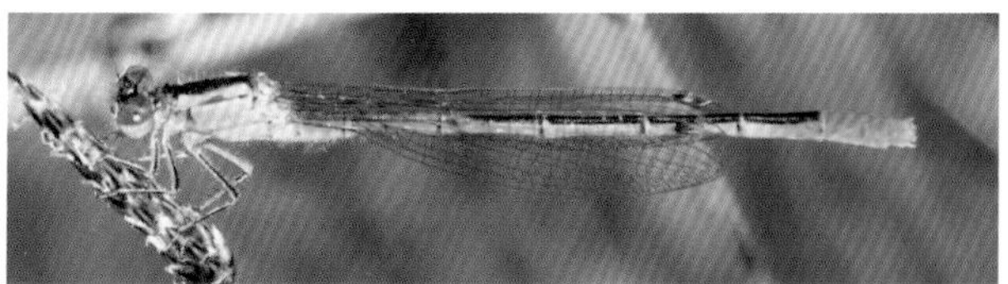

Juvenile male Painted Damsel (*Hesperagrion heterodoxum*).

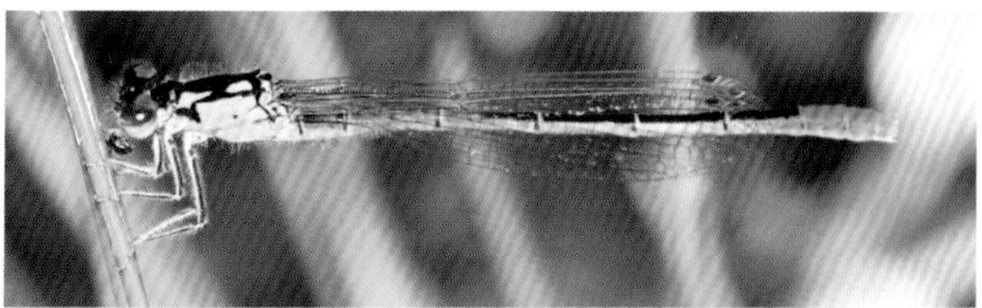

Juvenile male Painted Damsel with thorax turning blue.

Mature male Painted Damsel.

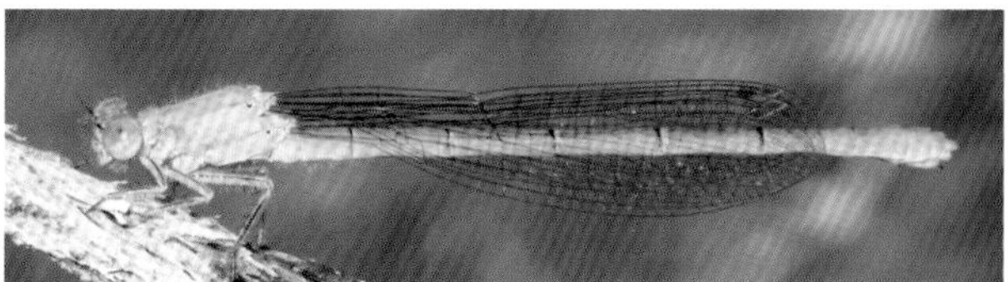

Juvenile female Painted Damsel.

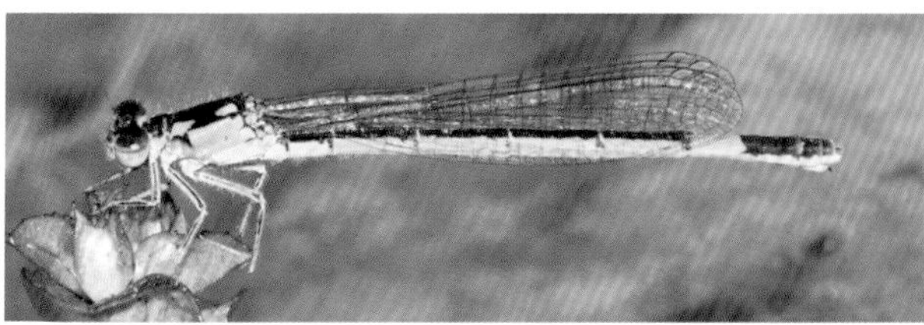

Mature female Painted Damsel.

Older male Powdered Dancer (*Argia moesta*) with bloom of white pruinescence.

Life History of Damselflies

EGG. Damselfly eggs are rod shaped and look like small grains of rice. Females have an ovipositor equipped with curved blades that are used to cut into plant tissues, soft wood, and even trash in some cases. This type of egg laying is called endophytic oviposition. Most species lay their eggs right at the water surface or just below it. Many species submerge themselves, often accompanied by the male, as they "walk" down a piece of vegetation, laying eggs. They may remain submerged for more than an hour, breathing air that has been trapped in a thin film around the body. Other species, like the spreadwings, lay their eggs in stems above the water surface. In some cases, eggs are laid in plants living in areas that will fill with rainwater. Mites prey on eggs, and several families of wasps are known to parasitize them. Mold is also known to kill eggs. Those that survive generally hatch in 1–6 weeks, but may take as long as several months in species whose eggs survive extended droughts or winter conditions. Eggs laid in temporary pools hatch more quickly.

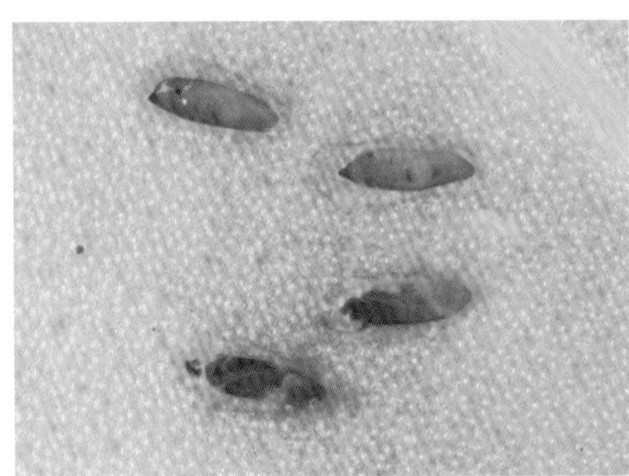

Eggs deposited in aquatic vegetation by a Comanche Dancer (*Argia barretti*).

Female Great Spreadwing (*Archilestes grandis*) laying eggs in a stem above water with the male in tandem.

Tandem pairs of *Argia orichalcea* from Trinidad laying eggs. Note all the eggs visible in the leaf underwater.

A pair of Burgundy Bluets (*Enallagma dubium*) laying eggs. The female's and the male's abdomens are submerged underwater.

NYMPH. Dragonflies and damselflies spend most of their time as aquatic immatures called nymphs (also referred to as larvae or naiads), which are common in ponds, marshes, lakes, and streams but exploit a wide range of permanent and temporary aquatic habitats, including brackish pools and estuarine habitats. Some nymphs are able to survive in moist substrates under rocks. When the nymphs hatch, they look very little like the adults they will eventually become. They are voracious predators, feeding on worms, small crustaceans, mosquito larvae, tiny fish, and even other damselfly nymphs. They capture their prey by extending their lower lip (the labium), which is equipped with 2 movable toothed palps. The labium, which may reach one-third of the nymph's body length, extends at lightning-fast speed (0.01 seconds). Because nymphs are gen-

Damselfly nymph: a Dusky Dancer (*Argia translata*).

Dragonfly nymph: a Pale-faced Clubskimmer (*Brechmorhoga mendax*).

erally shades of green and brown, they can blend in well with their environment. In fact, many species are capable of changing their color from green to brown and vice versa over several weeks. Many species, especially dancers, will cling to rocks and vegetation underwater.

Great Spreadwing (*Archilestes grandis*) nymph showing the long petiolate (stalked) labium.

Damselfly nymphs have 3 leaf-like gills at the tip of the abdomen. Because the gills are used in respiration, they become most important at times of low oxygen levels. Nymphs use their gills like fins for swimming, giving them great agility in the water. Nymphs have the ability to regenerate these gills, at least in part. Damselfly nymphs also have the ability to absorb oxygen through the walls of their rectums as well as other areas of the body where the skin (cuticle) is thin, such as the wingpads. Dragonflies, in contrast, lack external gills and respire through internal gills within the rectum. They siphon water through the anus, over these gills, where oxygen is extracted, and then forcibly expel the water back out, propelling them across the water column—a feat damselflies are incapable of.

Nymphs grow by shedding their skin (part of the exoskeleton) in a process called molting. This may occur 6–17 times over a period of typically 1–9 months in Texas, depending upon the species and environmental conditions. Most species in Texas have 1 generation a year, diapausing (going dormant) in an egg stage, but a number of species, such as many of the forktails, have multiple generations a year. The wingpads become more and more evident as nymphs grow in size and approach adulthood. As the damselfly nears the time for adult emergence, an internal change or metamorphosis occurs. At this point, the adult colors, eyes, and wings may be visible through the nymphal skin. The lower lip also shrinks to adult size a few days before emergence, leaving the nymph unable to hunt and feed. At this point, the nymph will often move to the surface of the water and begin breathing air.

The emergence of the adult generally occurs in the early morning and often under the cover of darkness, but many damselflies also emerge during the day. The nymph usually climbs out of the water onto some vegetation or a vertical rock face, on which it hangs. At this point it takes in air, causing the body to expand, and the skin splits on top of the thorax and back of the head. The adult pulls itself out of the nymphal skin (called the exuviae) while continuing to take in air. Thin, white, thread-like tracheal linings are visible at this point, as are the linings of the fore- and hindgut. The legs harden, and then the damselfly reaches forward and pulls its abdomen out of the exuviae. The wings and abdomen begin to inflate as blood is pumped to them. It is not uncommon to see damselflies with deformities that occurred as a result of difficulties during emergence. The damselfly will usually remain perched on the exuviae for 30 minutes to an hour or more while its muscles harden. At this point it is very vulnerable and barely able to fly. If the damselfly is knocked off the perch by a wave, the wind, or a predator, it will most likely die. The wings and body have a silky shimmer to them that lasts for a day or longer. This newly emerged state is called ***teneral***. As tenerals, most damselflies remain away from the water. Males usually mature more quickly than females and may make their way back to suitable egg-laying habitats, where they set up territories and wait for females.

ADULT. Most damselflies in Texas occur as adults from April or May through September and October. At least 6 species are known to occur as adults year-round in Texas (see Appendix C). Once an individual is no longer teneral, it may take from a day to more than a week to become a sexually mature and fully colored adult. I will use the term ***juvenile*** to describe these prereproductive adults and the term ***adult*** to describe sexually mature individuals. The maturation time mainly depends on the species, temperature, and food supply. They prey on small flying insects, mainly biting flies. As they feed and mature, they often become brighter in color; this is especially evident in males. Damselflies typically don't travel long distances from the bodies of water where they emerged. Unlike a number of dragonflies, damselflies are not known to engage in long-distance migration; however, there is considerable evidence to suggest that they can be carried long distances by storms and strong winds. An adult damselfly will typically live 2–4 weeks, but may last several months.

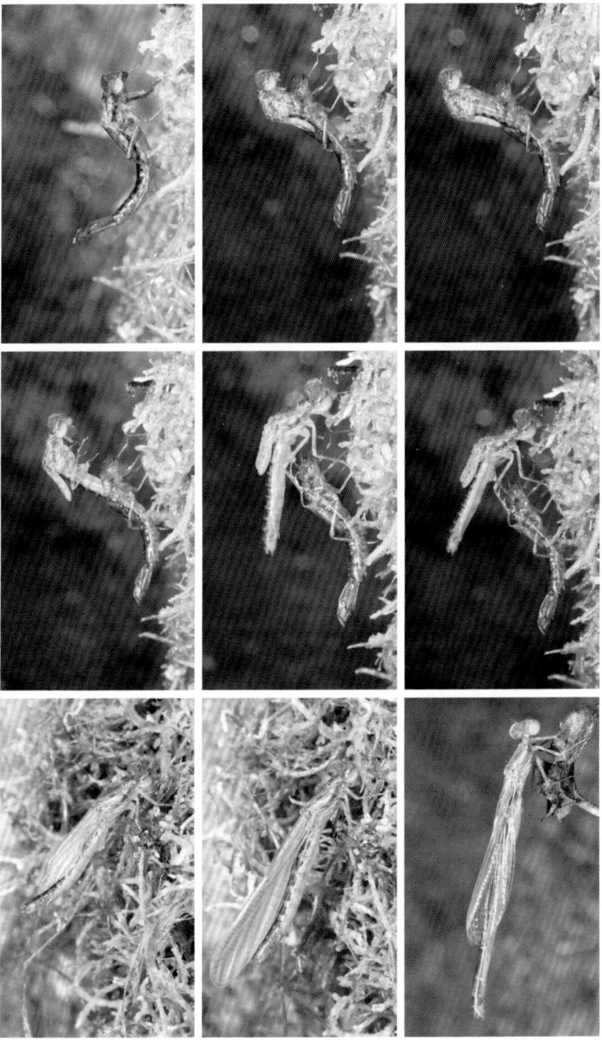

Desert Firetail (*Telebasis salva*) emerging.

REPRODUCTION. As it is for any living organism, reproduction is a critical stage in the life cycle of odonates. Eventually, they must find a suitable body of water where they can find a mate and females can lay their eggs. Some species require specialized habitats, such as unpolluted springs and streams, while others can breed in a wide range of habitats. Some species require certain types of plants to be in abundance. Others have narrow tolerances for acidity, alkalinity, and dissolved oxygen. In general, there are many more males at a given body of water than females. This is because, in most species, females come to the water only to mate, while males congregate there, waiting for females. Males defend their territories, so it is not unusual to see males chasing one another off in an attempt to hang on to the most desirable breeding sites.

In most species, the male will search for females in this territory and seize a receptive female looking for a suitable egg-laying habitat. This capture usually takes place in midair as the male flies over the female and grabs her with his terminal appendages. The only damselflies in North America that exhibit any kind of courtship behavior are some of the beautifully marked broad-winged damsels, like the jewelwings. In most species, the male initiates mating by grabbing the female's prothorax with his legs. Unreceptive females will either fly away or give a rejection display by curling their abdomens downward while beating their wings. If a female is receptive, the male then uses his terminal appendages to grab her prothorax. The male then releases his legs, and the pair are said to be in tandem. It is not uncommon to see males attack tandem pairs, trying to separate males and females.

In insects, the reproductive structures for the both the male and female are located at the tip of the abdomen. Male damsel-

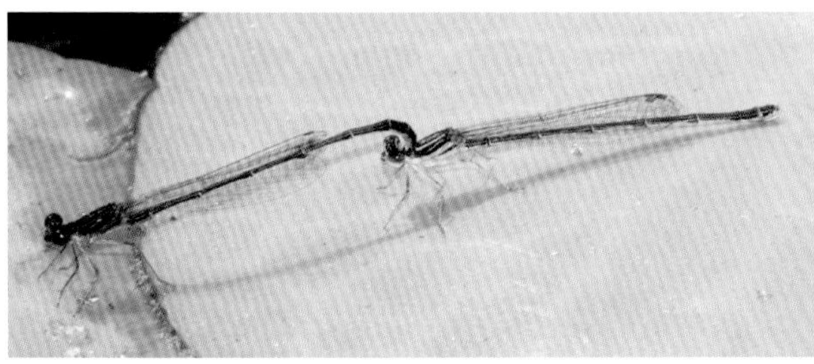

A pair of Burgundy Bluets (*Enallagma dubium*) in tandem.

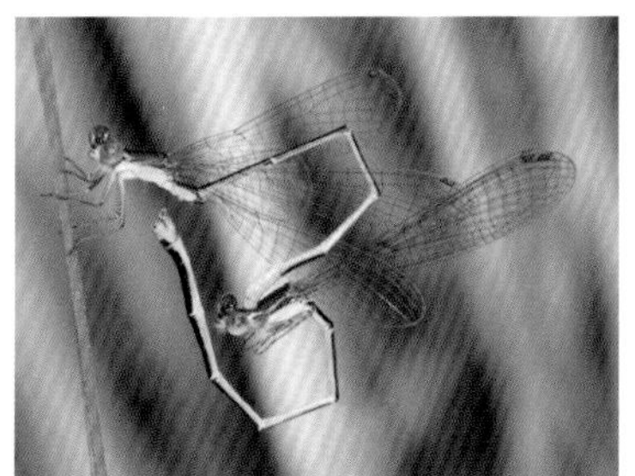

A pair of Sphagnum Sprites (*Nehalennia gracilis*) preparing to mate. The female is curling her abdomen up so that her genital opening comes into contact with the male's accessory genitalia on the ventral side of S2.

flies and all other odonates, however, have accessory genitalia located ventrally at the base of the abdomen. These structures are not connected to the internal reproductive system, but act as an intromittent organ. As a result, the male must transfer sperm from the tip of his abdomen to this accessory structure by curling his abdomen forward while in tandem or sometimes just before. The female then curls her abdomen forward until the genital opening at the tip of her abdomen comes into contact with the male's accessory genitalia. When pairs are in this position, they are said to be in copula or in the wheel position. It has not been lost on many observers that in damselflies this wheel position is heart shaped. They may remain in this position, usually protected within vegetation, for minutes or hours, depending on the species. Most females will mate more than once, while others use the sperm from a single male to fertilize eggs throughout their life. In at least some species, males are known to remove the sperm deposited by previous males before mating, by using special structures associated with the accessory genitalia.

A pair of Sphagnum Sprites in the wheel position. Note the heart shape.

To make sure only his sperm fertilize the eggs, the male damselfly of many species will stay in tandem with a female while she lays eggs. This behavior is known as contact guarding. The male may even partially or fully submerge himself underwater with the female while she lays eggs. Males of other species may exhibit noncontact guarding. This occurs when the male releases the female but hovers nearby or perches on vegetation above and defends the female from any intruding males. In forktails, most females lay eggs alone. Males may find themselves easy targets for prey when they are in tandem. Predation often occurs from dragonflies, but birds and lizards also go after pairs. On rare occasions, you may find a female damselfly with a male's abdomen still attached, but with the rest of the male absent due to predation.

Above, a female Eastern Pondhawk (*Erythemis simplicicollis*) feeds on a male Blue-fronted Dancer (*Argia apicalis*) that is still attached to a female. Left, the female, with the male's abdomen still attached to her prothorax.

FLIGHT. One of the many attractive qualities of odonates is their amazing aerial agility. Though dragonflies are the better fliers, damselflies are quite agile in flight. They can move each of their four wings independently. They can move so easily and quickly because they not only beat their wings, but also rotate them on their own axes. No other order of insect exhibits such fantastic aerial maneuverability. Most damselflies fly by alternating the two pairs of wings. This means that as one pair is on the way

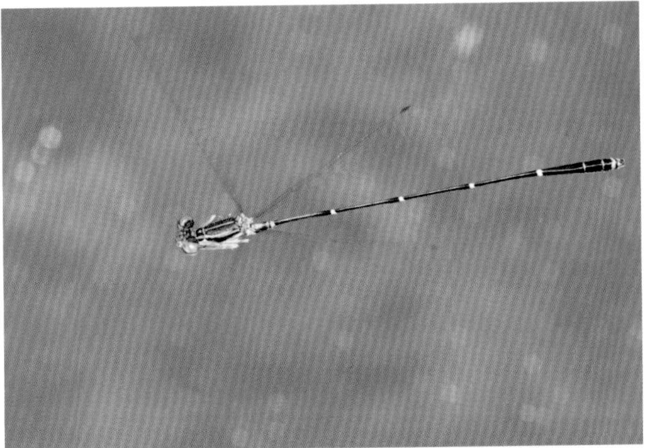

Orange-striped Threadtail (*Protoneura cara*) in flight.

Male Ebony Jewelwing (*Calopteryx maculata*) in flight. Photographed using multiple high-speed flashes.

down, the other is on the way up. The downward movement results in the thrust that propels the damselfly forward. Damselflies can beat their wings an average of 35 times a second. Despite this fast wingbeat, the actual velocity that damselflies can achieve (2–2.5 m/sec on average) is not that fast. The wings of most damselflies, other than the broad-winged damsels, are too narrow and short to produce fast flight.

Desert Firetail (*Telebasis salva*) in flight. Note the forewings in the up position and the hindwings in the down position. Photographed using multiple high-speed flashes.

VISION. The damselfly eye is made up of thousands of individual facets called ommatidia, which give odonates the best vision in the insect world, since the ommatidia act as individual receptors, forming essentially a mosaic image. This allows odonates to detect the smallest movements, including wing movement, potential prey, and mates, all during flight. The eyes of damselflies are well separated compared to those of dragonflies, which typically wrap around the head. Damselflies can see most of the same colors that we can, but as with most insects, their vision extends into the ultraviolet (UV) wavelengths, which many species reflect as a result. Damselflies that appear bright blue to us are also reflecting UV and may appear even brighter to other damselflies.

American Rubyspot (*Hetaerina americana*) showing large eyes.

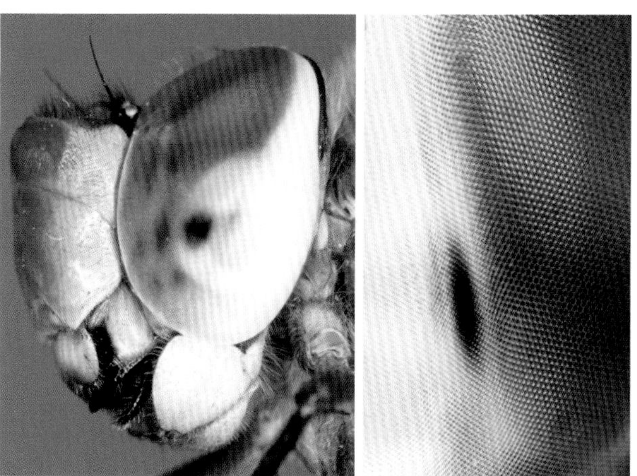

Eyes of a Common Green Darner (*Anax junius*). Large dragonflies like this one can have up to 30,000 individual ommatidia in each eye. The right image shows these individual facets.

Creating the Illustrations in the Book

The illustrations in this guide were inspired by the tremendous work of Ed Lam (see his book *Damselflies of the Northeast*). After much experimenting and after consulting with Ed and with another remarkable scientific illustrator, Steve Buchanan, we came up with the process used to create the illustrations found in this guide. As far as we know, the techniques we developed are original, and we thought readers would find the process interesting. It took more than two years to create the 417 color illustrations used in this book.

Scans were made of male and female specimens for all 77 species illustrated. The preserved specimens used were never positioned as desired. As a result, the typical procedure was to dissect each specimen, removing its wings, legs, and head, often separating its thorax and abdomen. These individual parts were scanned and reassembled digitally to achieve the uniform appearance of the illustrations. The head was positioned on a piece of wax to achieve the desired angle. Next, the scans were cleaned, and any unwanted elements were removed. At this point, antennae, leg spines, and tarsal claws were frequently redrawn because they were either broken or not picked up on the scans. Finally, each illustration was painted digitally. Scans were processed in Adobe Photoshop (CS2–4) using graphics tablets and a stylus (Cintiq or Intuos by Wacom).

This process involved several people, but without the help of Sara Pratt and the hundreds, even thousands, of hours she devoted to scanning and cleaning images, this project would not have been possible. We owe Sara tremendous thanks for her patience and diligence throughout the process.

The following are a few of the steps we took in creating the illustrations.

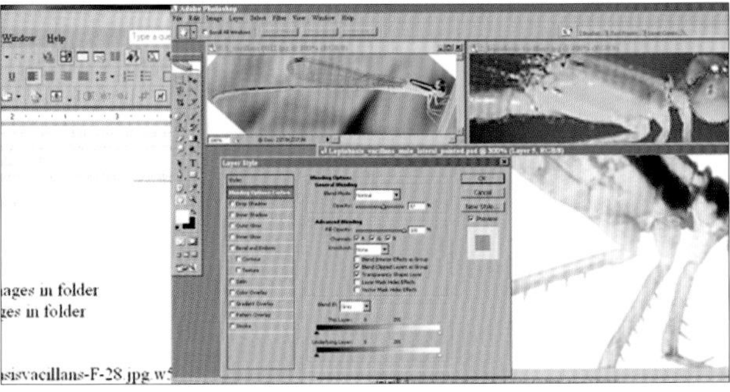

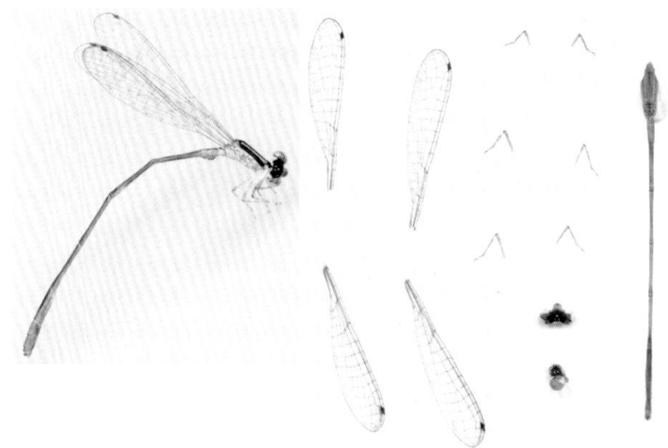

1. Select an intact specimen, in this case a male Red-tipped Swampdamsel, and place it on a flatbed scanner with its best side showing (i.e., the one with the least damage, exposing the dorsal side of the head and showing the thorax unobscured by the legs). Slightly prop the scanner lid and cover the specimen with white cardstock. This intact view will serve as a reference and contribute components to the illustrations. Using a microscope and forceps, carefully remove the wings, head, and legs and, if necessary, separate the thorax from the abdomen. Position the head and thorax with adhesive wax on the underside of the supported white cardstock and scan each component under high resolution (min. 300 dpi), with settings that offer sufficient detail but minimize darkness in the background.

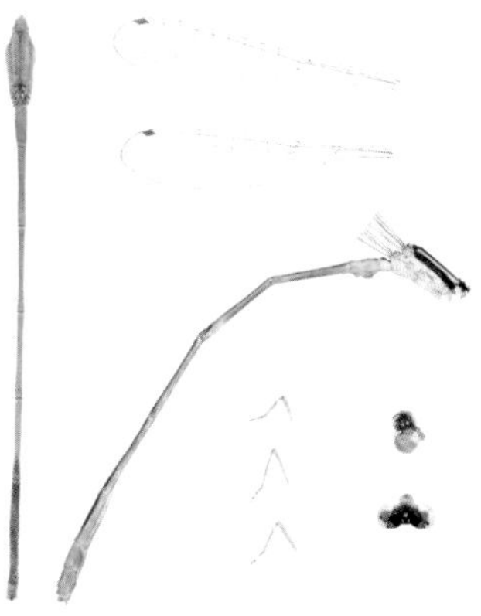

2. Using Adobe Photoshop or a comparable graphics program, clean each element separately by changing brightness/contrast levels, clearing areas by using appropriate selection tools (lassos, wand, etc.), and eliminating any extraneous elements (wax, frass, hairs) by using the eraser or clone-stamp tools. Select the clearest, cleanest, and least damaged forewing, hindwing, foreleg, midleg, and hindleg; these are the building blocks for dorsal and lateral views.

3. Select positions that will expose key diagnostic features and refer to photographs of live subjects to mimic natural, vivacious postures. Assemble the components into dorsal and lateral views. Replace or reposition missing components (antennae, spines, tarsal claws, venation) by using drawing tools, copying and pasting existing features when present and appropriate. Review photographs and other specimens for accuracy. Always create and maintain separate layers to facilitate subsequent editing.

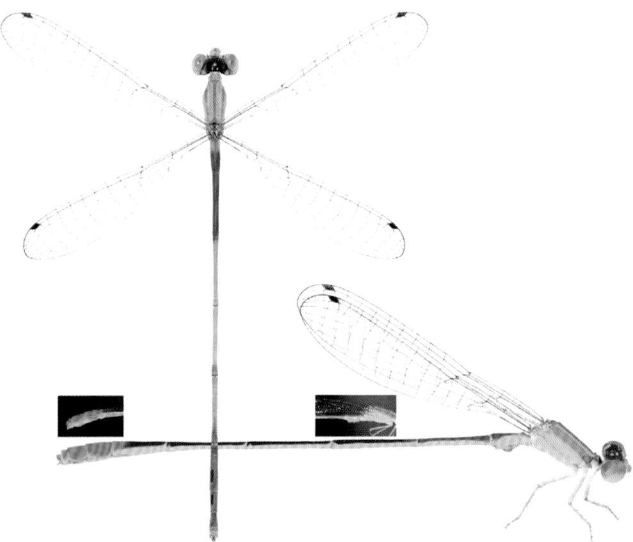

4. Paint base coats, each as a separate layer, pulling hues from photographs and referring to both photographs and specimens for patterning. Follow the morphological features visible within scans when applying paints. After base coats are painted and smudged into place, the drawings should match not just one photographed subject, but should represent an average within a population (e.g., young male Red-tipped Swampdamsels).

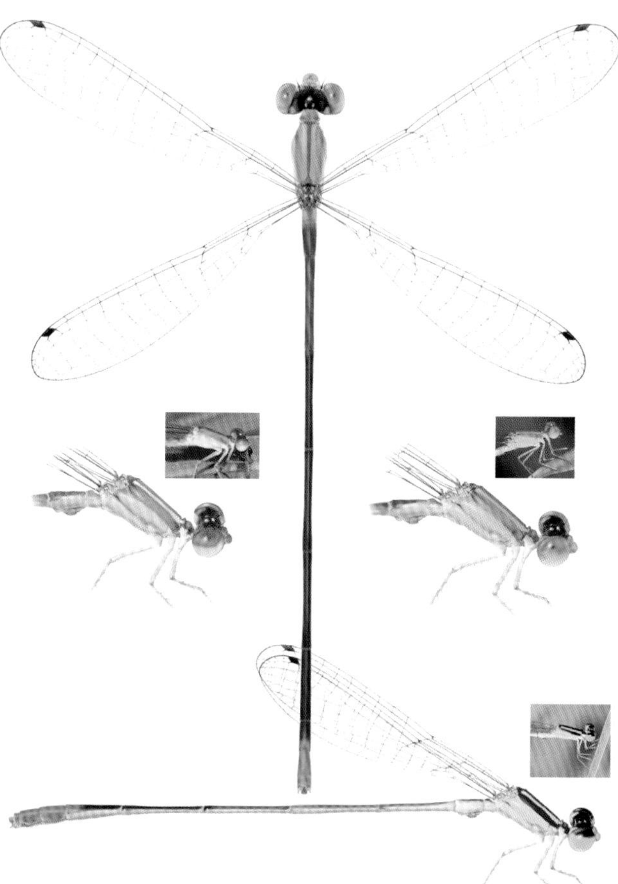

5. To create an illusion of three-dimensionality, produce areas where light would reflect and where less light would fall, given a consistent light source. For reflections, lay down white or another appropriate light color either as points or line segments (in the case of metallic or iridescent surfaces), or as smudges. For darker regions, lay down a darker version of the darkest color on the damselfly and smudge it in regions where less light would fall, leaving room for some back reflection. Play with the opacity level for light and dark areas separately until the abdomen looks somewhat tubular and the eyes pop. Finally, take the same male profile and change individual layers or repaint entire areas to match different morphs, ages, or degrees of pruinosity. Save a multilayered file for future use and modification.

Texas Biotic Provinces

Texas's size (268,581 square miles) and geographic position make it the ideal place to study and observe dragonflies and damselflies. Eastern and western species meet in the state, along with temperate and Neotropical species from the north and south. Biomes in the state range from wet deciduous forests to arid deserts, receiving as much as 60 inches of rain annually in the east and as little as 5 inches in the west. In the central and eastern parts of the state, most of the precipitation falls from March to May, while in the Trans-Pecos and western part of the state, the majority of the rains come during the late-summer and early-fall monsoons. Temperature is also an important factor in the distribution of plant and animal communities, and ranges from an annual average of 22.8°C (73.4°F) in subtropical Brownsville to 12°C (53°F) in the Texas Panhandle, resulting in a shorter growing season in the latter. Major vegetation types include eastern pines and hardwoods, central prairies and grasslands, western semidesert areas, and western montane forests. Elevation ranges from sea level along the coastal areas to 2,667 meters (8,749 feet) at Guadalupe Peak in the Guadalupe Mountains National Park of West Texas. The major watersheds drain eastward or southeastward. These stream systems provide important dispersal routes for the westward distribution of eastern species into more arid, treeless environments.

Seven biotic provinces are recognized within Texas, and are convenient for discussing the damselfly fauna of the state. These provinces differ in topography, temperature, vegetation, soil type, geology, and climate.

The Austroriparian province encompasses the Gulf coastal plain from extreme East Texas to the Atlantic Ocean. This biotic region's western boundary is demarcated by the availability of moisture. The typical vegetation types include longleaf pine (*Pinus palustris*), loblolly pine (*P. taeda*), and hardwood forests variously consisting of sweet gum (*Liquidambar styraciflua*), post oak (*Quercus stellata*), and blackjack oak (*Q. marilandica*). The lowland hardwood forests of the southeastern portion of this province are typically characterized by magnolia (*Magnolia grandiflora*), tupelo (*Nyssa sylvatica*), and water oak (*Q. nigra*) in addition to those trees mentioned above. Other plants typical of this region include Spanish moss (*Tillandsia usneoides*) and palmetto (*Sabal minor*).

The Texan biotic province constitutes a broad ecotone between the forests of the Austroriparian province in the eastern

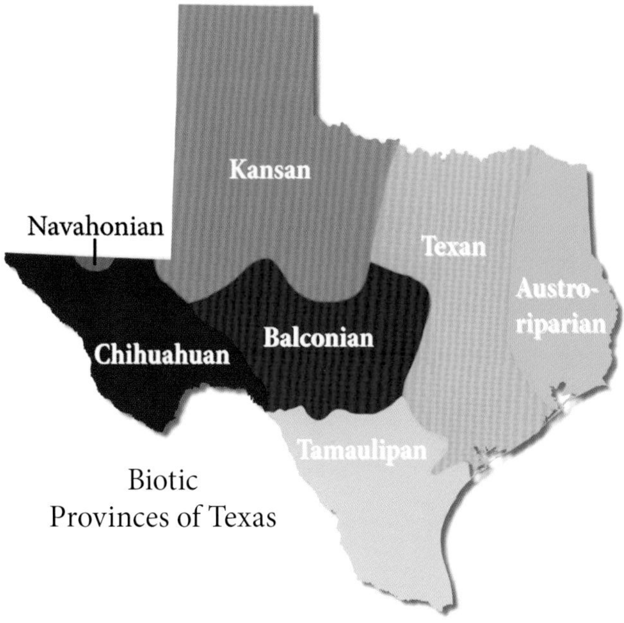

portion of this region and western grasslands. The Balcones Escarpment forms an abrupt boundary to the west, otherwise delineated by a line based on soil type. This area was once characterized by tall-grass prairies supported by clay soils, but cultivation of much of the area has led to sandy soils characterized by combination oak-hickory forests, dominated usually by post and blackjack oaks and hickory (*Carya texana*). This province is considered to have a moist, humid climate, receiving little water beyond that required for growth. The drainage pattern of the Texan province is an important biogeographic feature. The Red and Trinity rivers, along with their tributaries, drain the northern part of this province. Both of these rivers enter the Austroriparian province before emptying into the Gulf of Mexico. The southern portion of this province is drained largely by the Brazos, Colorado, San Marcos, and Guadalupe rivers.

The Kansan province is characterized by a mixture of eastern forest species and western grassland species. Notable exceptions to the monotonous prairies of this province are Palo Duro Canyon State Park and Caprock Canyon State Park, which have

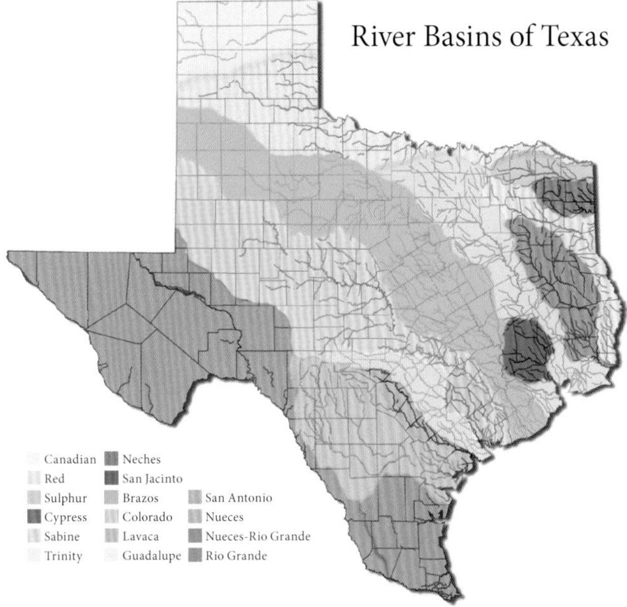

been characterized as relict habitats. Moisture decreases from east to west in this province, and the region is considered moisture deficient.

The Balconian biotic province is defined by the Edwards Plateau and derives its name from the Balcones fault zone, which forms its southern and eastern boundaries. It is characterized by scrub forests of juniper (*Juniperus* spp.) and oaks (*Quercus* spp.), including stunted live oak (*Q. virginiana*).

Farther south, the Tamaulipan province extends from southern Texas into eastern Mexico. This semiarid region is dominated by mesquite (*Prosopis glandulosa*), *Acacia* spp., *Mimosa* spp., and prickly pear cactus (*Opuntia* spp.). Thornthwaite (1948) noted a marked deficiency of moisture for plant growth, though some growth occurs year-round. This province is drained in the north largely by the Nueces River and its tributaries, and is poorly drained in the southern portion by minor tributaries of the Rio Grande. In the Brownsville region, to the south, the province becomes subtropical.

The Chihuahuan province includes the Trans-Pecos area of Texas, excluding the Guadalupe Mountains. It extends southward into the Mexican states of Chihuahua and Coahuila, and is drained largely by the Rio Grande. This province is the most diverse physiographically in the state. The climate in this area is arid and moisture deficient, and the vegetation is variable, but basin areas up to 1,350 meters (4,500 feet) in elevation include grasses, desert shrubs, and creosote bush (*Larrea tridentata*). Streams in this area are usually small and intermittent; those that are permanent are usually spring fed. Mountains, including the Chisos and Davis ranges, show a vertical zonation of plant communities, with elevations above 1,500 meters (5,000 feet) dominated by Emory oak (*Quercus emoryi*) and cedars (*Juniperus* spp.).

The Navahonian province, which includes most of New Mexico, barely enters the northern edge of western Texas (Culberson Co.) at the southern extension of the Guadalupe Mountains. A vertical zonation in elevation, similar to that of the Chihuahuan province, characterizes this area. Trees dominant at elevations above 2,250 meters (7,500 feet) include various pines (*Pinus* spp.), oaks (*Quercus* spp.), and Douglas fir (*Pseudotsuga menziesii*).

Damselfly Habitats

Damselflies are found in and around a wide variety of freshwater aquatic habitats. Some species may be present at nearly any body of water, but most will be more abundant at either ponds and lakes or streams and rivers. As a general rule, bluets are more common at standing bodies of water, while dancers are more common at flowing habitats. Some species are even more specialized, preferring certain types or forms of vegetation, spring seeps, or fast-flowing water, for example. Some species prefer small-cobble substrates, while others prefer sand substrates.

Damselflies that breed in flowing waters may often be seen perched on rocks along the bank or even out in the middle of the stream or river. Those species found in ponds and lakes are typically more dependent on riparian vegetation. As a result, ponds and lakes that have been mowed right up to the edge of the water typically don't support as diverse a damselfly community as others. I call this the "golf course" effect.

Another variable that affects where damselflies can breed is the permanency of a body of water. Farther south in Texas, many ponds and streams tend to become more ephemeral or temporary. Some species have life histories that allow them to take advantage of such temporary habitats. They usually survive the dry times in the egg stage and speed through the life cycle when it rains. Many species survive the winter months the same way, while others survive in the nymphal stage. Farther south, in the tropics, where the year is divided into rainy and dry seasons, many damselflies persist in the dry season as relatively inactive adults. There is evidence that some more southern species in Texas, which have come up from Mexico, may be surviving dry periods as adults as well.

Spring along Dolan Creek.

Small-cobble stream with water running over boulders.

Pintail Lake at Santa Ana National Wildlife Refuge. Note the surrounding vegetation, which provides perches for damselflies.

Temporary roadside pond that may provide habitat for a number of species.

American lotuses (*Nelumbo lutea*), like these at Caddo Lake, are unique habitats for damselflies.

Conservation

Odonates play a major role as beneficial predators of mosquitoes and other biting insects, both as adults and immatures. The nymphs also form an important link in food chains for fish and other aquatic vertebrates. Historically, the Odonata have not been acknowledged as good indicators of water quality, but recent studies are beginning to recognize that capacity.

It is estimated that 3%–6% of the damselfly species in North America have limited or restricted geographic ranges and may be at risk of extinction. Areas of particularly high endemism in the United States include the New England coast, Florida, the central Gulf coast, and the Pacific coast. Those species living in streams, rivers, and other flowing-water habitats are at greatest risk.

Bick (2003) listed 4 species as "at risk." One of them, the Everglades Sprite (*Nehalennia pallidula*), is a species essentially endemic to Florida. Two females, however, were recently discovered in the Smithsonian collection from Galveston, collected in 1913. There are no other records for this species outside Florida, but this suggests it is possible that this species was once more widespread. It is unlikely that this species still exists anywhere near Texas. Little is known of its biology, and the nymph remains unknown. A second species listed by Bick, the Coral-fronted Threadtail (*Neoneura aaroni*), occurs in Texas. It is also known from Mexico, but its distribution is centered on the Texas Hill Country. It is known from 22 counties in Central Texas southward. It is uncommon, but may be locally abundant in protected pools along slow-moving rivers and streams with emergent or floating vegetation.

Currently, the Texas Parks and Wildlife Department does not have a complete odonate-conservation plan. I have, however, assessed the damselflies in Texas and assigned state-level conservation ranks to them. I used the following criteria, which are based on the Wyoming Natural Diversity Database.

- **S1**: Critically imperiled because of extreme rarity (often <5 extant occurrences) or because some factor makes it highly vulnerable to extinction.
- **S2**: Imperiled because of rarity (often 6–20 extant occurrences) or because of factors making it vulnerable to extinction.
- **S3**: Rare or local throughout its range or found locally in a restricted range (often 21–100 known occurrences).

S4: Apparently secure, although it may be quite rare in parts of its range, especially at the periphery.
S5: Demonstrably secure, although it may be rare in parts of its range, especially at the periphery.

Some taxa receive nonnumeric scores, indicating special situations:

SH: Known only from historical records (typically pre-1970).
SA: Accidental or vagrant: taxon appears irregularly and infrequently.

This state-level status rank (S-rank) is given in the upper-right corner of each species treatment. Global status ranks (G-ranks) have been assigned to all but 2 of our species (Cream-tipped Swampdamsel [*Leptobasis melinogaster*] and Red-tipped Swampdamsel [*L. vacillans*]), both of which were only recently discovered in Texas and North America. These G-ranks, which are listed in the NatureServe Explorer Database (http://www.natureserve.org), are similar to the S-ranks, but take into account the global distribution of a species. Both the G-ranks and S-ranks are listed in Appendix B.

Eighty percent of Texas damselfly species are considered globally secure (ranked G5). Out of the remaining 15 species, all but 3 (Leonora's Dancer [*Argia leonorae*], Golden-winged Dancer [*Argia rhoadsi*] and Everglades Sprite [*Nehalennia pallidula*]) are rated G4. At the state level, 27 species, or 35%, are ranked S5 (demonstrably secure). Another 34 (44%) species are still considered secure, ranked either S3 or S4. Of the remaining 16 species, the Everglades Sprite (*Nehalennia pallidula*) is considered an accidental occurrence, and the Canyon Rubyspot (*Hetaerina vulnerata*) is a historical occurrence, though likely to be discovered in the state again. All 16 species considered imperiled (S1 or S2) at the state level are considered secure at the global scale, and most are ranked G5. The only 2 exceptions to this are the aforementioned swampdamsels, which have not been assessed at the global scale. It is always important to consider the global conservation status of a species when considering state-level conservation activities. Most of the species that are considered imperiled in the state are simply at the edge of their known distributions. Examples of these include the Furtive Forktail (*Ischnura prognata*) in the east, the Paiute Dancer (*Argia alberta*) from the west, the Mexican Wedgetail (*Acan-*

thagrion quadratum) from the south, and the Rainbow Bluet (*Enallagma antennatum*) from the north. These rankings can act as powerful and useful tools for quickly assessing management activities for species.

Ten species found in Texas occur nowhere else north of Mexico. They include all 3 members of the threadtail family found in North America: the Coral-fronted Threadtail (*Neoneura aaroni*), Amelia's Threadtail (*N. amelia*), and the Orange-striped Threadtail (*Protoneura cara*). The other 7 species are the Mexican Wedgetail (*Acanthagrion quadratum*), Comanche Dancer (*Argia barretti*), Coppery Dancer (*A. cuprea*), Golden-winged Dancer (*A. rhoadsi*), Neotropical Bluet (*Enallagma novaehispaniae*), Cream-tipped Swampdamsel (*L. melinogaster*), and the Red-tipped Swampdamsel (*L. vacillans*).

The single most important factor in the conservation of Odonata, and damselflies in particular, is the protection of land and aquatic habitats. The efforts needed for the protection of these resources vary with the type of habitat. Removing the surrounding vegetation from streams by mowing completely alters the composition of the water, effectively removing some species. A buffer zone of vegetation on either side of a stream (generally, at least 30 meters is recommended) helps prevent erosion. The construction of dams poses a real challenge to stream species. In Texas, there is only one natural lake (Caddo Lake), which indicates how prevalent dams are in the state. The numerous man-made reservoirs provide habitat for those few species that can breed in lakes, but they take away habitat from other damselflies. Rivers are seldom protected from human impact and disturbances, but conservation organizations like the Big Thicket National Preserve in East Texas are working hard to secure these areas by purchasing riparian lands and creating corridors between their preserve units.

For some species, especially those living in more arid conditions, a small area of suitable habitat may be all that is needed for their continued existence. For most species, however, larger areas of suitable habitat are necessary. This is why a good network of local, state, and national parks is so important. These areas provide protected habitats for odonates on relatively little land. Private groups like the Nature Conservancy are crucial for securing and protecting land. Time is of the essence, for whereas observations have shown some species expanding their ranges because of global warming, many others are left to compete for fewer, poorer quality habitats.

In addition to the preservation and management of natural habitats, the creation of new habitats, especially ponds, can play an important role in conservation. An artificial pond, especially one in an arid area, that has an assortment of aquatic vegetation and a lush riparian zone protected from livestock will provide productive breeding habitats for many species. Many Odonata can coexist with fish in smaller ponds (as long as there is plenty of vegetation to hide in), but the presence of fish will prevent some species from persisting in the habitat.

Sewage and other organic wastes that run off into streams promote bacterial growth, which depletes the oxygen content of the water and in turn stresses or kills damselfly nymphs. Fertilizer runoff from agricultural fields leads to eutrophication, a condition that promotes algal growth, which may lead to blooms that remove oxygen from the system and prevent sunlight from penetrating the water. Pesticide runoff kills nymphs. Those species of damselflies living in ponds and lakes are generally at less risk. In fact, the construction of new ponds, lakes, borrow pits, and even stock tanks may provide some damselflies with a new competition-free habitat to colonize. However, allowing livestock access to these areas can severely disrupt these pond species.

We still have a lot to learn about the specific microhabitat requirements of individual damselfly species. While many species are at risk, others, for example the Great Spreadwing (*Archilestes grandis*) and the Double-striped Bluet (*Enallagma basidens*), seem to be expanding their ranges. It is unclear in most instances whether the expansion of these species is coming at the expense of others. We need more refined methods of population estimation, ones that rely on exuviae and nymph counts rather than adult counts, if we are to begin getting at these questions. The collection and photographing of individuals will also play a critical roll in filling gaps in our knowledge and understanding of species distributions.

Both nymphs and adults are recreationally important; fly fishermen have patterned tied flies after them, and adults are observed and studied by laymen and scientists because of their colors, flying ability, and curious habits. Odonates have also served for centuries as favorite subjects of poets, naturalists, artists, and collectors. Particularly during this time of growing interest in the group, we should be vigilant in our attempts to conserve aquatic habitats.

Odonate Names

All species are given a Latin scientific name made up of a genus and a specific epithet. The derivation of these names is usually Latin or Greek, and often the name is somehow descriptive of the insect. The scientific name is always italicized (underlined if written by hand) and in lowercase letters except for the first letter of the genus (e.g., *Hetaerina americana*). Most insects do not have common names, but all North American odonates have been given a common name officially recognized by the Dragonfly Society of the Americas. A full list of these names is available on the society's website, which is hosted by OdonataCentral (http://www.odonatacentral.org). I have used these names as the primary way of referring to species in this book because the audience to which this guide is aimed generally prefers them.

I strongly encourage anyone interested in Odonata to learn the scientific names as well as the common names. You will not only be able to communicate more easily with professional odonatologists (keep in mind there are no official common names for Mexican Odonata species), but you will also find that a lot of useful information can be derived from the scientific name. Genera (the plural of genus) are groups of species that are usually well defined by a suite of characteristics. These characteristics are almost always morphological, but may also involve ecological and behavioral traits as well.

One example of the usefulness of scientific names can be seen within the spreadwings, or family Lestidae. Most Texas species belong in the genus *Lestes*, but one species, *Archilestes grandis,* is placed in a different genus. This fact (and therefore the relationship between the species) is lost when only common names are used, since you can't tell that the Great Spreadwing and the Rainpool Spreadwing, for example, are in different genera and therefore not as closely related as, say, the Southern Spreadwing and the Rainpool Spreadwing. It is also fun to learn the derivations of these scientific names. *Archilestes* means "ancient *Lestes*" and refers to its primitive position in the family, while *Lestes* is Latin for "robber," which may refer to the predatory nature of the group.

Two of the biggest reasons given by amateurs for not wanting to learn the scientific names is that they are hard to pronounce and their meanings are hard to decipher. A checklist of North American Odonata with the known derivations for all the species is available on http://www.odonatacentral.org. Pronouncing scientific names can be challenge, but I have provided the generally accepted pronunciation for each species on the species-account pages. In addition, below are a few basic rules that will help with the pronunciation of scientific names.

1. "ch" (as in *Chromagrion*) is pronounced as a hard *K*.
2. "ae" (as in Coenagrionidae) is pronounced *EE*.
3. "ii" (as in *daeckii*) is pronounced *EE-eye*.
4. Most vowels (including "y") are pronounced short rather than long (as in *math, ethics, fish, box, bus*, and *cyst*).

Latin biological names in English speech are usually pronounced with English letter sounds. For example, *virus* is pronounced *vye-rus* in English, but would have been pronounced *wee-ros* in the Latin of ancient Rome. An Anglo-Latin pronunciation in use for centuries incorporates features of late Roman dialects that differ from the corresponding forms in classical Latin. Several authors (Chandler 1889, Else 1967, Kelly 1986) have identified rules that describe the traditional English pronunciation of scientific names. Usage varies among individuals and continues to evolve, but the descriptive rules serve as a convenient pronunciation benchmark.

I have tried to use the most commonly accepted pronunciations for the scientific names in this book. Therefore, they may not always strictly adhere to the rules given in some of the references above.

HOW TO INTERPRET THE PRONUNCIATIONS. I have indicated the stressed syllable in uppercase letters. I have also used a schwa "ə" in the pronunciations. The schwa is pronounced like the:

a in *about* [əbaut]
e in *taken* [teikən]
i in *pencil* [pensəl]
o in *eloquent* [eləkwənt]
u in *supply* [səplai]
y in *sibyl* [sibəl]

Photographing Damselflies

It probably won't be long after you start observing odonates that you will want to photograph them. Given their beauty, this is a natural extension of one's interest. With the advent of digital cameras, the number of high-quality odonate images has steadily increased. Generally, damselflies are easier to photograph than dragonflies because they don't move as quickly and are more easily approached. On the other hand, they are generally smaller, requiring you to get closer or use additional magnification.

I switched from film to digital camera bodies early on and have never regretted the decision. The first question you will have to ask yourself when purchasing equipment is whether to go with a "point and shoot" or an SLR (single-lens reflex) camera. Many very good point-and-shoot cameras available now have exceptional macro capabilities and are very affordable. The benefit of choosing one of these is portability and affordability. The downside is a loss of flexibility and perhaps quality. Digital SLR systems are much more expensive (though they continue to increase in quality and decrease in price), but provide superior flexibility, which should improve the quality of your images.

I typically use an SLR system and will provide some details based on my experience. My standard equipment for damselfly photography generally consists of a midlevel digital body with a 1.6× magnification factor. The smaller the chip that gathers the light in the camera, the larger the magnification (this is not the same as the digital-zoom feature on point-and-shoot cameras) and generally the less expensive the camera. For landscape or portrait photography, a 1.6× built-in magnification is considered a detriment, but to a wildlife photographer, it is a huge plus. It means that a 100 mm lens effectively becomes 160 mm, without any tradeoffs.

When photographing odonates in general, I prefer a 70–200 mm *f*/2.8 lens (minimum focusing distance of 1.4 m) with a 2× teleconverter and a 25 mm extension tube between the teleconverter and camera. This means I am effectively shooting between 224 mm (70×2×1.6) and 640 mm (200×2×1.6). The zoom lens allows me to change magnification without physically moving, and the extension tube allows me to get closer than the 1.4 m minimum focusing distance. I almost always use a good, solid tripod and a flash on the camera to fill in shadows. Though a tripod certainly takes away some flexibility in the field and can make it very easy to scare off an odonate when one of its legs hits a bush, I think the benefits are worth it. Especially with a telephoto lens, shooting from a good, stable platform really pays off. I shoot manual, usually at 1/125–1/200 sec at *f*/14–*f*/18. One of the many advantages of digital photography is the ability to shoot at higher ISOs than you can with film. My default ISO is 400. I would never think of shooting at this ISO with film, but with digital you see little noise and get the benefits of greater light sensitivity. The setup above works well for both dragonflies and larger damselflies, but for smaller damselflies, I will use a 180 mm macro lens with a 1.4× or 2× teleconverter and flash. You must get closer to the subject with this setup, but for damselflies that is usually not difficult.

When I first started photographing odonates, I used a 100 mm macro and got less than pleasing results. I learned that although such a close macro is required to photograph many smaller insects, the benefits shooting odonates with a telephoto setup are innumerable. You do not have to get as close, and thus risk scaring them, and by having your camera positioned farther away from the subject, the background immediately behind the subject is more easily blurred, making the subject itself stand out.

Additionally, it is important to make sure your line of sight is perpendicular to the body surface you are photographing so that the entire individual is in sharp focus. This is generally easy to do when photographing damselflies from the side, but it is easy for the tip of the abdomen to be out of focus if your sight line isn't perpendicular. Another important criterion is the background. You may not always be able to choose this, but good photographs have contrasting backgrounds (blue sky, green vegetation) that are out of focus and not distracting. The telephoto setup above will help with this, but look for individuals that are already perched in these sorts of situations.

When photographing nymphs, I use two different setups. If you want to photograph a nymph in a controlled situation, you can place it in a homemade aquarium with a very narrow (1.0 cm–1.5 cm) width. Using gravel and vegetation, create a natural scene and place the nymph in the aquarium. Lighting can be tricky, but the time invested in setting the scene will be worth it. You will need to have your light sources (typically flashes) positioned at a 45° angle to the glass to avoid reflections. I typically also position a flash above the aquarium and point it directly downward. The second method I use for shooting nymphs involves a snoot I have built; it goes over the lens so that I can submerge the lens in a shallow stream or pond. This method requires you to submerge a flash underwater. This can be done by building your own housing or by purchasing an underwater flash housing. This method is more elaborate than the aquarium setup, but allows you to photograph odonates in their natural environment with little to no alteration of their normal behaviors. In both of these cases, I use a 100 mm macro lens equipped with extension tubes as needed, depending on the size of the subject.

The photos of the male appendages and female mesostigmal plates included in this book were taken using a microscope because the structures are very small. A microscope, however, has a very shallow depth of field. Modern software has provided a way of dealing with this by allowing you to stack images. This is a technique in which you take many photographs of the same object at multiple focuses. You then stack or compile the images using special software to generate a single image with a much deeper depth of field. There are several systems that allow you to do this, but I have found the Helicon Focus software to be the best.

Finally, make sure that in addition to your camera equipment, you take a healthy dose of patience. Odonate photography can be rewarding, but it is not without frustrations!

The Value of Odonate Collections

Insects were probably one of the earliest groups of organisms to be collected and catalogued. There are many reasons for this, including their beauty, availability, and abundance. Odonates have become a popular group of insects among amateur enthusiasts. As a result, there are a number of field guides now for odonates in different parts of the world. Most, perhaps all, would not have been possible without the library of specimens that make up odonate collections. These collections have provided and continue to provide invaluable information. There is simply no replacement for them, even in this age of abundant high-quality photographs. No matter how good a photograph is, it is still only a two-dimensional rendition of the actual specimen. Having said that, I understand that most readers of this book will not be interested in collecting. As a photographer myself, I also recognize the value that photos play in our understanding of odonate distributions. The website OdonataCentral (http://www.odonatacentral.org) is a community-based website that documents distributional data for species in the New World. These records must be documented with either a specimen or a photograph. The site has been very well received and now includes thousands of images of odonates that provide additional distributional data points.

Unlike most insects, many dragonflies and damselflies can be identified in the field without catching them, but there are a number of species that require careful examination for an accurate determination. Many enthusiasts enjoy catching odonates, examining them in hand (sometimes photographing them in hand as well) and then releasing them. Again, this is a very valuable way of learning the group; however, be careful not to catch teneral individuals (those soft-bodied individuals just emerged from the exuviae) because they are easily damaged when handled. For those who would like to build a reference collection or donate collected specimens to a collection, I have provided some guidelines and procedures below.

In Texas, you typically do not need a permit to collect odonates. Collecting odonates on protected lands requires special permission and sometimes a scientific permit. I have found that land stewards or agencies in charge of these protected areas generally have no problem with the collection of voucher specimens to ensure proper documentation and identification. Often, they encourage this practice in order to properly document the fauna of the lands they manage and protect. In Texas, as in most other states, scientific collecting permits are required for any gathering of specimens on state park property or preserve; these are administered by the Texas Parks and Wildlife Department. Because national parks administer their own scientific collecting permits, each park must be contacted separately. City and municipal parks may also be protected, and you should contact the appropriate administering agency in these areas to inquire about collecting. To obtain a scientific collecting permit, you will need to provide a proposal of the research being conducted to the relevant administering agency, which will mandate the deposition of vouchers (specimens accessioned or numbered) in a legitimate and publicly accessible collection.

You should also familiarize yourself with any rules governing the use of local or municipal parks. It is also best to ask when in doubt. There are no endangered damselflies or dragonflies in Texas, and there are no species rare enough that the collection of one or two specimens would cause an impact on the population, but collecting should be done only for research or educational purposes.

Catching an odonate can be quite challenging, but damselflies are typically much easier to net than dragonflies. They do not fly as fast and tend to perch more readily. Whether you are after a damselfly or a dragonfly, remember that they have superb vision, and so it is always best to approach from behind. Slowly move your aerial net within swing distance of the odonate and then swing forward with a decisive action, following through by flipping the net bag so that the excess rests on the rim and traps the odonate inside. It is often easier, especially with dragonflies, to collect them while they are engaged in some activity such as feeding or mating. When you collect a pair of odonates, be sure to keep them together, since having examples of the sexes associated is helpful.

You should now be able to gently work your hand into the net and grab the odonate by the wings folded over the abdomen. Most winged insects will tend to fly upward when given the opportunity, and odonates are no exception, so be careful not to open the net widely with the exit pointed up. Odonates can't do you any harm, but some larger dragonflies have strong mandibles and may attempt to bite a finger if given the opportunity. Damselflies are much more delicate, and you will need to practice more caution when handling them. The legs in particular are easily broken off. Once you have a secure hold on the odonate, remove it from the net and place it in a glassine envelope (commonly available from hobby stores and sold as stamp-collecting envelopes) with the wings folded back over the abdomen. Pairs caught in tandem or in copula can usually be placed in the same envelope, but it is best to face them away from each other in order to avoid any unwanted predation. Label the envelope with the date, locality, your name, and the species, if known. With pairs, be sure to note whether they were taken in copula or in tandem. It is helpful to have a 3 × 5 inch card file or similar box that you can store specimens in while collecting. Don't leave the specimens exposed to severe temperatures or sunlight. Ideally, the specimens will remain alive long enough to void their guts of any frass or excrement. This improves the preservation process by removing fats and oils.

Once you have returned home, it is time to acetone the specimens. We treat odonates with acetone because it does a good job of removing fats and oils, which will cause the specimen to

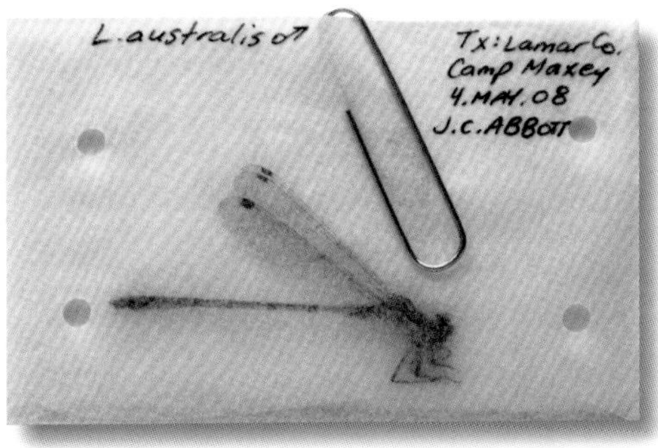

grease up. It also fixes the colors to some degree, though odonates, unlike beetles and butterflies, don't retain their beautiful colors. It is important to not let the acetone touch your skin; use forceps to remove specimens and always work with acetone in a well-ventilated area. Remove the specimens from the envelopes (making sure to not lose the continuity of the label data and the specimen itself) and drop them in acetone to kill them. This will take only a minute. Remove the specimen and carefully straighten the abdomen, arrange the legs so they are pointed downward, and gently rotate the head so you are looking at the top when the odonate is lying on its side. Finally, separate the forewings from the hindwings so they are not overlapping. This makes for a much easier examination of wing venation. Place the specimens back in their labeled glassine envelopes and either punch a few small holes (an eighth of an inch) in the envelope or cut off the corners to allow the acetone to diffuse and ultimately drain out. Make sure if you cut the corners that you do not cut so much that a small damselfly might slip out. I then place a paper clip over the flap of the envelope to ensure it will not open accidentally. Leave the specimens in the acetone overnight.

Use forceps to remove the specimen envelopes from the acetone and then allow them to dry. Separate the envelopes and drain off as much acetone as possible. I find that placing a fan on the envelopes forces the acetone to evaporate more quickly and that I ultimately get better specimens. Once the specimens are removed from the acetone, they are dehydrated, and as a result very brittle, so handle them carefully.

The final step is to remove a completely dried specimen from its envelope and place it in front of a data card inside a clear envelope. Because damselflies are so delicate, I place each one in a small envelope inside a bigger one so that it can be easily removed. These enveloped specimens can then be stored in sealed containers (plastic shoe boxes) or in drawers housed in cabinets. However you store them, it is important to make sure that they are well sealed in order to guard against pest species (dermestid and anobiid beetles) that will attack and destroy preserved insect collections. In Appendix C, I have provided sources for both types of envelopes mentioned above, forceps, aerial nets, and other supplies.

The odonate collection at the University of Texas at Austin contains nearly 20,000 specimens at the moment and is the largest collection of dragonflies and damselflies in the south-central United States. I welcome contributions to the collection as well as visitors who would benefit from examining it.

One of the metal cabinets in the University of Texas at Austin odonate collection with envelopes housed in Cornell-style drawers.

How to Identify Damselflies

When people first get interested in odonates, they almost invariably focus on dragonflies. They are bigger, generally more easily seen, and often easier to identify than the smaller damselflies. I myself struggled to learn many of the similar-looking damselflies when I first started studying them, but now I find damselflies more fascinating than dragonflies and so tend to focus more on them. There are currently 77 species of damselflies known from Texas; that is more than half of the 138 species known from North America. I think the Texas fauna is manageable, however, even for beginners. The four families represented in Texas are reasonably easy to tell apart. One of them, however, the pond damsels, which is by far the largest, contains the most species that look alike—all the little blue ones.

When trying to narrow down the identification of a species, consider everything, including where you found it and its behavior. For example, some species are found at ponds, others at streams, but few are found at both. Some good questions to ask include the following: Is the damselfly perching on the ground, down in vegetation, or in the open on a branch? How are the wings oriented when the individual is perched? How long is the abdomen in proportion to the wings? Does the damselfly have prominent eyespots? What is the color pattern on the thorax and abdomen?

With a little practice, you will be able to identify most of Texas's species just by using binoculars, but sometimes, especially with females, it may be necessary to net an individual and examine it more closely, with either a hand lens or a microscope. Detailed photos of male terminal appendages, female mesostigmal plates, and female ovipositors are provided for the appropriate groups. I encourage you to study these and to try to recognize these structures on the species, especially as you begin observing damselflies.

Use the color-coded key on the right to help place species in a particular group. Especially with the pond damsels, the silhouettes and habitat descriptions are meant to be only a general guide and to cover only the most commonly encountered groups.

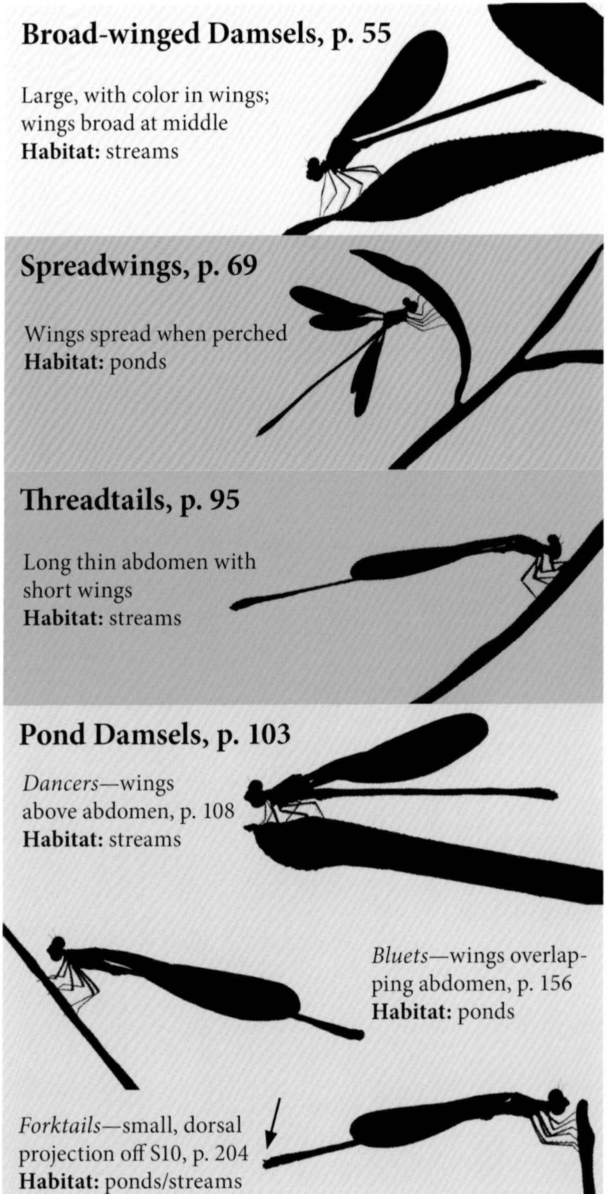
Broad-winged Damsels, p. 55
Large, with color in wings; wings broad at middle
Habitat: streams
Spreadwings, p. 69
Wings spread when perched
Habitat: ponds
Threadtails, p. 95
Long thin abdomen with short wings
Habitat: streams
Pond Damsels, p. 103
Dancers—wings above abdomen, p. 108
Habitat: streams
Bluets—wings overlapping abdomen, p. 156
Habitat: ponds
Forktails—small, dorsal projection off S10, p. 204
Habitat: ponds/streams

How to Use the Species Accounts

All 77 species of damselflies that have been reported in Texas are treated in this book. They are organized by family in phylogenetic order. Most species are organized alphabetically by the scientific name, but occasionally I have deviated from this in order to place the most similar-looking species next to each other for easy comparison. Each family is color coded for easy reference and introduced with a brief discussion of its characteristics. That is followed by a synopsis of each genus found in the family. I have concentrated on morphological characteristics, but have included behavioral and natural history information whenever space permitted. Each species is then discussed and illustrated on a two-page spread in a standardized format.

The heading for each species contains the officially accepted common name for the species and the scientific name below that. The pronunciation of the scientific name is provided in parentheses. The remainder of the left side of the page contains illustrations of the species with key features highlighted. I have tried to include as many color forms as practical. The left and right sides of each species account, along with the Key Features section, are color coded by family. The top of the right side of the page contains a map showing the range of the species as determined by known points of occurrence but generalized to include areas of expected occurrence as well.

To the right of the map is a colored box containing the Key Features section. For each sex, a brief set of characteristics is given for quick reference in identifying the species. For a full description, you should consult the Identification section. This section provides a more thorough description of the species; the male is discussed first, then the female. The descriptions typically start at the head and work backward to the thorax and abdomen. I use the term "juvenile" to refer to younger adults that are typically not reproductively mature. When referring to individual segments of the abdomen, I have used the following notation: S1 = segment 1, S3–6 = segments 3 through 6. Damselflies, like most insects, are quite variable, and it is important to read the entire description when first encountering a species. You may also find helpful characteristics mentioned in the family- and generic-level write-ups found at the beginning of each family section.

In the Similar Species section, the species is compared to others that are likely to be confused with it. I have tried to include all such species in this section, but you will want to refer to the individual species accounts mentioned in this section for additional information. In some cases, it may be necessary to consult the microscope photographs of terminal appendages and mesostigmal plates (found at the end of each group) in order to definitively identify a species. This will require the use of a hand loupe or a microscope.

The Texas Status section indicates how likely one is to encounter the species (rare, uncommon, or common), followed by a brief elaboration of where the species may be found. The Habitat section provides a description of where the species is commonly encountered, and generally breeds. The Discussion section typically includes what is known about the species' biology, behavior, and natural history.

Along the right side of the page is a box showing the state-level conservation status ranking. This is meant to provide a quick idea of whether a species is imperiled (S1-2) or secure (S3-4) within Texas. For a complete discussion of these rankings, see the Conservation section in the introduction to this book. Following this is a life-size silhouette with a range of measurements for the total length of the individual from the head to the tip of the abdomen. These measurements were largely taken from *Damselflies of North America* by Westfall and May and supplemented with measurements from the University of Texas Insect Collection. The silhouette represents the median length of the species. Keep in mind that damselflies can vary quite a bit in size and that although females can be a bit bulkier in overall appearance, males typically have longer abdomens. Along the bottom of the right-hand side of the page is a seasonal histogram. This concisely indicates when the species has been seen in Texas. The early and late dates for a species are constantly changing, and you should not be concerned if you find a species outside these dates. I have provided a list of the actual early and late dates for Texas species in Appendix C.

There are relatively few photographs used in this book. Rather, I have tried to let the beautiful illustrations stand on their own. I have added photographs to species accounts when space allowed and generally when a photo showed the damselfly exhibiting a particular behavior. I have also used photos throughout the introductory material at the front of each chapter.

Species Accounts

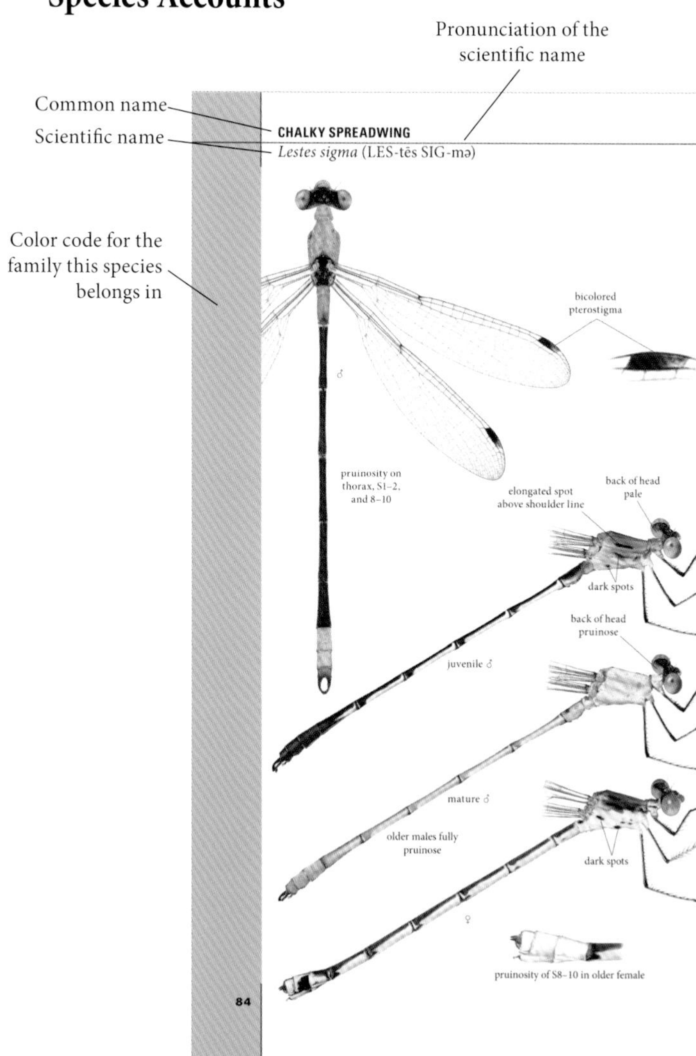

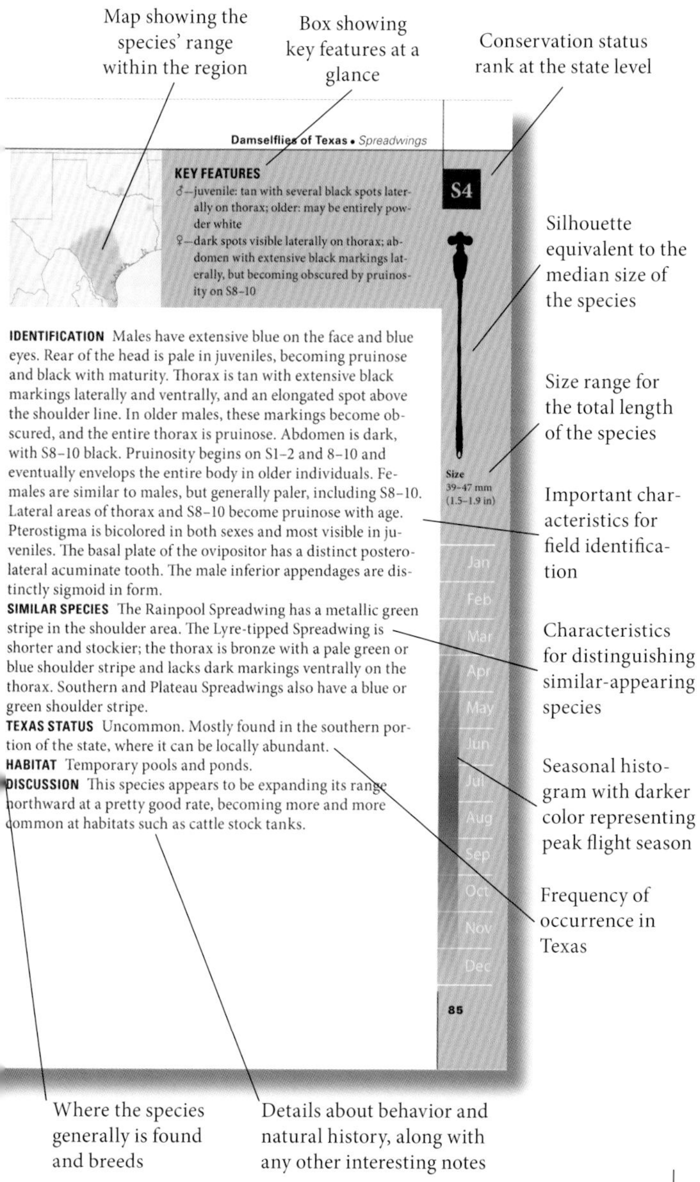

Map showing the species' range within the region
Box showing key features at a glance
Conservation status rank at the state level
Damselflies of Texas • Spreadwings
KEY FEATURES
♂—juvenile: tan with several black spots laterally on thorax; older: may be entirely powder white
♀—dark spots visible laterally on thorax; abdomen with extensive black markings laterally, but becoming obscured by pruinosity on S8–10
S4
Silhouette equivalent to the median size of the species
Size range for the total length of the species
Size
39–47 mm
(1.5–1.9 in)
IDENTIFICATION Males have extensive blue on the face and blue eyes. Rear of the head is pale in juveniles, becoming pruinose and black with maturity. Thorax is tan with extensive black markings laterally and ventrally, and an elongated spot above the shoulder line. In older males, these markings become obscured, and the entire thorax is pruinose. Abdomen is dark, with S8–10 black. Pruinosity begins on S1–2 and 8–10 and eventually envelops the entire body in older individuals. Females are similar to males, but generally paler, including S8–10. Lateral areas of thorax and S8–10 become pruinose with age. Pterostigma is bicolored in both sexes and most visible in juveniles. The basal plate of the ovipositor has a distinct posterolateral acuminate tooth. The male inferior appendages are distinctly sigmoid in form.
Important characteristics for field identification
SIMILAR SPECIES The Rainpool Spreadwing has a metallic green stripe in the shoulder area. The Lyre-tipped Spreadwing is shorter and stockier; the thorax is bronze with a pale green or blue shoulder stripe and lacks dark markings ventrally on the thorax. Southern and Plateau Spreadwings also have a blue or green shoulder stripe.
Characteristics for distinguishing similar-appearing species
TEXAS STATUS Uncommon. Mostly found in the southern portion of the state, where it can be locally abundant.
HABITAT Temporary pools and ponds.
DISCUSSION This species appears to be expanding its range northward at a pretty good rate, becoming more and more common at habitats such as cattle stock tanks.
Jan
Feb
Mar
Apr
May
Jun
Jul
Aug
Sep
Oct
Nov
Dec
Seasonal histogram with darker color representing peak flight season
Frequency of occurrence in Texas
85
Where the species generally is found and breeds
Details about behavior and natural history, along with any other interesting notes

Species Accounts

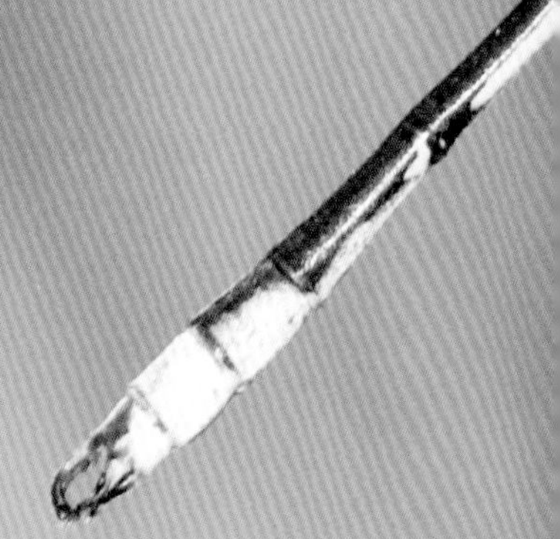

Lyre-tipped Spreadwing

Ebony Jewelwing

Broad-winged Damsels
Family Calopterygidae

This family contains some of Texas's largest and most brilliantly colored damselflies. They can be separated from all other North American damselflies by broad wings, nonstalked or petiolate, that don't narrow extensively at their base and the numerous (5 or more) antenodal crossveins found in both wings. The postnodal crossveins are also not lined up. The pterostigma is weakly formed or absent, especially in males. They have extensive color in the wings. This is the only damselfly family in North America that engages in courtship. They typically perch horizontally on vegetation or rocks at relatively low heights, and are often seen flying low over the water, sometimes even skating downstream short distances on the surface.

JEWELWINGS, GENUS *CALOPTERYX*. Large, with brilliant, iridescent green and blue bodies and long black legs armed with numerous spines. Wings of females are more uniformly colored and not as dark as males. A true pterostigma is absent in both sexes, but females have a white area covering numerous cells that is called a pseudostigma. Adults stay close to the streamside, moving from one bush or limb to another in a characteristic fluttering flight.

RUBYSPOTS, GENUS *HETAERINA*. The common name, rubyspots, refers to the basal red patch in the wings of males. Females usually have amber-colored wings and are more robust than males. The simple, small white pterostigma is often absent in one or both sexes outside of the United States, but is generally present in Texas species. The wings are narrower and the body is more slender than in jewelwings.

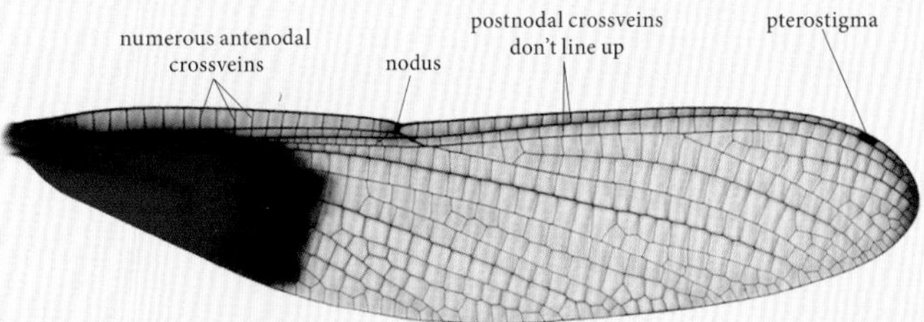

Broad-winged damsel forewing showing characteristic venation.

SPARKLING JEWELWING

Calopteryx dimidiata (ca-LOP-tə-rix də-mid-ē-A-tə)

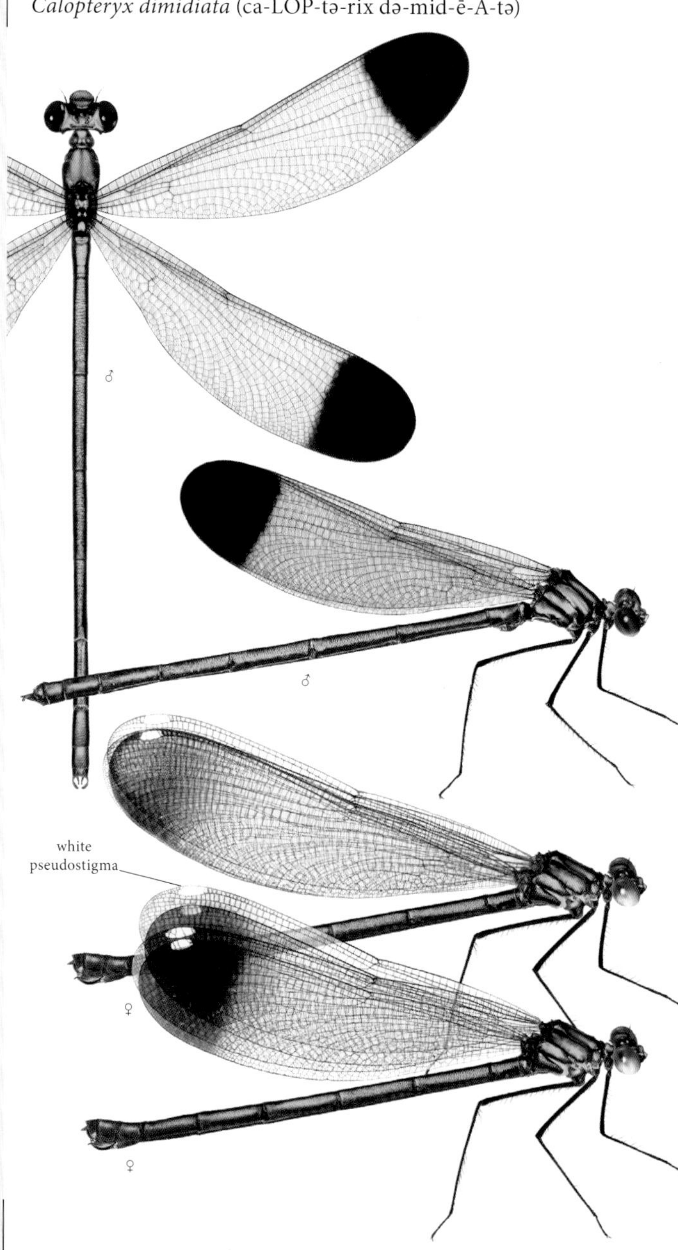

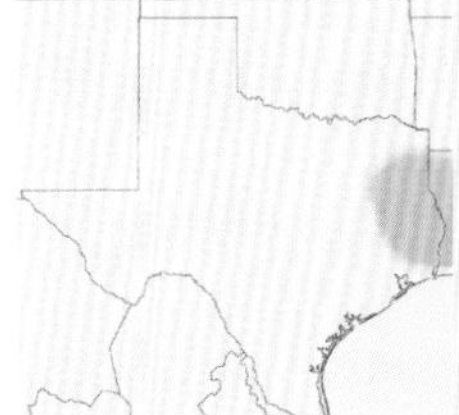

KEY FEATURES

♂—metallic green body; wings clear to amber with dark tips, lacking a white pseudostigma

♀—metallic green body; wings clear to amber with or without dark wing tips, but generally with a white pseudostigma

Size
37–50 mm
(1.5–2.0 in)

Jan Feb Mar Apr May Jun Jul Aug Sep Oct Nov Dec

IDENTIFICATION This is a large, iridescent green species. Males are easily recognized by their size, green body, and clear to amber wings with contrasting black wing tips in the outer quarter or fifth of the wing. They lack a white pseudostigma. Females are not as brilliantly colored as males and have clear to amber wings with the outer band varying from as dark as the male to barely darker than the rest of the wing. In females, there is generally a white pseudostigma that covers 3–5 cells. The wings are 3.5–4 times as long as wide.

SIMILAR SPECIES Ebony Jewelwing is larger and has uniformly darker and broader wings. The wings of the Smoky Rubyspot vary, but at least have an extensive dark patch basally in each wing.

TEXAS STATUS Uncommon. Restricted to the southeastern part of the state.

HABITAT Small, clear, sandy-bottomed streams with vegetation. Occasionally found in rivers with little canopy cover.

DISCUSSION Sparkling Jewelwings do not travel far from the stream they inhabit, and are generally found perching on low vegetation along the side of the stream and hanging over it. Both sexes are often found together at a stream. Males actively defend territories by giving chase in spiral flights over the water. Males court approaching females by dropping to the water and floating short distances with their wings partially spread and their abdomens curled up; a behavior known as the "floating cross display." Females indicate receptiveness by flipping their wings. After a brief courtship of wing whirring by the male, they typically copulate for 2 minutes. Females lay eggs while walking down vegetation and eventually submerging themselves for around 20 minutes.

Calopteryx maculata (ca-LOP-tə-rix mac-ū-LA-tə)

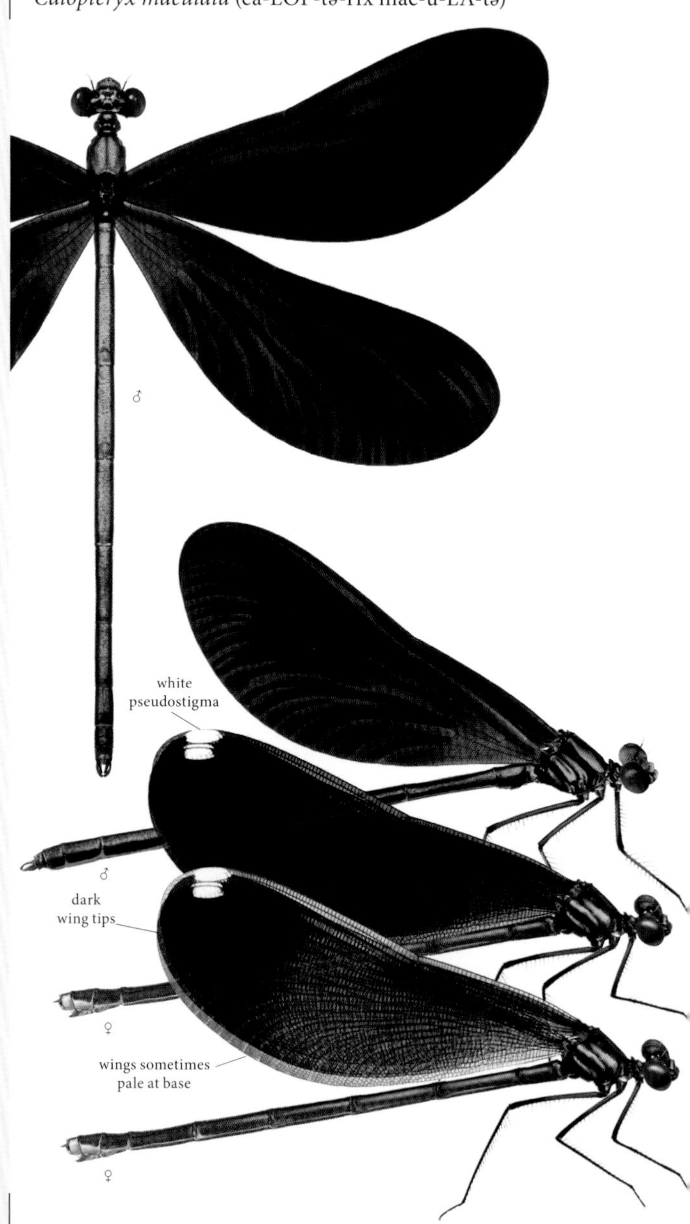

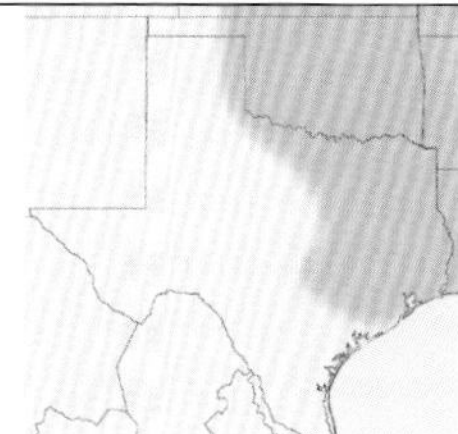

KEY FEATURES

♂—metallic green or blue body; wings broad and uniformly dark, lacking a pseudostigma

♀—metallic green or blue body; wings may have darker tips; always with a white pseudostigma

S5

Size
33–57 mm
(1.5–2.2 in)

Jan Feb Mar Apr May Jun Jul Aug Sep Oct Nov Dec

IDENTIFICATION This is a large, iridescent green or blue species with uniformly dark wings. Older, mature males have solid black wings, while wings in juveniles are lighter brown. Wings of females are usually paler, becoming progressively darker apically with a conspicuous white pseudostigma that is distinctively widened at its middle. The wings are 3 times as long as wide. The abdomen is iridescent blue-green on top and black on bottom except for a white (in males) or brown (in females) area starting posteriorly on the bottom of S8 and continuing to S10. Wings of females generally have darker tips.

SIMILAR SPECIES In the Sparkling Jewelwing, only the wing tips are black. The Smoky Rubyspot is the only other damselfly that may have completely dark wings. It is much smaller, lacks the blue-green iridescence on the body, and has wings that are only about a fifth as wide as long.

TEXAS STATUS Common. Found in the eastern part of the state.

HABITAT Small, slow-moving woodland streams and occasionally exposed streams and rivulets often associated with nearby trees for roosting at night.

DISCUSSION Males vigorously compete for territories with submergent vegetation, the prime egg-laying habitat for females. Males attract females with a "cross display" in which the male faces the female with his hindwings deflected downward at right angles to his body, and the forewings and abdomen raised, revealing the pale area on the ventral side of the abdomen. Mating and egg laying generally occur in the early afternoon, and a single male may guard multiple females, resulting sometimes in large aggregations. Females lay their eggs in submergent vegetation for 10–120 minutes and may submerge themselves.

AMERICAN RUBYSPOT

Hetaerina americana (het-ə-RĪN-ə a-mare-i-CĀN-ə)

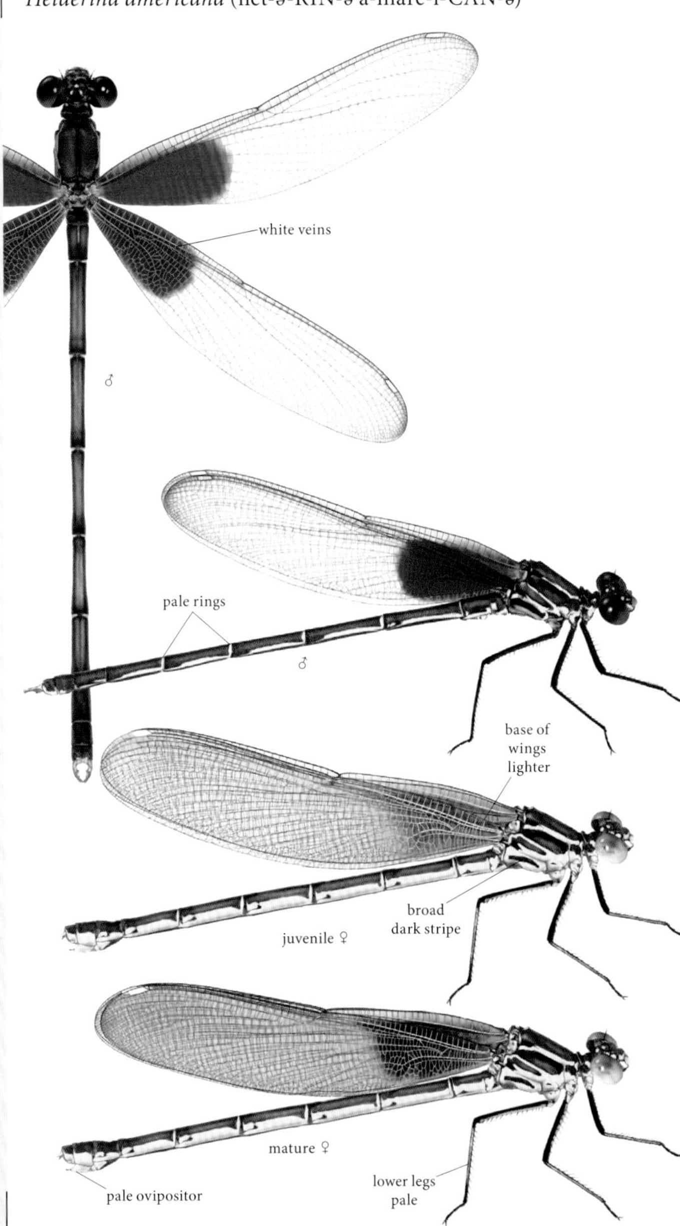

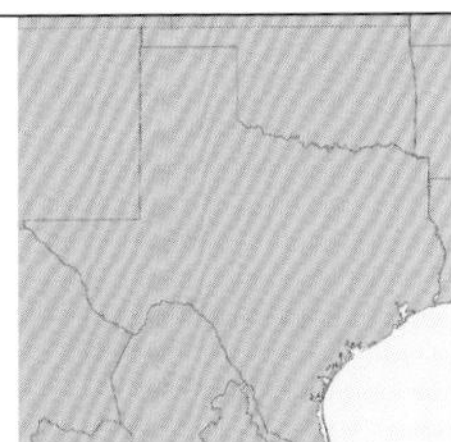

S5

KEY FEATURES

♂—metallic red face and thorax; large red patch basally on wings; pale abdominal rings; pale abdominal appendages

♀—metallic brown-green head and thorax; extensive pale areas on thorax; pale ovipositor

Size
36–51 mm
(1.4–2.0 in)

Jan
Feb
Mar
Apr
May
Jun
Jul
Aug
Sep
Oct
Nov
Dec

IDENTIFICATION This is a large species, with striking red patches and white veins in the base of the wings. Males have a metallic red thorax and metallic green abdomen. The vivid red patches at the base of the wings become larger with age (ranging from 20%–50% of the wing length). Females have a duller green-brown thorax and abdomen with metallic reflections. The basal red patch is present, but not nearly as pronounced as in males. Females also have a thin pale middorsal line running the length of the abdomen, and the lower legs are pale. A pale pterostigma is generally present in both sexes, but populations in southwestern New Mexico have been found lacking a pterostigma. The underside of the abdomen is extensively pale in both sexes.
SIMILAR SPECIES Smoky Rubyspots are much darker, and the wing tips almost always show at least a hint of dark color. The wings are narrower in shape and variable in color; males have red or white veins on dark patches basally in the hindwing. Females have dark lower legs, and the underside of the abdomen is dark in both sexes. Canyon Rubyspots lack a pterostigma, the basal red patch is generally not as extensive, and the lowest lateral dark stripe on the thorax is narrower.
TEXAS STATUS Common. Found statewide.
HABITAT Open streams and rivers of varying sizes and current.
DISCUSSION Both sexes are often found in good numbers streamside and perch horizontally on twigs and leaves of riparian vegetation; females often perch higher than males. There is no courtship, but males aggressively defend territories through circular flights. Females lay eggs on vegetation at the surface or by submerging themselves. Although this species is primarily found on streams, it has been shown experimentally that nymphs and teneral adults exposed to still water return to still water habitats after they mature.

CANYON RUBYSPOT

Hetaerina vulnerata (het-a-RĪN-a vul-nuh-RĀT-ə)

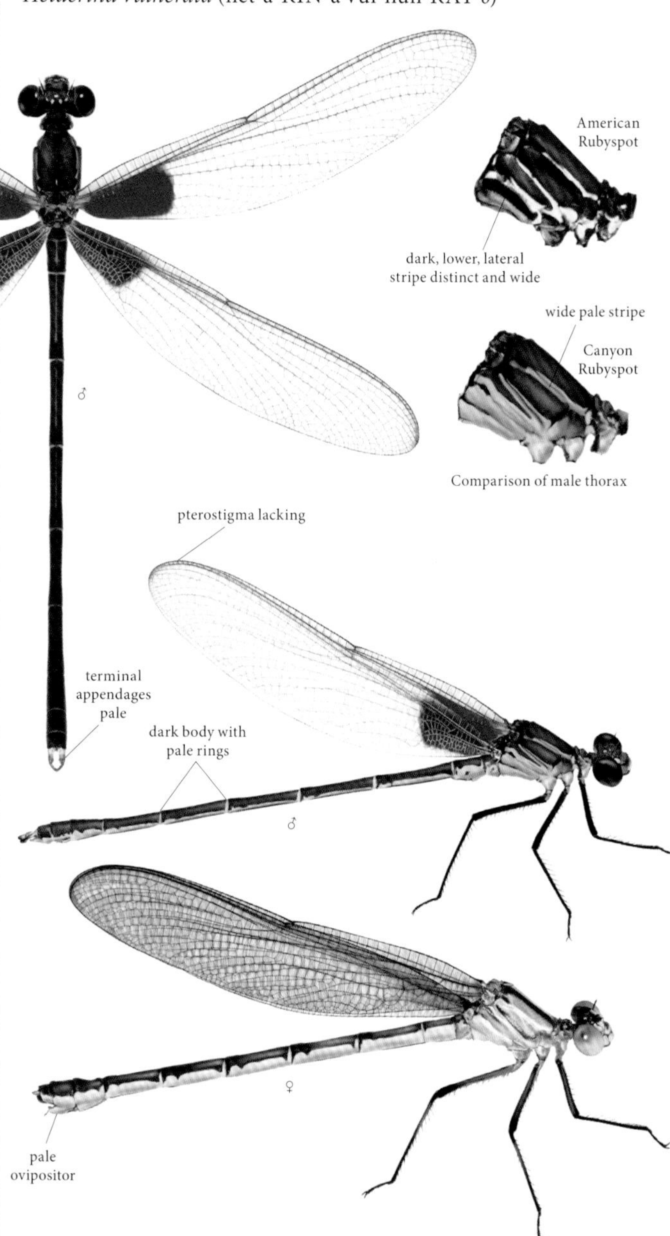

Comparison of male thorax

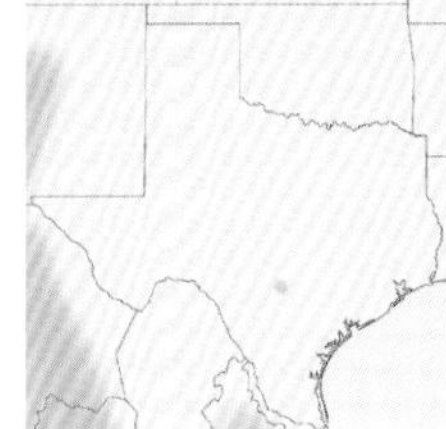

KEY FEATURES

♂—bright red patches at base of wings; brown body with pale rings; wings without a pterostigma

♀—thorax with iridescent green reflections; wings with diffused orange basally, lacking pterostigma; pale ovipositor

IDENTIFICATION Male's lower lip is pale yellow with a central, dark brown spot. The thorax is deep, iridescent red dorsally with a black middorsal stripe and a pale shoulder stripe. Basal red patch in both wings becomes more intense with age. Veins in the red patch are white on the underside. Wing tips are often edged with brown and generally lack a pterostigma. Females are similar to males, but paler overall. Thorax is iridescent green dorsally with lateral, iridescent green stripes, but these are less extensive than in males and may be absent. Wings lack the intense basal red patch, but are suffused with orange basally.

SIMILAR SPECIES Closely resembles the American Rubyspot, but that species generally has pterostigmas and often a more pronounced basal red patch, and the lowest dark stripe laterally on the thorax is distinctly wider. Smoky Rubyspots are darker overall, they can have extensive brown in the wings, and the abdomen is uniformly dark, without pale rings. Male caudal appendages may need to be checked for positive identification.

TEXAS STATUS Historical. Potential populations in West Texas.

HABITAT Wooded canyon streams and rivers with riffles.

DISCUSSION Canyon Rubyspots were thought to completely lack pterostigmas, but individuals from El Cañon de la Huasteca, a national park in Nuevo Leon, Mexico, have been found with them. The ranges of American and Canyon Rubyspots overlap, and they are known to occur together. Males engage in circling flights to defend territories. They remain with the female after mating and even adopt the unusual behavior of leaving their territory to accompany females in tandem on a search for egg-laying sites elsewhere. They then perch and guard the female while she submerges to lay eggs in vegetation. There are two historical records of male Canyon Rubyspots in Bexar County, Texas. This is considerably east of the normal range for this species, but populations in West Texas are not unexpected.

Size
36–49 mm,
1.4–1.9 in

Jan
Feb
Mar
Apr
May
Jun
Jul
Aug
Sep
Oct
Nov
Dec

SMOKY RUBYSPOT

Hetaerina titia (het-a-RĪN-a TISH-ə)

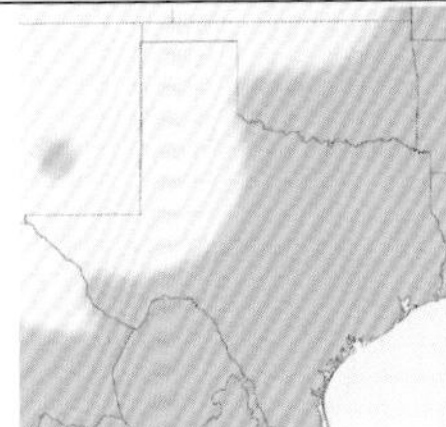

KEY FEATURES

♂—dark with metallic green reflections; base of forewing red, base of hindwing dark with red veins, rest of wings variable

♀—tan or brown with metallic green reflections on thorax and abdomen; wings smoky brown

S5

Size
39–53 mm
(1.5–2.1 in)

Jan
Feb
Mar
Apr
May
Jun
Jul
Aug
Sep
Oct
Nov
Dec

IDENTIFICATION This is a large dark species with variable wing markings. Males have a dark thorax and abdomen with metallic green stripes occasionally visible on the thorax. Forewings have at least some red basally, and coloration of the hindwings can vary from dark brown wing patches basally with reddish or white veins to entirely dark wings, sometimes with extensive clear areas in the middle and toward the outer edge. Wings have dark pterostigmas and nearly always have dark tips. Females often have more green on the thorax than males. Wings are generally smoky throughout, though not as dark as males, and usually with a pale pterostigma that darkens with age. Lower legs and the underside of the abdomen are dark in both sexes.

SIMILAR SPECIES American Rubyspots have bright red wing patches basally in both wings and never have dark wing tips. The thorax and abdomen are darker in the Smoky Rubyspot and lack extensive pale markings on the underside of the abdomen. The Canyon Rubyspot lacks a pterostigma. Ebony Jewelwings have black wings, but their wings are much broader.

TEXAS STATUS Common. Widespread except in northwest Texas.

HABITAT Slow, shaded streams and rivers with aquatic vegetation for egg laying.

DISCUSSION Mark and recapture experiments have shown that wing color in males does not change over time. Individuals recaptured up to 35 days later showed no change in the amount of dark color in the wings. All forms are present throughout the season, but those with darker wings are more evident later in the season. Both sexes perch horizontally on vegetation along the shore, preferring higher perches than the less wary American Rubyspot. Females invite mating by hovering and reject males by spreading the wings and bending the abdomen upward.

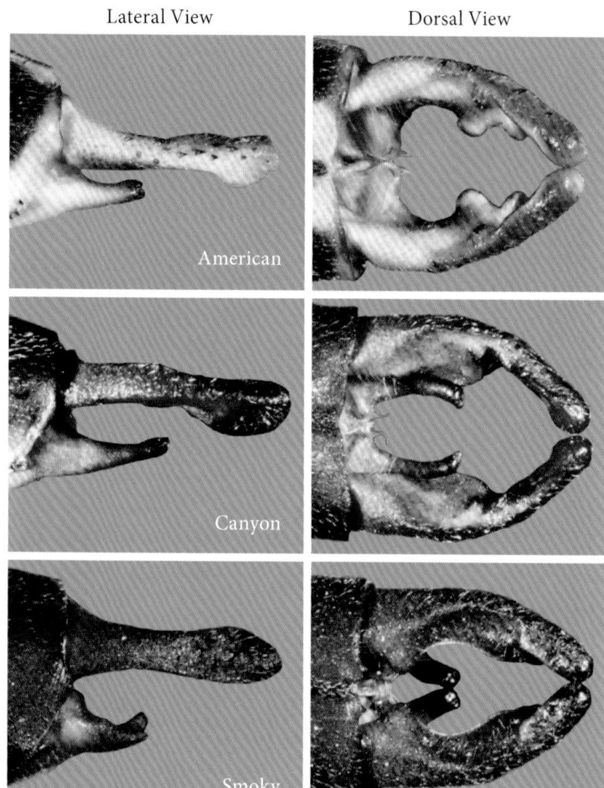
Lateral View
Dorsal View
American
Canyon
Smoky

Smoky Rubyspot

Great Spreadwing

Spreadwings
Family Lestidae

Spreadwings can generally be recognized by their relatively large and stocky bodies coupled with their unique resting posture. They typically perch with their clear wings slightly apart (at a 45° angle) and their bodies angled obliquely on vertical or occasionally horizontal stems. They are nearly always found around standing bodies of water. The eyes and face, especially in males, are blue; the terminal abdominal segments are generally covered with a white pruinescence. The thorax and abdomen are generally metallic bronze or green. Females usually lay eggs in vegetation just above the waterline, while in tandem.

STREAM SPREADWINGS, GENUS *ARCHILESTES*. This is a small group of rather large damselflies—only 2 species are found in North America. The California Spreadwing (*A. californicus*) is found only in the Southwest. The larger Great Spreadwing is much more widely distributed, occurring from southern Canada to Venezuela.

POND SPREADWINGS, GENUS *LESTES*. Together, the metallic green and bronze colors, elongated abdomen, and distinctive perching habit serve as good field-recognition characteristics for this group. Males have a characteristic blue face and eyes and often develop a distinct pruinose appearance toward the rear of the head, on the thorax, between the wings, and posteriorly on S9–10. Females have brown eyes and are generally less pruinose and paler in color. The thoracic color pattern is often characteristic and useful for making identifications in the field. In Texas, most species undergo an egg diapause and hatch in response to the warming temperatures of the approaching spring.

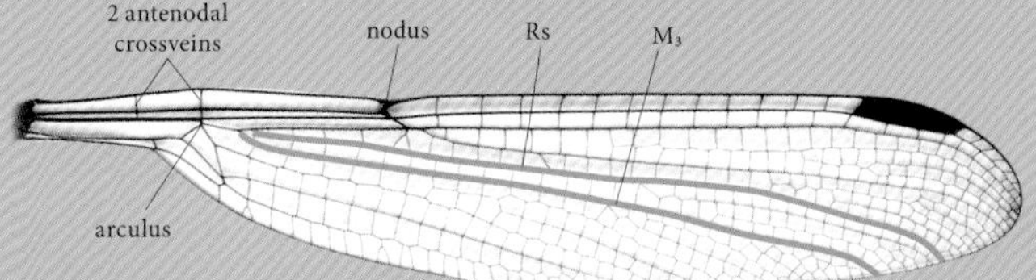

Spreadwing damselfly forewing showing characteristic venation. The Rs and M_3 veins arise closer to the arculus than to the nodus.

GREAT SPREADWING

Archilestes grandis (ark-i-LEST-ēs GRAN-diss)

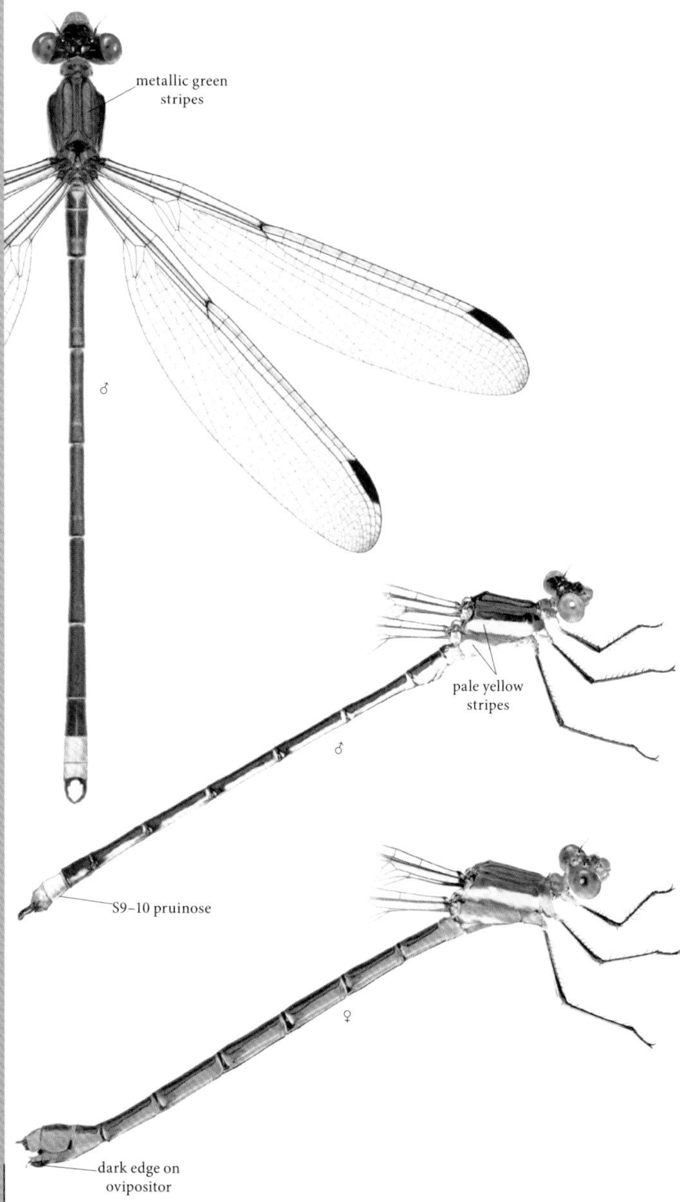

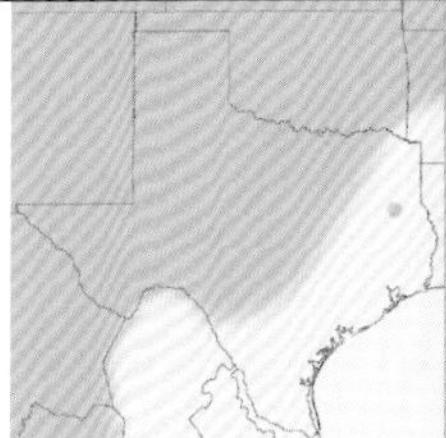

KEY FEATURES

♂—thorax with metallic green stripe dorsally and pale yellow stripes laterally; S9–10 white with pruinosity

♀—thorax with metallic green stripe dorsally and pale yellow stripes laterally

S5

Size
50–62 mm
(2.0–2.4 in)

Jan Feb Mar Apr May Jun Jul Aug Sep Oct Nov Dec

IDENTIFICATION The largest damselfly in Texas and the United States, it is easily recognized by its size and distinctive thoracic pattern. The thorax is brown with broad pale yellow stripes laterally followed by a thinner bronze-green stripe just above and below the shoulder line. The eyes and labrum are blue, and the abdomen is dark with the last two segments pruinose. Females have the same thoracic pattern and dark abdomen, but lack pruinosity at the tip. Wings in both sexes are clear or smoky, often with dark tips.

SIMILAR SPECIES Pond spreadwings (*Lestes* spp.) are smaller, and though they may superficially resemble Great Spreadwings, none possess the distinctive thoracic pattern of this species.

TEXAS STATUS Widespread. Found from the Blackland Prairie west.

HABITAT Small permanent ponds or streams with moderate flow.

DISCUSSION This species was known only from the southwest United States until the 1920s, but it has since undergone a dramatic range expansion northward. It now occurs as far northeast as western New England. Males perch over water while defending small territories. Neither males nor females exhibit any type of courtship behavior, and unreceptive females show no refusal signs; rather, they simply leave the water or escape by rapid flight.

Great Spreadwing nymph.

Lestes alacer (LES-tēs AL-a-sir)

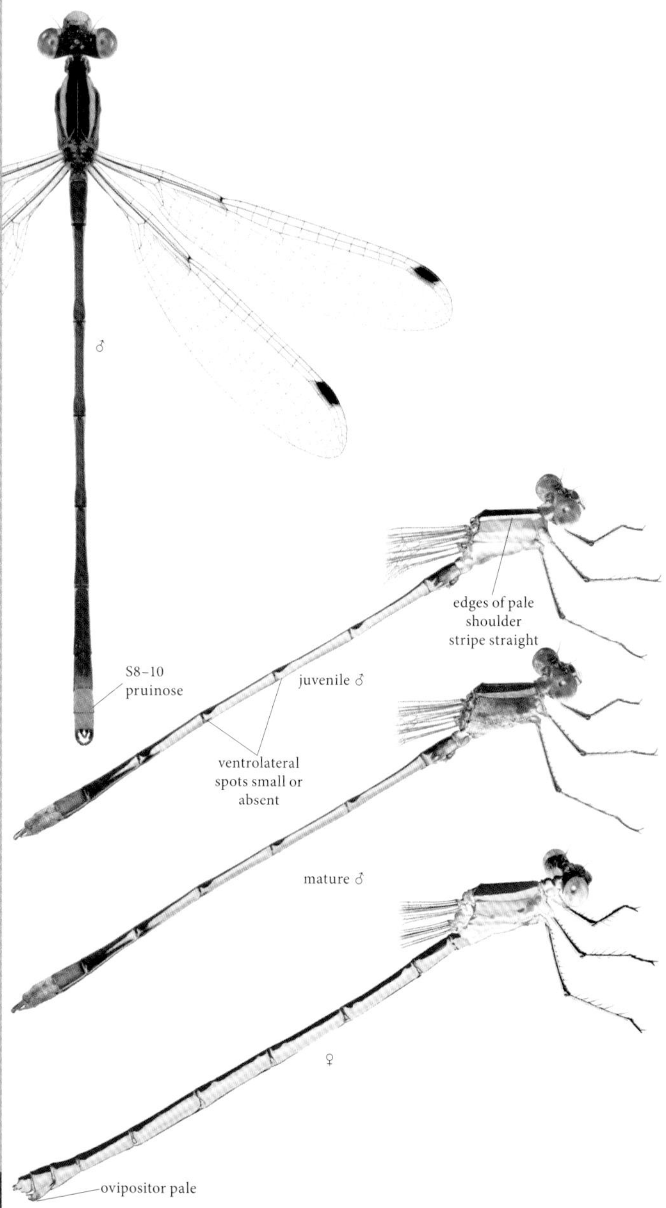

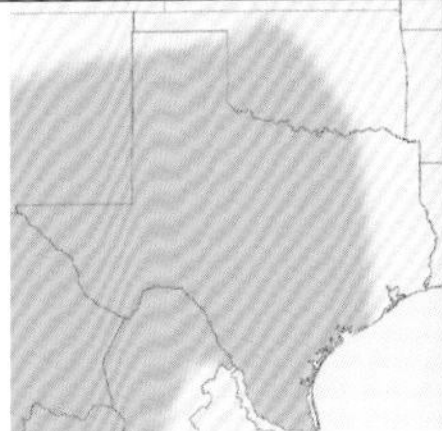

KEY FEATURES

♂—median black stripe on thorax; blue or yellow shoulder stripe; abdomen largely pale on sides; S8–10 pruinose

♀—median black stripe on thorax; pale shoulder stripe as in male; abdomen pale on sides; ovipositor mostly pale

Size
34–45 mm
(1.3–1.8 in)

Jan Feb Mar Apr May Jun Jul Aug Sep Oct Nov Dec

IDENTIFICATION Males have blue eyes and a blue face with a dark head. The top of the thorax is bronze or black with a pale blue or yellow shoulder stripe. The whitish lower thorax becomes dark and pruinose with age. The abdomen is slender, especially toward the middle. Ventrolateral spots are scarce, usually absent, on S3–5. S1–2 and 8–10 become pruinose along with ventrolateral spots on S6–7. Females are colored similarly to males, but the thorax remains pale laterally. The posterolateral margin of the ovipositor basal plate is acutely angulate. Tips of the valves of the ovipositor usually extend to a point between posterior margin of S10 and the paraprocts.

SIMILAR SPECIES The Southern Spreadwing is darker overall and has a more robust build. The abdomen in particular is thicker, S3–5 have distinct dark ventrolateral spots, and S10 is not entirely pruinose. Both sexes of the Southern Spreadwing have more irregular pale shoulder stripes. Both sexes of the Lyre-tipped Spreadwing are darker, more robust, and have metallic green dorsally on the abdomen.

TEXAS STATUS Locally common. Absent in the eastern part of the state.

HABITAT Still, slow-moving waters, including temporary and permanent ponds and spring seeps. Occasionally found in more saline waters.

DISCUSSION Can be found year-round in the southern part of the state. Prefers laying eggs in rushes well above the waterline in irregular vertical rows.

Lestes australis (LES-tēs awl-STRAL-iss)

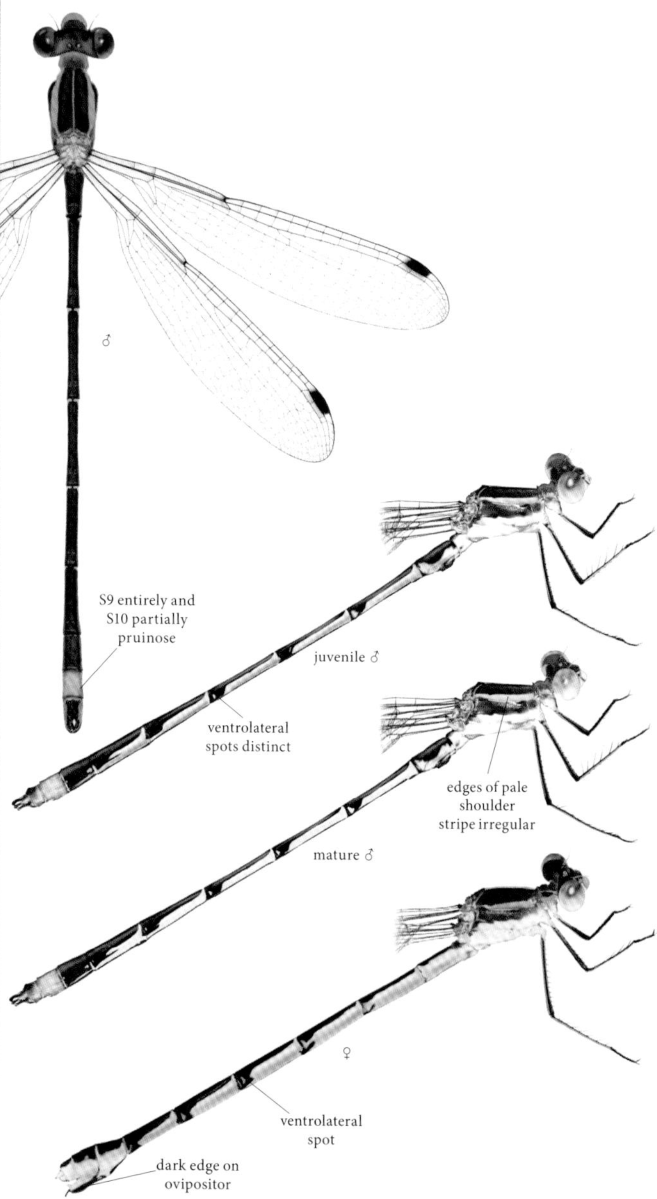

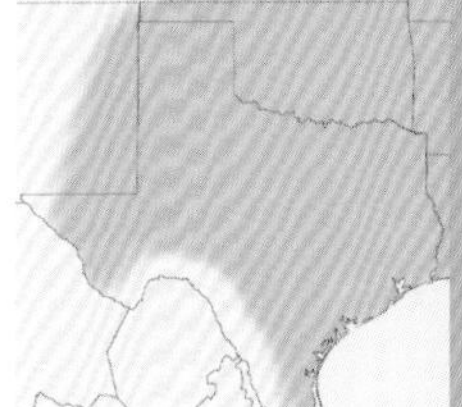

KEY FEATURES

♂—yellow or blue shoulder stripe with irregular sides; dark ventrolateral spots on S3–5; S9 and some of S10 pruinose dorsally

♀—pale shoulder stripe with irregular sides; dark ventrolateral spots on S3–5; lower half of ovipositor dark

Size
36–46 mm
(1.4–1.8 in)

Jan
Feb
Mar
Apr
May
Jun
Jul
Aug
Sep
Oct
Nov
Dec

IDENTIFICATION Males have blue eyes and a blue face, and the top of the head has coppery reflections. The thorax is dark with a tan shoulder stripe that quickly turns blue-green with age; the lower sides of thorax are whitish. Thorax may become dark in older individuals. Stout abdomen is dark, coppery brown with distinct ventrolateral dark spots on S3–5, most pronounced distally. S9 is completely pruinose in older males; S10 is variable, but generally not entirely pruinose. Females are similar to males, with brown eyes, a coppery thorax, and a pale brown shoulder stripe. Females lack pruinosity on the abdomen, but the rear of the head becomes pruinose. Small dark spot present ventrolaterally on S3–7. S8–10 is uniformly pale laterally. Ovipositor is pale in upper half with dark edge on lower half.
SIMILAR SPECIES Female Slender Spreadwing is larger and has white veins at wing tip. The Plateau Spreadwing is not as dark, has a thinner abdomen, and generally lacks distinctive ventrolateral spots on S3–5; older males have S9–10 completely pruinose. The abdomen of the Lyre-tipped Spreadwing is metallic green dorsally.
TEXAS STATUS Widespread. Found commonly statewide except along much of the Rio Grande.
HABITAT Still, slow-moving permanent ponds, marshes, and lakes with emergent vegetation. Also found in temporary ponds.
DISCUSSION Formerly considered a subspecies of the Northern Spreadwing (*L. disjunctus*). Males are not territorial, and individuals are often seen a considerable distance, several hundred meters, from any body of water. Mating activity tends to peak in late afternoon, around five. Egg laying occurs in tandem in green stems of cattails and similar plants, above the waterline. Females usually lay over 100 eggs. Nymphs can tolerate considerable salinity and may be a common inhabitant of saline lakes.

RAINPOOL SPREADWING

Lestes forficula (LES-tēs for-FIC-ū-lə)

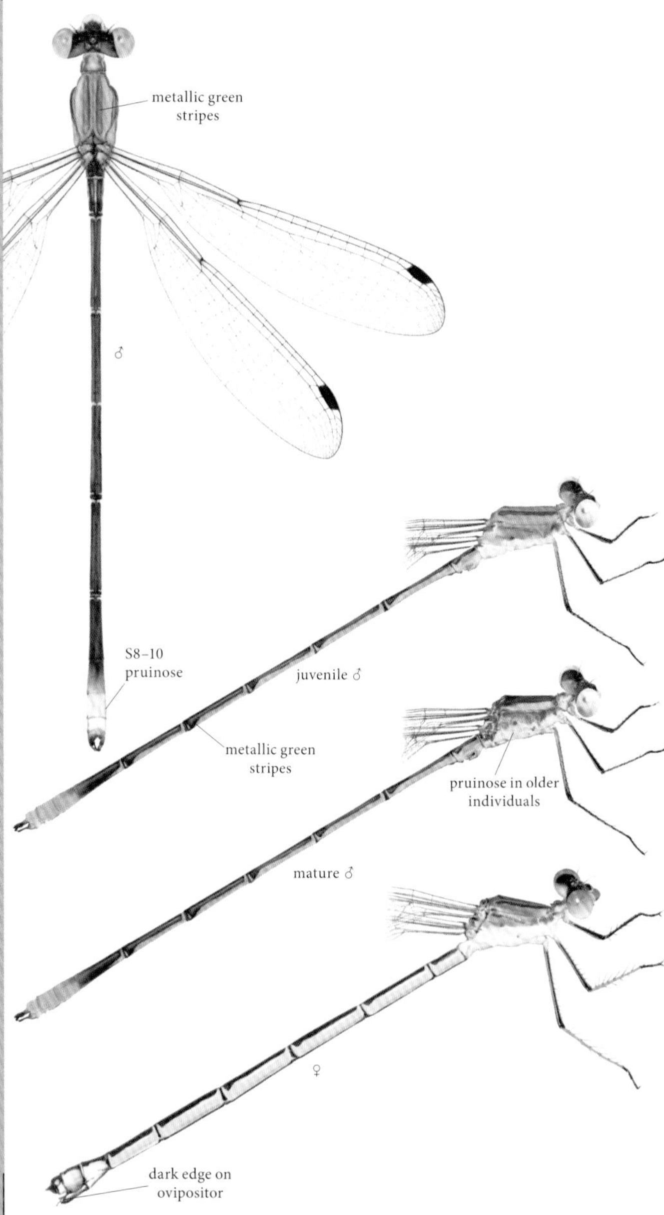

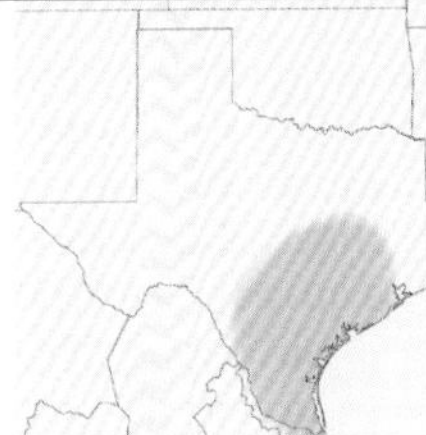

KEY FEATURES

♂—paired metallic green stripes dorsally on thorax; green dorsally on abdomen; S8–10 and sides of thorax pruinose

♀—paired metallic green stripes dorsally on thorax; green dorsally on abdomen; lower edge of ovipositor dark

S4

Size
35–43 mm
(1.4–1.7 in)

Jan Feb Mar Apr May Jun Jul Aug Sep Oct Nov Dec

IDENTIFICATION Males have the typical blue eyes and face. Thorax is pale blue with metallic green stripe on either side of middorsal line. Second, thinner, less prominent green stripe present below shoulder stripe. Upper green stripe is always present and widens slightly posteriorly. Lower stripe often obscured by heavy pruinosity that envelops lower portions of thorax and S1. Legs pale with dark stripe on femora and front tibia. Abdomen is metallic green dorsally. S9 is always pruinose; S8 and/or S10 are usually pruinose. General coloration of female head and thorax tan with same pattern of metallic green stripes as male. Rest of abdomen similar to male except S7–S10. These segments are dark brown dorsally, becoming paler laterally with some pruinosity. Basal plate of the ovipositor is produced into long, acuminate tooth.

SIMILAR SPECIES The Swamp and Elegant Spreadwings are both larger than the Rainpool Spreadwing and have almost completely metallic green thoraxes.

TEXAS STATUS Uncommon. May be locally abundant in the southern and eastern portions of the state.

HABITAT Permanent and temporary ponds, pools, and other standing bodies of water, as well as slow reaches of streams, with heavy emergent vegetation.

DISCUSSION Females lay eggs both accompanied and unaccompanied by males, in vertical sedges 8–10 inches above the water surface. Females also lay eggs at the water surface and sometimes submerge their abdomens. This tropical species spends the dry season away from water and may overwinter the same way in Texas, returning to ponds after spring rains. It appears to be expanding its range northward and eastward, having recently turned up all along the Gulf coast in Louisiana, Mississippi, Alabama, and Florida. It is likely to expand into East Texas as well.

Lestes tenuatus (LES-tēs ten-ū-WĀT-us)

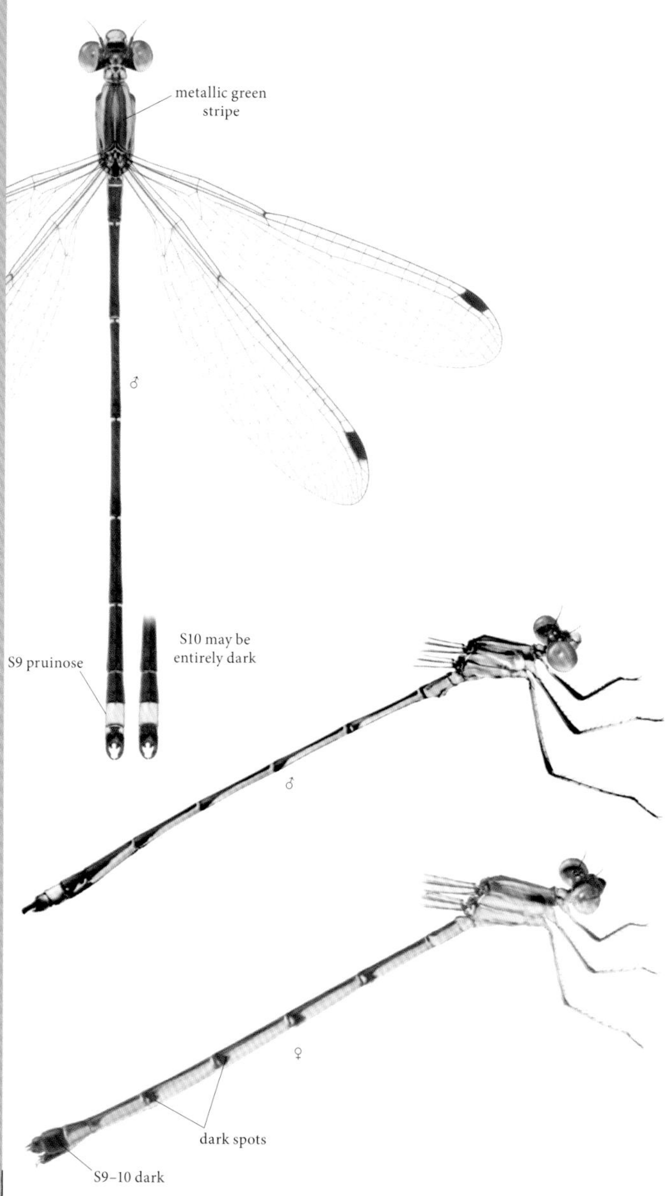

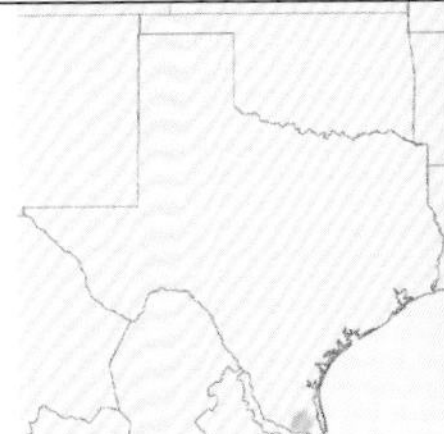

KEY FEATURES

♂—thorax largely bright blue with broad, dark, metallic green middorsal and shoulder stripes; S9 pruinose

♀—thorax either like male or pale blue with metallic brown stripes; most of S8 and all of S9–10 dark brown

S2

Size
39–44 mm
(1.5–1.7 in)

Jan Feb Mar Apr May Jun Jul Aug Sep Oct Nov Dec

IDENTIFICATION Males have blue face and eyes. Top of head is dark with metallic green reflections. Rear of head is pale. Thorax is blue with broad brown middorsal and shoulder stripe when juvenile, becoming metallic green in older individuals. Metallic green middorsal stripe is divided by a brown ridge. Abdomen is dark metallic brown or green above except for narrow blue basal rings. Sides of abdomen are pale with a dark apical spot. S9–10 are largely dark, with S9 becoming pruinose in older individuals. Female similar to male, but generally not as bright blue, and dark thoracic and abdominal stripes are metallic brown. Legs pale in both sexes, with dark stripe on femora and front tibia only. In older females, most of S8 and all of S9–10, dark. S10 may be pale above in juveniles. Posterior margin of ovipositor basal plate is smoothly rounded.

SIMILAR SPECIES The Rainpool Spreadwing has a metallic green stripe on either side of middorsal line, but the shoulder stripe, if present, is much narrower. Male Chalky Spreadwings lack metallic green stripes. In females of Chalky and Rainpool Spreadwings, S8–10 are largely pale, and the basal plate of the ovipositor has a distinct tooth. Male Southern and Plateau Spreadwings lack the metallic green stripe and show at least some pruinosity on S10.

TEXAS STATUS Rare. Only known from the Santa Ana National Wildlife Refuge in the Lower Rio Grande Valley.

HABITAT Wooded pools and ponds.

DISCUSSION This tropical species occurs as far south as Venezuela. Previously only known from southern Florida within the United States, in September 2008 a population was discovered at Santa Ana National Wildlife Refuge.

Lestes inaequalis (LES-tēs in-ē-QUAL-iss)

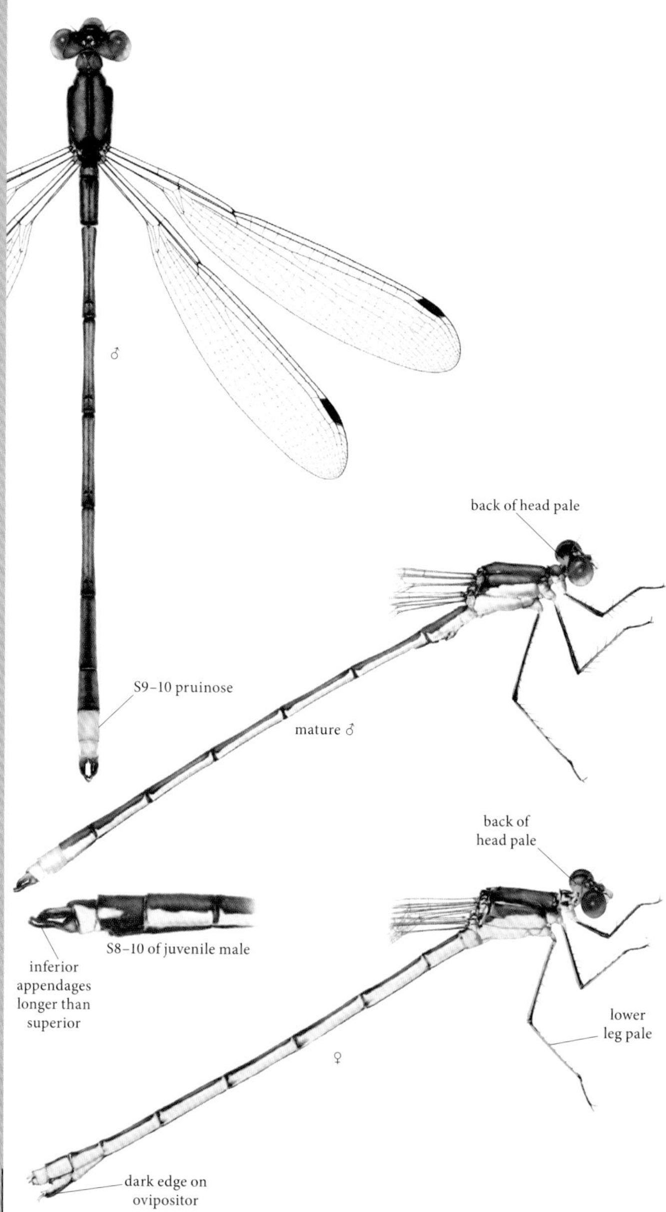

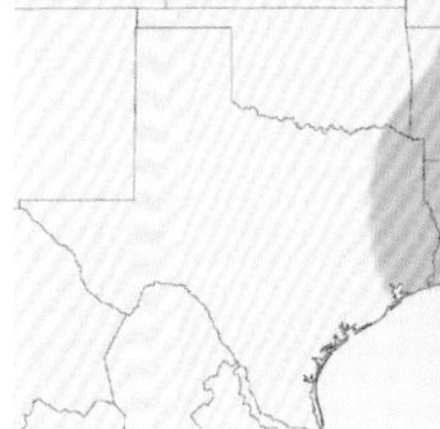

KEY FEATURES

♂—long abdomen; metallic green thorax and abdomen; side of thorax yellow; S9–10 pruinose; inferior terminal appendages longer than superior

♀—long abdomen; back of head pale; lower part of legs pale; lower edge of ovipositor dark

S3

Size
45–60 mm
(1.8–2.4 in)

Jan Feb Mar Apr May Jun Jul Aug Sep Oct Nov Dec

IDENTIFICATION A striking species with a long abdomen. Males have a blue face and blue eyes on top, contrasting with green below. The top of the head is metallic green, and the back is pale yellow. The thorax is metallic green on top and pale yellow on the sides. Juvenile males have a thin pale middorsal and shoulder stripe. The legs are darker above and pale below. The abdomen is green on top except for S9–10, which becomes pruinose. In males, inferior terminal appendages are longer than superior ones. Females are similar to males, but the metallic green on the thorax is less extensive, revealing more brown or bronze areas. The brown middorsal and shoulder stripes are more distinct. The abdomen is metallic green to brownish on top, contrasting with yellow laterally. The upper half of the ovipositor is pale, contrasting with the darker lower half. The posterolateral margin of the ovipositor basal plate is truncate and lacks a tooth.

SIMILAR SPECIES In Swamp Spreadwings, the legs and back of head are dark, and the female has a pale ovipositor. Slender Spreadwing males don't develop white pruinescence on S8–10, females have a broad pale shoulder stripe, and both sexes have pale veins at the wing tips. The Rainpool Spreadwing is smaller and has metallic green stripes on the thorax.

TEXAS STATUS Rare. Found in the eastern part of the state.

HABITAT Canopy-covered permanent ponds, lakes, slow-moving streams, and marshes with plenty of emergent vegetation and heavily wooded shorelines.

DISCUSSION The diet of this large species includes smaller damselflies. They are easily disturbed and are generally found perching in shady areas during the heat of the day. They have the unique behavior of laying eggs in tandem on the upper surface of lily pads.

Lestes rectangularis (LES-tēs wreck-tang-ū-LAIR-iss)

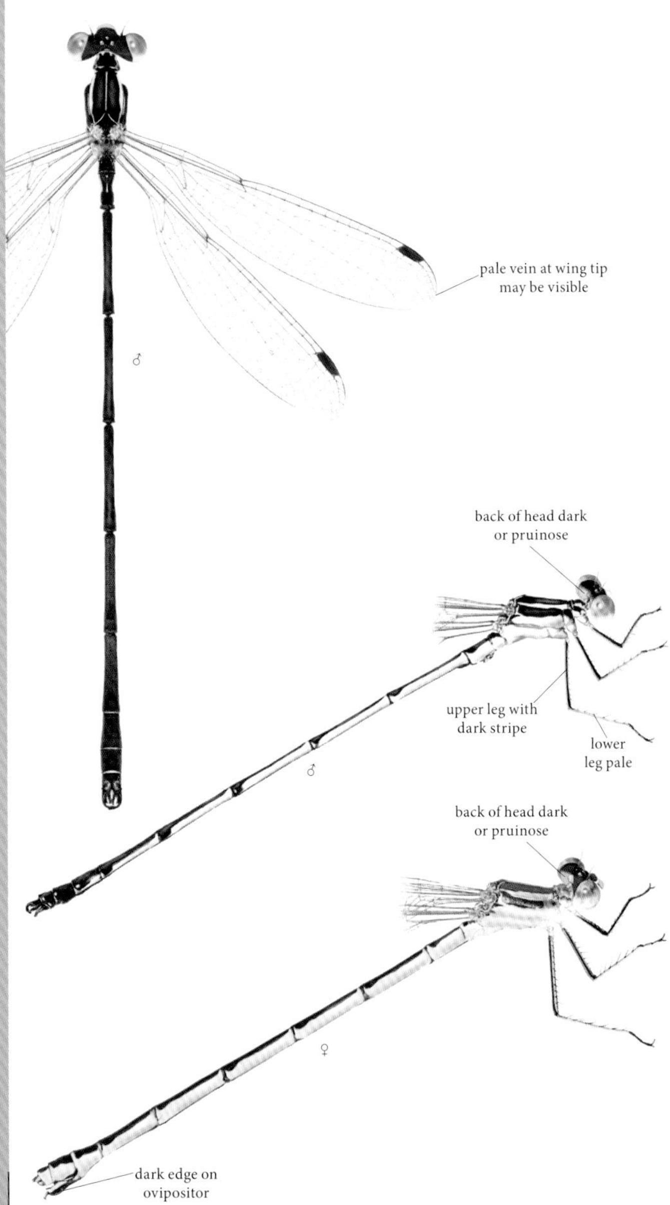

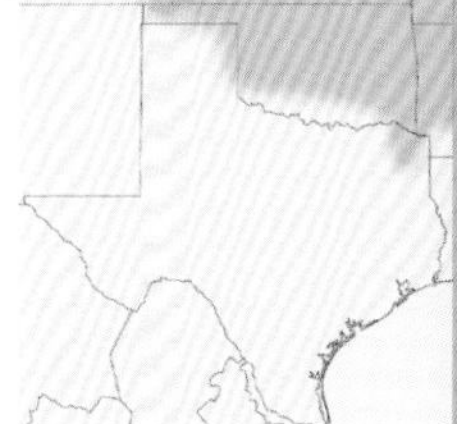

KEY FEATURES

♂—long slender abdomen; blue or green shoulder stripe; no pruinosity on abdomen

♀—long abdomen; back of head dark or with pruinescence; dark stripe on upper leg; lower edge of ovipositor dark

S2

Size
37–52 mm
(1.5–2.1 in)

Jan Feb Mar Apr May Jun Jul Aug Sep Oct Nov Dec

IDENTIFICATION A long slender species, as its common name suggests; it has an unusually long abdomen. Males have a blue face and blue eyes. Rear of the head is black, becoming pruinose at maturity. Thorax is dark bronze with a pale green or blue shoulder stripe. Lower part of the thorax is pale white or yellow. Long abdomen gives an overall short-winged appearance. It is brown dorsally and lacks pruinescence on S8–10. Females are similar, with a pale shoulder stripe that turns blue. Upper legs in both sexes have a dark line on their outer surface and pale lower legs. Wing tips have a white vein that is usually more prominent in males. The ovipositor is pale on its upper half and dark on its lower half. This is the only male spreadwing in Texas with paraprocts distinctly and strongly curved downward.
SIMILAR SPECIES Southern Spreadwing females have dark tarsi and shorter, stockier abdomens. Elegant and Swamp Spreadwing males have a white pruinescence on S9–10. The Rainpool Spreadwing has a shorter abdomen and one or two metallic green thoracic stripes. The Slender Spreadwing is the only species in Texas with pale veins in the wing tips.
TEXAS STATUS Rare. Two populations known along western edge of species range.
HABITAT Lakes or ponds with regular shade and dense emergent vegetation; often found in sand-bottomed lakes.
DISCUSSION Individuals are most active in midafternoon and females will lay eggs in tandem or alone, usually in cattail leaves. They are reluctant to fly over open water, and the female never submerges herself during egg laying. Adults are most abundant in shade and readily take shelter in thick vegetation during the heat of the day.

CHALKY SPREADWING

Lestes sigma (LES-tēs SIG-mə)

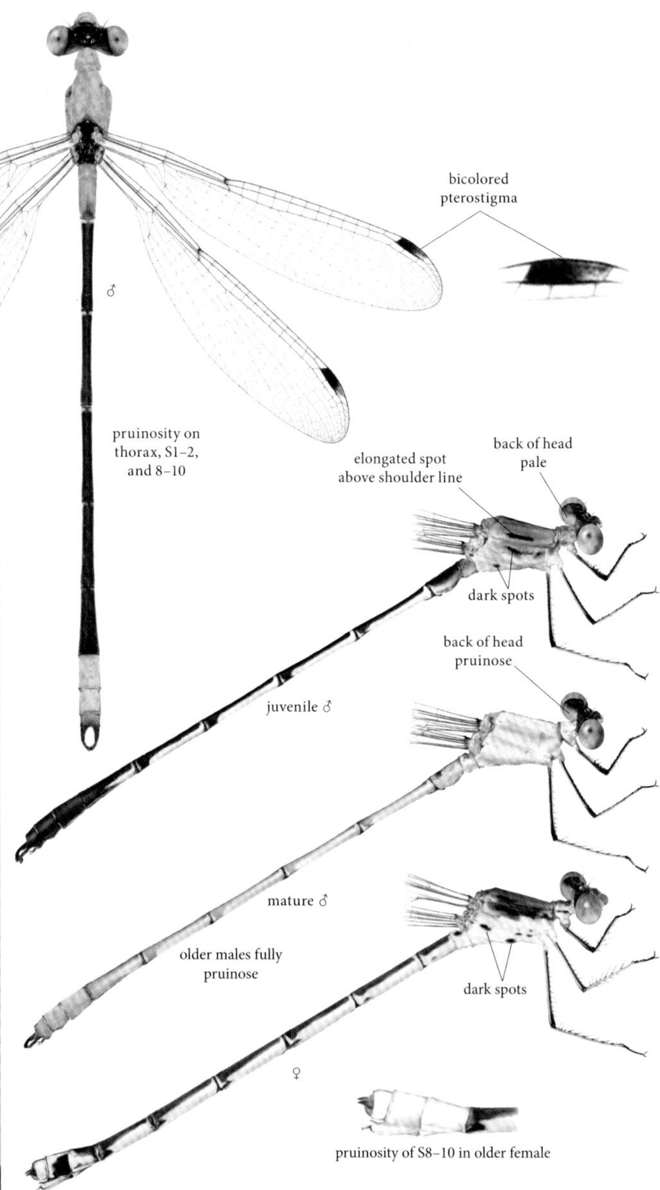

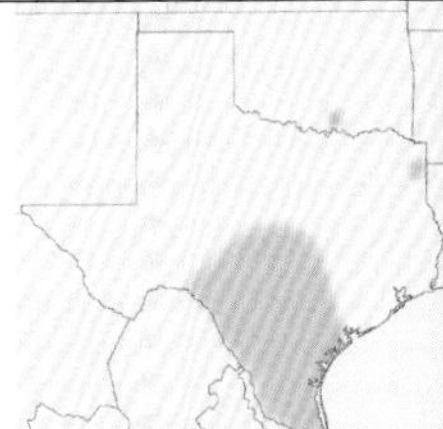

KEY FEATURES

♂—juvenile: tan with several black spots laterally on thorax; older: may be entirely powder white

♀—dark spots visible laterally on thorax; abdomen with extensive black markings laterally, but becoming obscured by pruinosity on S8–10

S4

Size
39–47 mm
(1.5–1.9 in)

Jan Feb Mar Apr May Jun Jul Aug Sep Oct Nov Dec

IDENTIFICATION Males have extensive blue on the face and blue eyes. Rear of the head is pale in juveniles, becoming pruinose and black with maturity. Thorax is tan with extensive black markings laterally and ventrally, and an elongated spot above the shoulder line. In older males, these markings become obscured, and the entire thorax is pruinose. Abdomen is dark, with S8–10 black. Pruinosity begins on S1–2 and 8–10 and eventually envelops the entire body in older individuals. Females are similar to males, but generally paler, including S8–10. Lateral areas of thorax and S8–10 become pruinose with age. Pterostigma is bicolored in both sexes and most visible in juveniles. The basal plate of the ovipositor has a distinct posterolateral acuminate tooth. The male inferior appendages are distinctly sigmoid in form.

SIMILAR SPECIES The Rainpool Spreadwing has a metallic green stripe in the shoulder area. The Lyre-tipped Spreadwing is shorter and stockier; the thorax is bronze with a pale green or blue shoulder stripe and lacks dark markings ventrally on the thorax. Southern and Plateau Spreadwings also have a blue or green shoulder stripe.

TEXAS STATUS Uncommon. Mostly found in the southern portion of the state, where it can be locally abundant.

HABITAT Temporary pools and ponds.

DISCUSSION This species appears to be expanding its range northward at a pretty good rate, becoming more and more common at habitats such as cattle stock tanks.

Lestes unguiculatus (LES-tēs un-guick-ū-LOT-us)

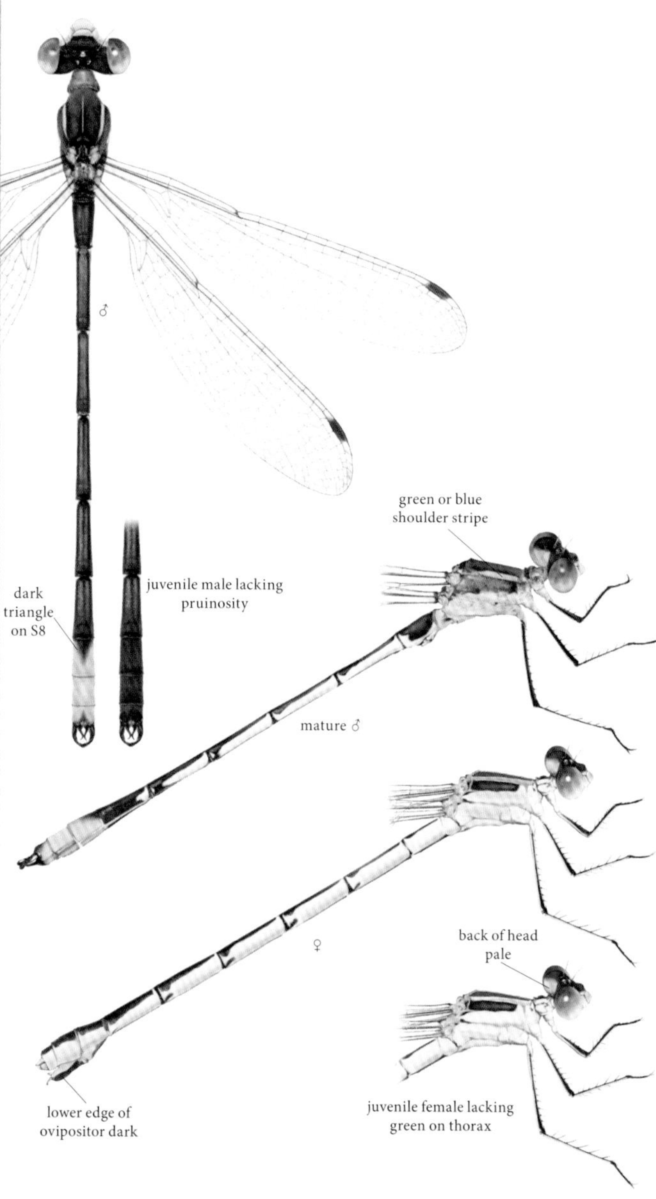

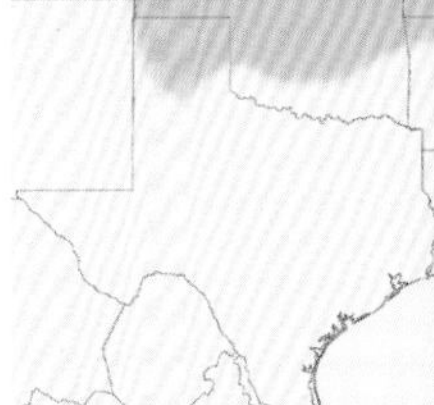

KEY FEATURES

♂—dark triangle on top of S8 in mature males; green or blue shoulder stripe

♀—back of head pale; greenish shoulder stripe usually visible; lower edge of ovipositor dark

S3

Size
31–44 mm
(1.2–1.7 in)

Jan
Feb
Mar
Apr
May
Jun
Jul
Aug
Sep
Oct
Nov
Dec

IDENTIFICATION Male has a blue face and eyes and a bronze head. Thorax is bronze with a green or blue shoulder stripe. Usually, a green stripe is visible laterally, and the lower part of the thorax is pale yellow or white. The abdomen is metallic green dorsally. S1–2 and 8–10 develop white pruinescence, often revealing a dark triangle on the upper surface of S8. Female is similar to male, but the rear of the head and the overall body are generally paler. Ovipositor has a dark lower half and pale upper half. Legs in both sexes are pale with a dark stripe on the outer surface.

SIMILAR SPECIES The Chalky Spreadwing has dark marks laterally on the thorax, and older males have an entirely white thorax. Abdomens of Southern and Plateau Spreadwings lack metallic green dorsally. Pruinosity does not form a dark triangle dorsally on S8 in any males of these species. The back of the head in Southern Spreadwing females is dark.

TEXAS STATUS Uncommon. May be locally abundant in the extreme northern portion of the state.

HABITAT Open pools, ponds, sloughs, and slow reaches of streams.

DISCUSSION Unpaired males may shift perch sites for no detectable reason about once a minute. Mating occurs in the early afternoon, between one-thirty and three and involves no courtship or display signals. Mating lasts an average of 25 minutes with pairs often momentarily breaking contact. Egg laying generally occurs in tandem, but may occur alone, and lasts an average of 1.5 hours. Pairs generally lay eggs in vegetation, about 10 inches above the water surface, as is typical in pond spreadwings. Females, however, may submerge themselves for short periods.

SWAMP SPREADWING

Lestes vigilax (LES-tēs VIJ-i-lax)

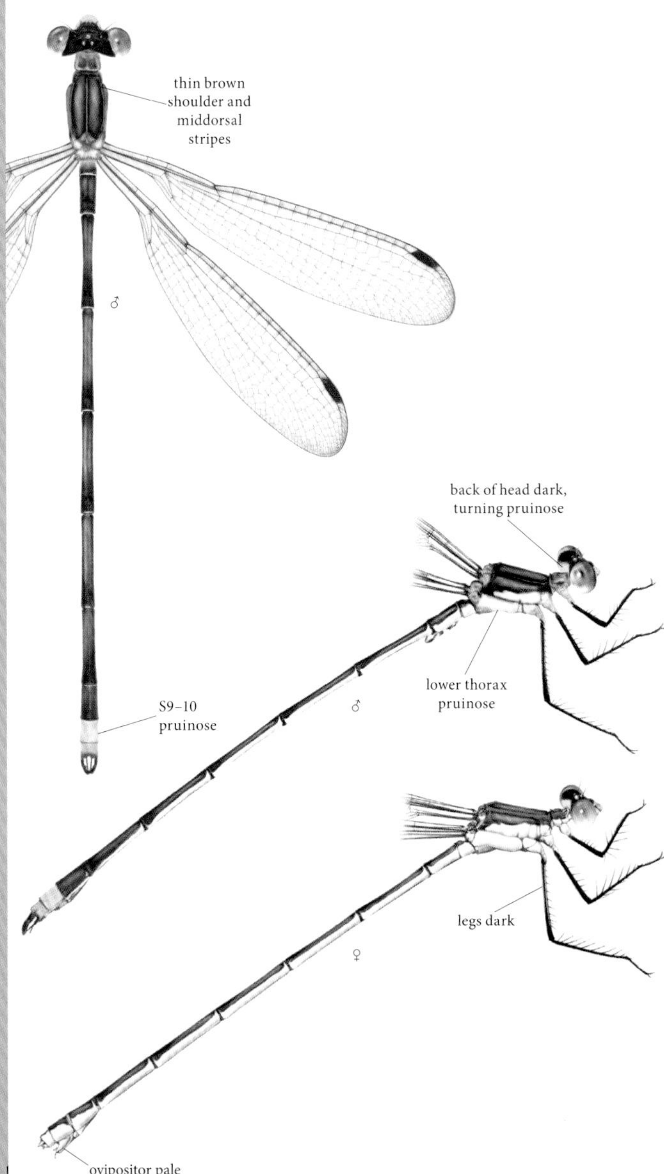

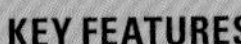

S4

KEY FEATURES

♂—thin brown shoulder and middorsal stripes; lower thorax pruinose; S9–10 pruinose

♀—thin brown shoulder stripe; dark legs; pale ovipositor

Size
43–55 mm
(1.7–2.2 in)

Jan Feb Mar Apr May Jun Jul Aug Sep Oct Nov Dec

IDENTIFICATION Males have a blue face and eyes. The back of the head is dark, becoming pruinose. Thorax is metallic green with brown middorsal and shoulder stripes. Sides of thorax are pale, becoming pruinose white. The top of the abdomen is metallic green; S9 and usually S10 are pruinose in older individuals. Female is similar, but greener overall. Ovipositor is pale. Legs in both sexes are dark. There is a distinct posterolateral tooth on the basal plate of the ovipositor. Older females are dull with brown abdomens and generally appear unremarkable.

SIMILAR SPECIES The Elegant Spreadwing has some pruinosity on S8 and a greener thorax in females; the lower rim of the ovipositor is dark. The Rainpool Spreadwing has a thinner green stripe on the thorax. The Slender Spreadwing has white veins in the wing tips and a bronze thorax; males lack any pruinosity on the tip of the abdomen.

TEXAS STATUS Uncommon. May be locally abundant in the eastern part of the state.

HABITAT Generally found in shaded acidic waters such as bogs, lakes, swamps, oxbows, and slow streams.

DISCUSSION Females lay eggs while in tandem within pickerelweed stems and other emergent vegetation at the water surface, but not in submergent plants. This species, especially males, prefers heavily shaded areas, often with tangled vegetation.

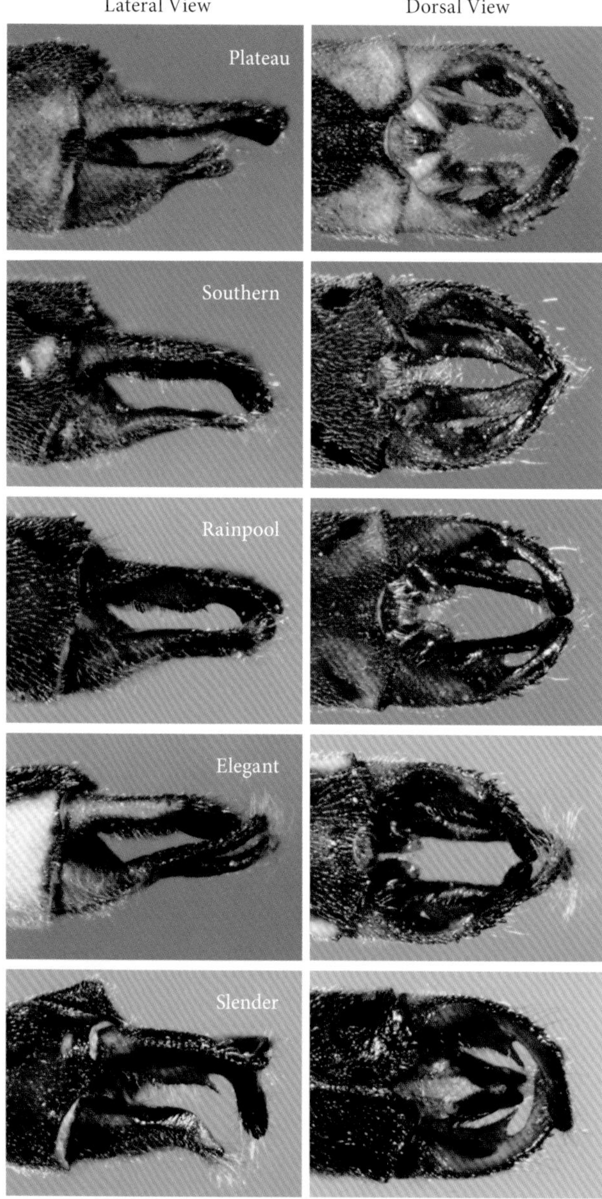
Lateral View
Dorsal View
Plateau
Southern
Rainpool
Elegant
Slender

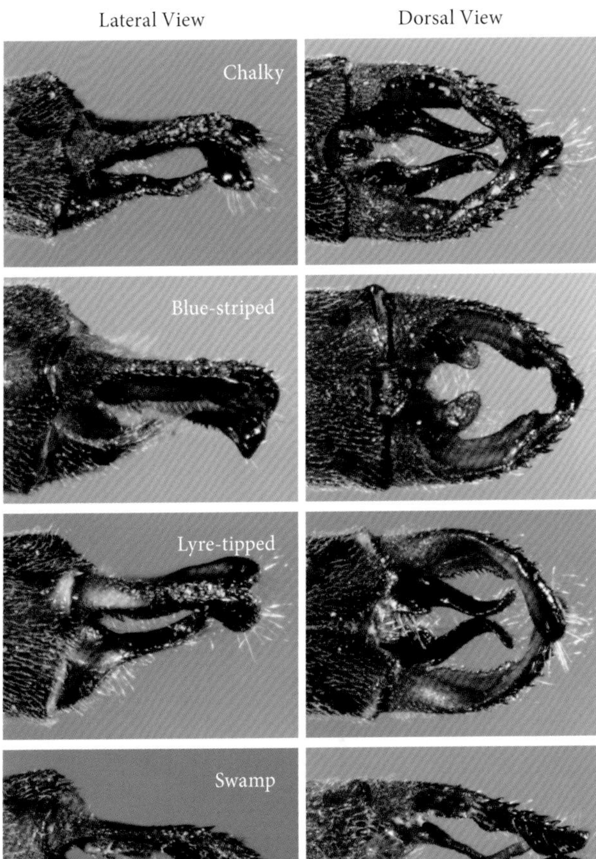
Lateral View
Dorsal View
Chalky
Blue-striped
Lyre-tipped
Swamp

Lateral View

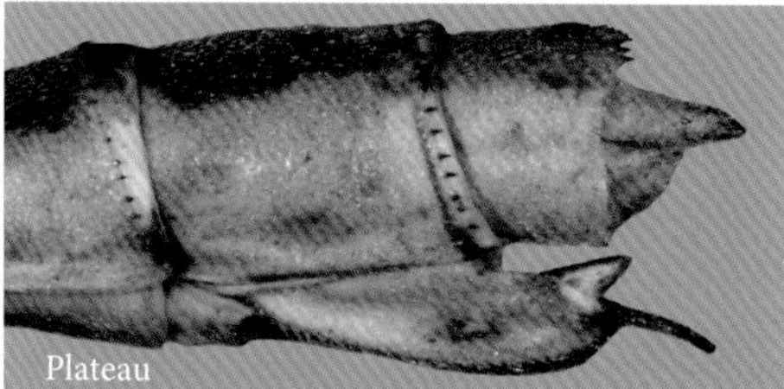
Plateau

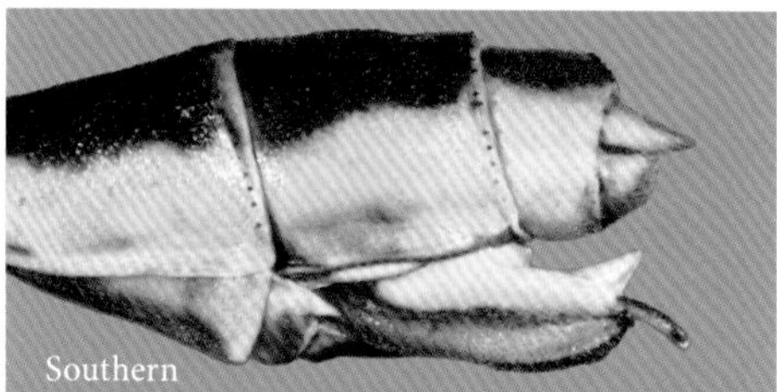
Southern

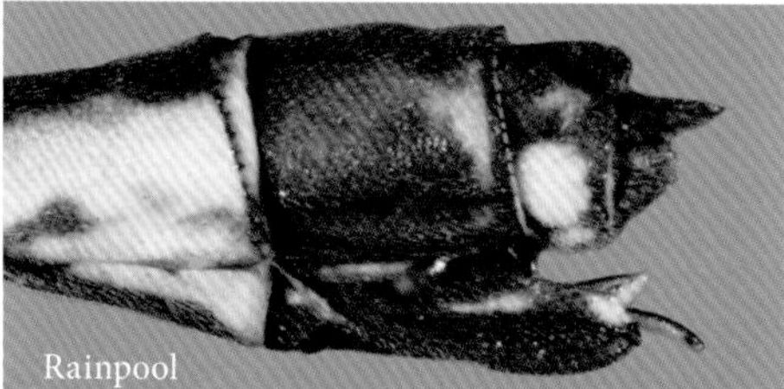
Rainpool

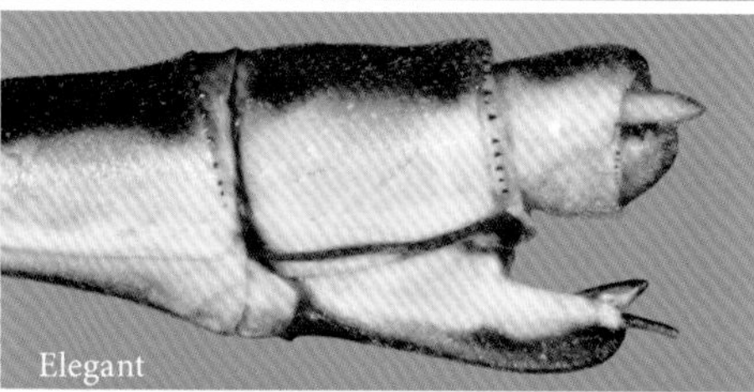
Elegant

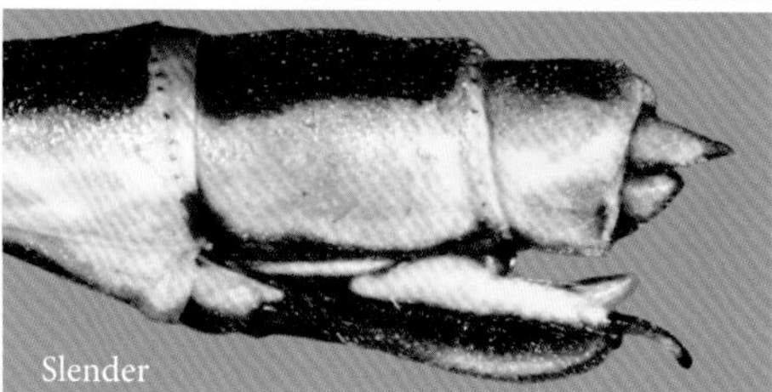
Slender

Lateral View

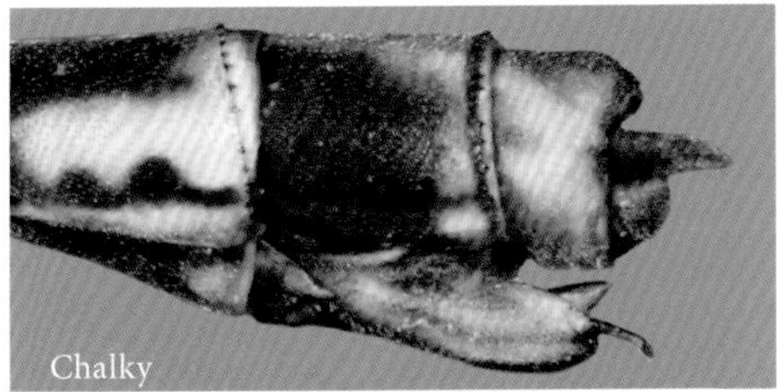
Chalky

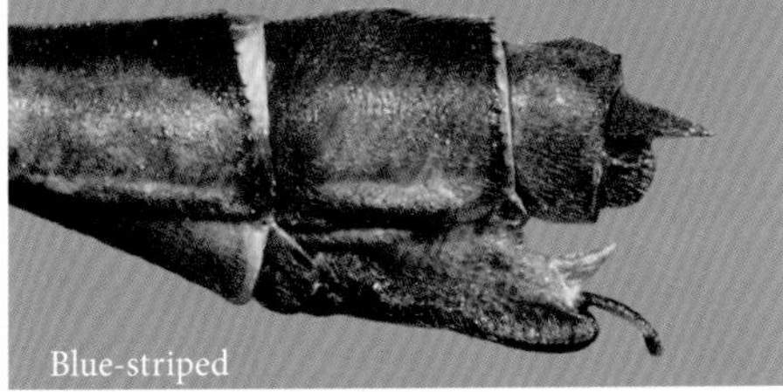
Blue-striped

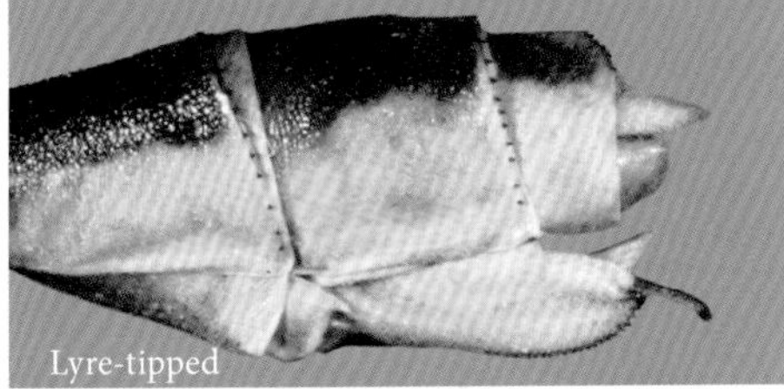
Lyre-tipped

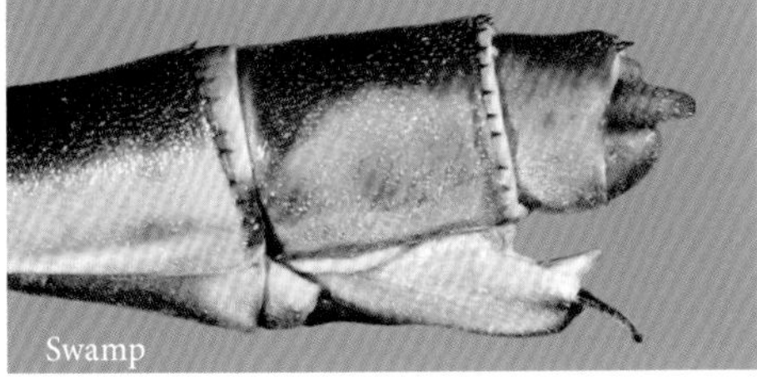
Swamp

Coral-fronted Threadtails

Threadtails
Family Protoneuridae

Threadtails are slender damselflies found in the tropics world-wide. In the Northern Hemisphere, they are mainly restricted to Central America. Only 3 species, in 2 genera, occur in North America, and all are limited to central and southern Texas. Adults and nymphs generally resemble those of the closely related pond damsels. This group has a characteristically reduced venation and a thin elongated abdomen, making the wings look proportionately smaller than in other damselflies. Males of Texas threadtails are generally orange or red, though older Coral-fronted Threadtails are dark with a red face and thoracic stripe.

ROBUST THREADTAILS, GENUS *NEONEURA*. Robust threadtails are a large group of brightly colored damselflies. Two species occur in Texas. Because of their relatively thick abdomens, members of this genus more closely resemble pond damsels than do other threadtails. Nymphs of this group are restricted to running waters, where they may be associated with leaf litter or cling to rocks. Adults prefer shaded areas of floating or emergent vegetation near the nymphal habitat.

SLENDER THREADTAILS, GENUS *PROTONEURA*. A single species of slender threadtails reaches as far north as the Hill Country. Males are readily distinguished in the field by an overall slender stature and a long, thin, characteristically ringed abdomen. Females are more robust and duller in color than males. They inhabit small slow streams, ditches, and seepages as well as larger streams, and are often found on ponds or sheltered lake shores with abundant litter or submerged vegetation.

CORAL-FRONTED THREADTAIL

Neoneura aaroni (nē-ō-NUR-a AIR-un-ī)

♂

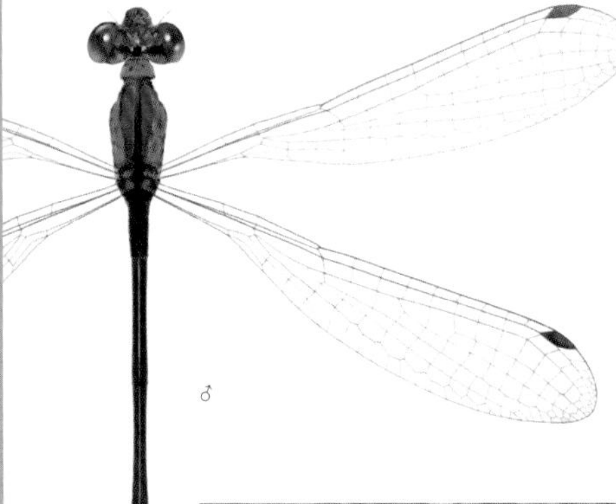

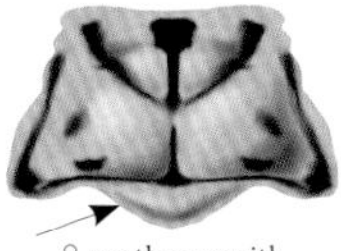

♀ prothorax with
single median flange

Aggregation of egg-laying pairs.

♂

S8–9 dark
on sides
♀
thin dark line

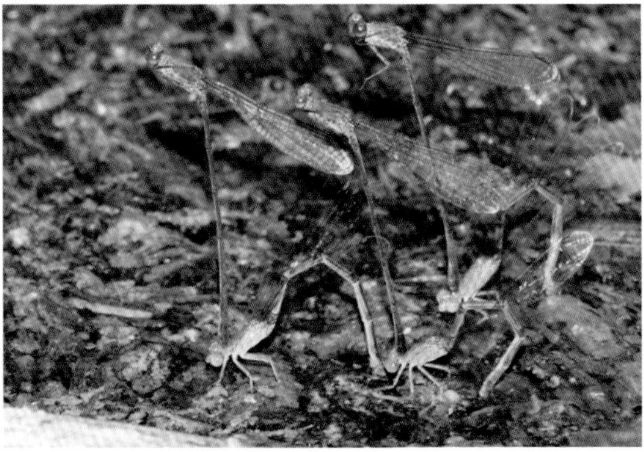

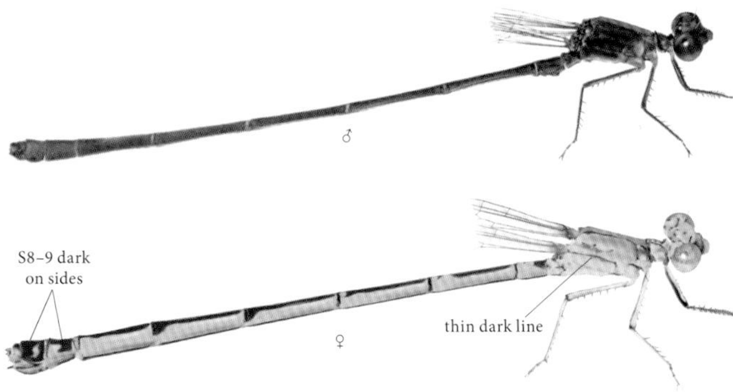

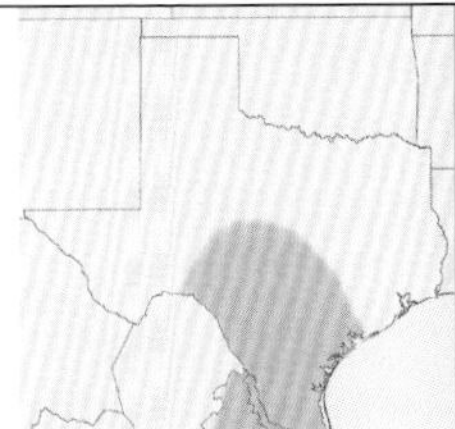

KEY FEATURES

♂—face and top of thorax red-orange; dark legs; thin body with wings proportionately small

♀—thin, pale tan body; legs pale; S8–9 dark laterally

S4

Size
30–37 mm,
1.2–1.5 in

Jan Feb Mar Apr May Jun Jul Aug Sep Oct Nov Dec

IDENTIFICATION Males have a bright red-orange face. Dorsally, the thorax bears two broad red-orange stripes separated by a dark medial line. The rest of the thorax and the back of the head are dark with heavy pruinosity. The upper part of the legs are dark, but become paler at the tibia. The abdomen is dark throughout its length, with no discernible rings or color. Juvenile males have light brown abdomens with dark apical bands on S3–6. S9–10 are nearly all black dorsally. The female's head and thorax are pale brown. Prothorax has a median flange on the posterior margin. Dark middorsal thoracic stripe is broken up and looks like a series of small spots that may be connected. Thin black shoulder stripe may be incomplete. A second thin dark stripe is present lower on the thorax. Legs are pale. S8–9 and sometimes S10 have dark sides.

SIMILAR SPECIES Male Amelia's Threadtails have more extensive orange on the thorax and on the upper surfaces of S1–3. Female Amelia's Threadtails are very similar, but often have a hint of orange visible on top of the head, generally lack extensive dark markings on the thorax and abdomen, and have a pair of dark spots on the margin of the pronotum. Male and female Orange-striped Threadtails have longer, thinner abdomens, more black than orange on the thorax, and pale legs. The male Orange Bluet has an orange stripe across the back of the head, and extensive orange laterally on the thorax; S9 is orange.

TEXAS STATUS Uncommon. Found from Central Texas southward.

HABITAT Protected pools along slow-moving rivers and streams with emergent or floating vegetation or detritus.

DISCUSSION Coral-fronted Threadtails may aggregate while laying eggs in floating vegetation. They fly only a few inches above the water and usually some distance from the shoreline. This species has been documented in Nuevo León, Mexico, but its range is largely restricted to the central and southern parts of Texas.

AMELIA'S THREADTAIL

Neoneura amelia (nē-ō-NUR-a a-MEAL-yə)

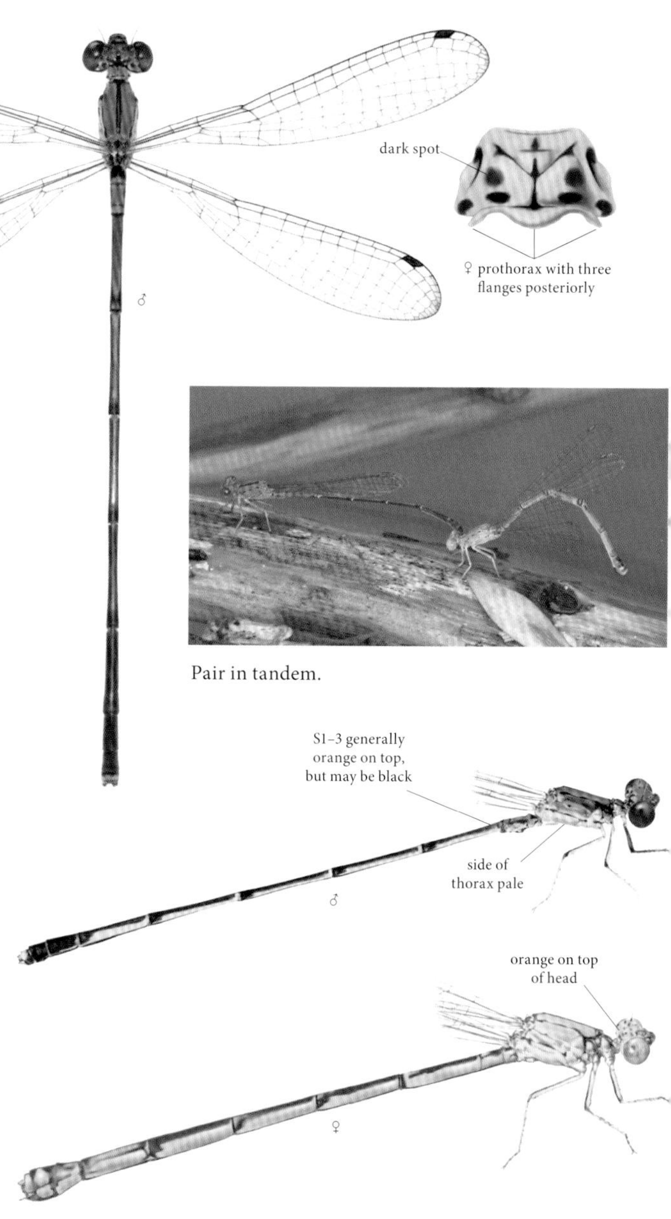

Pair in tandem.

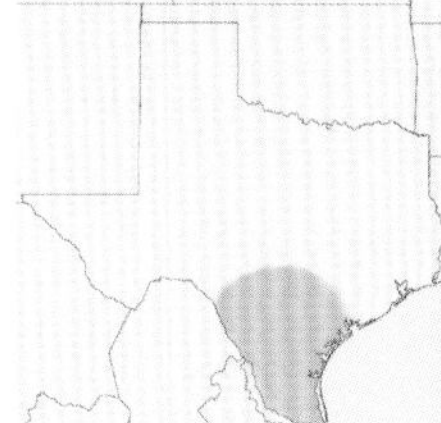

KEY FEATURES

♂—face and top of thorax red-orange; pale legs; sides of thorax pale

♀—thin, pale tan body; top of head with hint of orange; legs pale; S8–9 dark laterally

S3

Size
30–35 mm
(1.2–1.4 in)

Jan Feb Mar Apr May Jun Jul Aug Sep Oct Nov Dec

IDENTIFICATION Males have extensive red-orange on the face and head. Thorax is orange, becoming paler on the sides and has a dark middorsal and shoulder stripe. S1–3 variable, but generally with orange on the upper surface. The rest of the abdomen is black with pale narrow rings on S3–9. Females' head and body are tan with a thin black middorsal stripe, sometimes appearing as a series of dots. There is a thin shoulder stripe. Pronotum has a black spot on each side at the posterior margin and posteriorly projecting flanges at each corner. The abdomen is darker on the upper surface, with dark subapical rings and lateral stripes on the middle segments.

SIMILAR SPECIES Male Coral-fronted Threadtails generally lack orange on the upper surface of S1–3, and the sides of the thorax are dark. Female Coral-fronted Threadtails are very similar, but never have a hint of orange on top of the head and generally lack a pair of spots on the posterior margin of the pronotum. Male and female Orange-striped Threadtails have longer, thinner abdomens, more black than orange on the thorax, and pale legs. The male Orange Bluet has an orange stripe across the back of the head, and extensive orange laterally on the thorax; S9 is orange.

TEXAS STATUS Uncommon. May be locally abundant, especially in the Lower Rio Grande Valley.

HABITAT Prefers protected, well-shaded areas of slow-moving rivers and streams with emergent or floating vegetation, detritus, or debris.

DISCUSSION They perch on emergent vegetation in clear lakes in the immediate vicinity of stream outlets. Males are variable in the degree of black on the head, thorax, and first 3 abdominal segments. I have seen individuals lacking any evidence of orange on the initial abdominal segments. Females are generally not encountered except in mating pairs.

ORANGE-STRIPED THREADTAIL

Protoneura cara (prō-tō-NUR-ə CAR-ə)

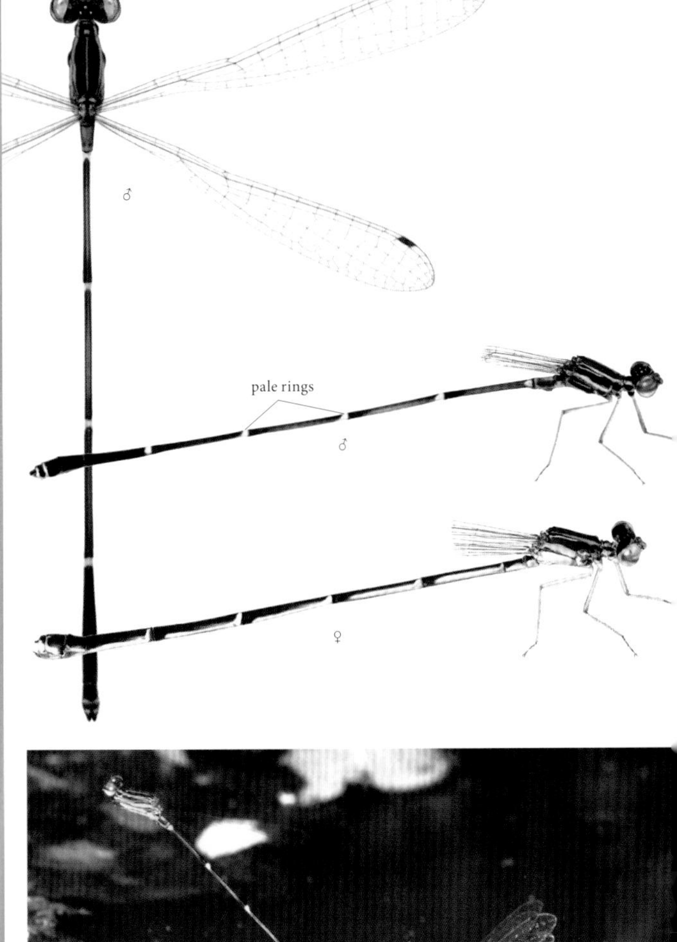

Pair in tandem, laying eggs in floating detritus.

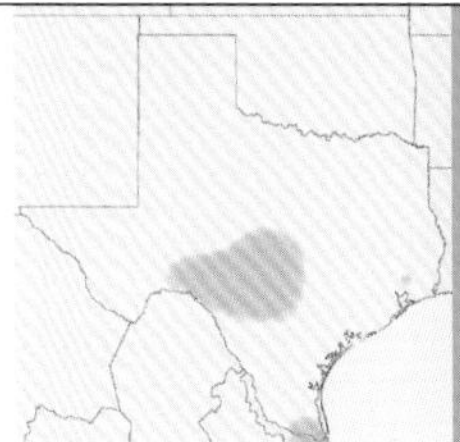

KEY FEATURES

♂—bright orange face and thorax; pale legs; long thin abdomen with pale basal rings and proportionately small wings

♀—bright orange face and thorax; long thin abdomen with pale basal rings

S4

Size
34–38 mm
(1.3–1.5 in)

Jan
Feb
Mar
Apr
May
Jun
Jul
Aug
Sep
Oct
Nov
Dec

IDENTIFICATION Male has a very long, thin abdomen; eyes are red-orange on their upper surface. Face is bright orange with a dark black central spot. Top of head is largely black. Thorax is black with metallic luster. There is a thin orange middorsal stripe as well as an orange shoulder stripe and a lower lateral pale stripe. S2 has orange on its upper surface; rest of abdomen is black with pale rings. Female is stockier and duller in color, but otherwise similar to male. S2 lacks orange. Legs pale in both sexes.

SIMILAR SPECIES Coral-fronted and Amelia's Threadtails have more orange on the face and the top of the thorax, and have proportionately shorter abdomens. Male Orange Bluets have an orange stripe across the back of the head and extensive orange on the sides of the thorax; S9 is orange. The male Burgundy Bluet has less distinct abdominal rings and a shorter abdomen, and does not overlap in distribution.

TEXAS STATUS Uncommon. Found in Central Texas and the Lower Rio Grande Valley.

HABITAT Well-shaded slow-moving streams with ample leaf litter and debris.

DISCUSSION Egg laying typically occurs in tandem near the margin of slow-moving water in floating and submerged vegetation and debris. Females curve their abdomens up between the wings while laying eggs. Males typically hover just above the water for extended periods of time. Males will aggregate in trees overhanging the water. Their dainty appearance can make them very difficult to spot as they hover against the water or perch. A photograph was taken of an egg-laying pair at the Houston Arboretum in 1988. These were probably an accidental introduction with aquatic plants, though, and they have not been seen there since.

Turquoise Bluet

Pond Damsels
Family Coenagrionidae

Pond damsels are found worldwide, and as the most diverse family of damselflies, they account for nearly 50% of the species. This book covers the 59 species currently known from Texas, which represent 57% of the North American fauna. Pond damsels are generally not metallic (exceptions include the sprites), but males may be marked with bright blues, greens, yellows, oranges, or reds. Most are small and dainty compared with broad-winged damsels and spreadwings. Many are found around ponds where they can be numerous, but others, including most dancers, are found on streams. Many species are a challenge to identify in the field because their general markings are similar. Females often have 2 color forms: an andromorphic, or "male-like," form and a distinct, gynomorphic form. To accurately identify many of these species, careful examination in the hand with a loupe or other optical aid may be necessary. Texas pond damsels have clear, petiolate wings that are held closed over the abdomen when at rest. There are only 2 antenodal crossveins, and the postnodal crossveins are generally in line with those below them. The pterostigma is short and generally surmounts only 1 or 2 cells. The legs are shorter than those of other damselflies in North America, except the threadtails. The male superior appendages are shorter than S10 and are not forcep- or "pincer"-like, as they are in spreadwings.

WEDGETAILS, GENUS *ACANTHAGRION.* Wedgetails are a diverse tropical group that has been recognized as the ecological equivalent of the bluets in North America. A single species is found in Texas. Males may be readily distinguished by the characteristic downward-sloping appearance of the abdomen tip, which provides the basis for this group's name. Females may be readily separated from all other groups in Texas by the cerci, which touch or nearly touch medially, and the distinctive pronotal pits, which touch the midline of the thorax.

DANCERS, GENUS *ARGIA*. Dancers are a large group with 21 species known from Texas. They can be distinguished from other pond damsels by the long spines on the tibia (some sprites have long spines as well). Most members perch horizontally, often on the ground, with their wings above the abdomen, unlike most other pond damsels. They can inhabit a wide variety of habitats, but are most often seen associated with streams and rivers. Females lay eggs in tandem or solitarily. Some species, such as the common Powdered Dancer of big rivers, may completely submerge themselves, remaining underwater for periods of more than a half hour. Many species are difficult to distinguish, but careful examination of thoracic and abdominal patterns will permit identification of most. Examination, in hand or under a microscope, may be necessary to reliably separate some species, particularly females. Some species have more than one color form of female, usually a juvenile tan or green form and an older blue form. Texas species can be broken up into 4 useful groups:

tibial spines longer than spaces between them

1. Red-eyed: Coppery and Fiery-eyed
2. Predominately blue abdomens: Apache, Aztec, Comanche, Leonora's, Seepage, and Springwater
3. Predominately violet abdomens: Amethyst, Kiowa, Lavender, and Violet
4. Predominately dark abdomens: Blue-fronted, Blue-ringed, Blue-tipped, Dusky, Golden-winged, Paiute, Powdered, Sooty, and Tezpi

Blue-tipped Dancer perching with its wings above the abdomen.

BLUETS, GENUS *ENALLAGMA*. This large group of damselflies comprises nearly 50 species found mostly in temperate North America. They are among the damselflies most familiar to the casual observer and the most speciose group of damselflies in North America. Eighteen of the 32 species in North America have been documented in Texas and are treated in this guide. As one might guess, most bluets are blue, but 3 species in Texas are not. Texas species can be broken into the following 3 groups:

1. Abdomen predominately red, orange, or yellow: Burgundy, Orange, and Vesper
2. S3–6 with at least half their length blue: Alkali, Arroyo, Atlantic, Big, Double-striped, Familiar, and Tule
3. Abdomen predominately dark: Attenuated, Azure, Neotropical, Rainbow, Skimming, Slender, Stream, and Turquoise

Most species possess conspicuous pale eyespots. Bluets are as diverse ecologically as they are morphologically. Some species, like the Big Bluet, live in brackish waters, while others, like the Alkali Bluet, are more commonly found in desert alkaline ponds. Many species commonly fly close to the water's surface, often making them difficult to photograph or collect. Mature adults are commonly found around standing water and are most active during midday. Recently emerged, teneral adults fly away from the water after 30 minutes. This is probably an effort to avoid predation and contact with mature adults during this vulnerable time. These recently emerged adults go through a maturation period of 1–3 weeks, during which they forage away from the water. Mature males congregate around pools and

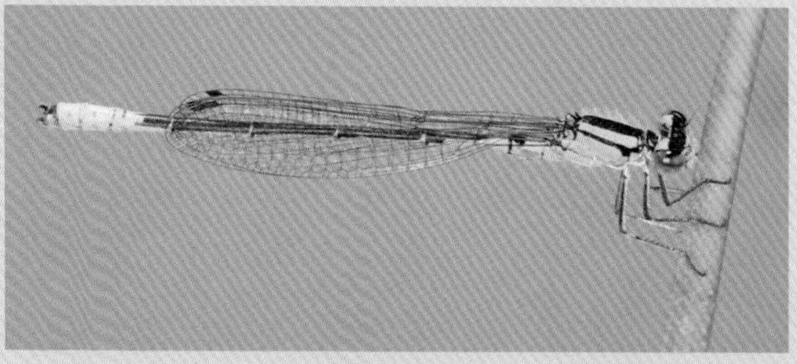

Azure Bluet perching with its abdomen through the wings.

ponds, while females tend to remain away from the water, approaching only to mate and oviposit. Adults typically perch on standing sedges, cattails, and other riparian vegetation. Both sexes will leave their perching sites near the water in late afternoon, probably to roost. Mating generally takes place during the active midday hours. Females, by themselves or in tandem, commonly lay eggs in living plant material, rotting wood, and algal mats. Females may submerge themselves for as much as an hour while laying their eggs. Most species, however, oviposit at or near the surface of the water.

PAINTED DAMSEL, GENUS *HESPERAGRION*. There is a single species in this genus, which may be closely related to the forktails. Beyond superficial affinities, though, adults share few similarities with that group. Both males and females of this species can be readily identified by a combination of color, thoracic pattern, and abdominal pattern. Some red females look similar to firetails. Painted Damsels are found in streams of the arid southwestern part of Texas.

SWAMPDAMSELS, GENUS *LEPTOBASIS*. Two species of this small Neotropical genus have been discovered in the Lower Rio Grande Valley. They are long slender species that generally undergo a dramatic color change as they mature. Females have long ovipositors. It is known that some species survive the extended dry season in the tropics as juveniles. There is some evidence to suggest that the Texas Cream-tipped Swampdamsel does this as well.

FORKTAILS, GENUS *ISCHNURA*. These often brightly colored damselflies are among the smallest and most studied in North America. Ten of the 14 species found in the United States occur in Texas. The species in Texas have distinctively eastern or western distributions, except for the Eastern Forktail in the north. The common name, forktails, refers to the forked projection arising from the apex of S10 in most males. This projection, lacking in Lilypad Forktails, gives the characteristic appearance of the group. Forktails may be abundant around the dense vegetation of their typical habitat, generally including ponds, lakes, and marshes. Some species, however, prefer creeks and streams. Although many of the species are widespread in distribution, they are relatively weak fliers. Forktails are fairly distinct, but resemble other groups, such as bluets and painted damsels. The eyespots are particularly well represented in some species, and an occipital bar may be present in some females. The thoracic color pattern of the group always includes a black middorsal stripe and usually a black shoulder stripe. The pale shoulder stripes, when present, of some males may be reduced to anterior and posterior spots. The pterostigma in most males is a different color and/or shape in the different wings. The presence of a vulvar spine on S8 is helpful for separating some difficult-to-identify females. All females, except Fragile Forktails, have multiple color forms. Members of this group typically have multiple generations, and compared to other pond damsels, longer flight seasons. The wide variation in size of many of the species is directly correlated to this. Larger specimens are predominantly encountered in the spring, when nymphal durations are longer. Smaller individuals occur in the summer and fall. Most females of this genus lay eggs alone, not in tandem, in emergent plant stems. Exceptions in the region include the Black-fronted and Plains Forktails. Females typically mate in the early morning and often only once.

SPRITES, GENUS *NEHALENNIA*. Three species of these dainty, metallic green damselflies have been documented in Texas. One of these, the Everglades Sprite, is known from only one historical occurrence. These species can be readily distinguished from other Texas damselflies by the combination of a metallic green thorax and a blue-tipped abdomen. This is also the only genus of damselflies other than dancers to hold their wings above the abdomen when perched.

YELLOWFACES, GENUS *NEOERYTHROMMA*. This is a small tropical genus comprising only 2 species, one of which ranges north to the Lower Rio Grande Valley. The other species, *N. gladiolatum*, is found in western Mexico. Males of both species are recognizable by their bright yellow faces. Females lack a vulvar spine on S8, and the ovipositor is short, not extending past the terminal abdominal segment. Both sexes also have characteristic yellow subapical bands on the femora.

FIRETAILS, GENUS *TELEBASIS*. This is a species-rich group extending from Argentina to the southern United States. Most species are predominantly red, but a few are blue. Both species known in the United States occur in Texas. Males are red, females tan or red, and both are easily identified from other pond damsels by their thoracic pattern and the lack of eyespots. They are commonly found on floating vegetation. The 2 species occurring in Texas are very similar and can be distinguished with certainty only by in-hand examination.

PAIUTE DANCER

Argia alberta (AR-gē-ə al-BUR-tə)

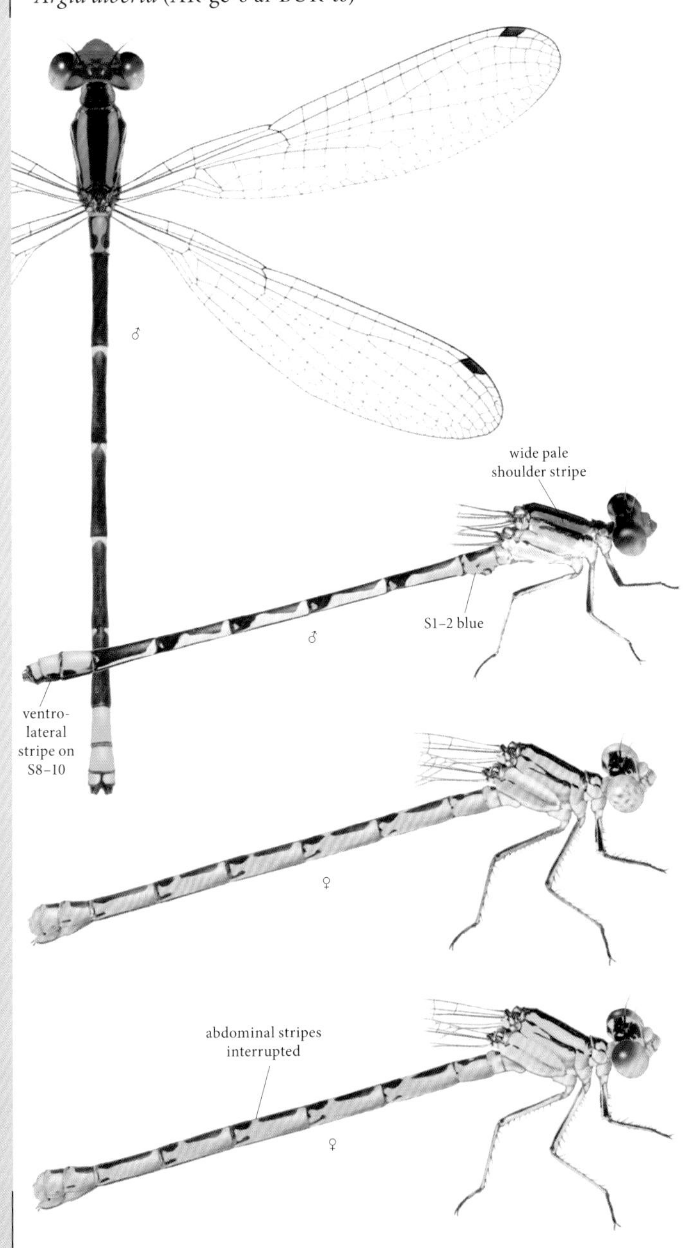

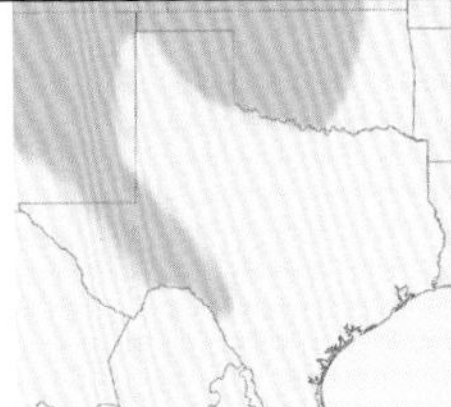

S3

Size
27–32 mm
(1.0–1.3 in)

Jan Feb Mar Apr May Jun Jul Aug Sep Oct Nov Dec

KEY FEATURES

♂—broad black middorsal thoracic stripe; abdomen largely black, with blue on S8–10

♀—brown or blue; forked shoulder stripe; abdomen with interrupted dark stripes; pale ovipositor

IDENTIFICATION Males have a blue face and eyes. Eyespots are narrow. Dark blue thorax has a broad black middorsal stripe and a broad black shoulder stripe, which is forked at its upper end. The fork is nearly always present and may extend up to a third the length of the stripe. Legs are pale with a dark stripe on the femur. Dark abdomen is mostly blue on S1–2, occasionally S3, and S8–10. Blue on the middle segments is limited to rings, at most. S8–10 has a black ventrolateral stripe. Females have either a brown or blue thorax. Dark stripes on the thorax are not as broad as in the male, and dark stripes on the femur are much less visible. Abdomen is brown or olive. The dark abdominal stripe is usually broken up in middle. Ovipositor is mostly pale.
SIMILAR SPECIES The Blue-ringed Dancer is very similar but with the following differences: in males, the lower fork of the shoulder stripe connects to the posterior margin of the thorax, blue rings on the abdomen are more pronounced, and the abdomen has wide basal blue rings; in females, wings are generally tinted brown, the abdomen is greener, and its tip is entirely pale (partly black in Paiutes). Male Leonora's Dancers are bluer and have a different abdominal pattern. Females have a single black lateral stripe on S3–6.
TEXAS STATUS Uncommon to rare.
HABITAT Small flowing streams or marshy springs.
DISCUSSION The Paiute Dancer is primarily a Great Basin species. It is most commonly seen at creeks, but northern specimens have been observed at hot springs, and it may be found associated with saline waters. Egg laying occurs in tandem, and pairs are often seen in the midafternoon.

BLUE-RINGED DANCER

Argia sedula (AR-gē-ə SĒ-jew-lə)

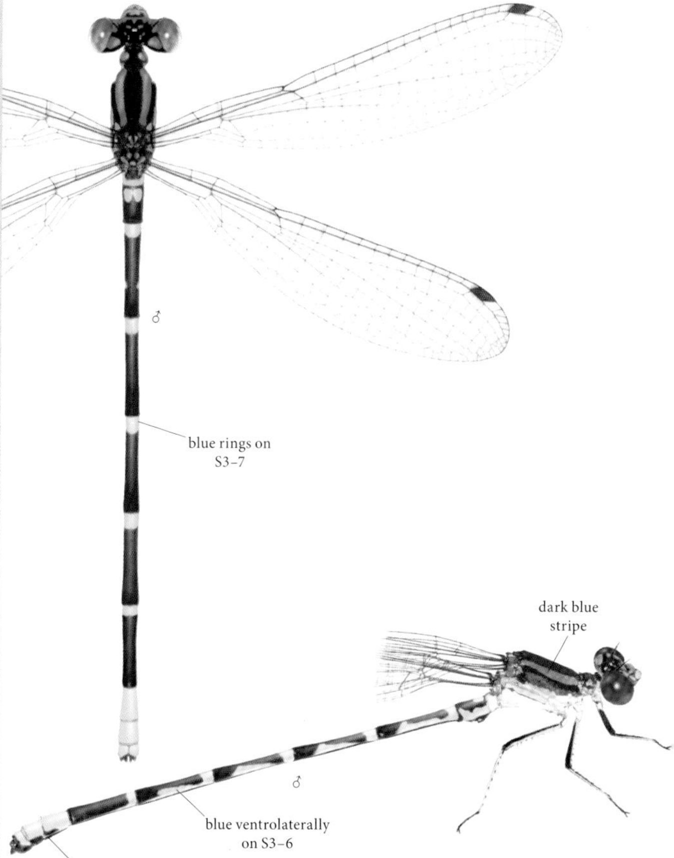

♂

blue rings on S3–7

dark blue stripe

♂

blue ventrolaterally on S3–6

ventrolateral stripe on S8–10

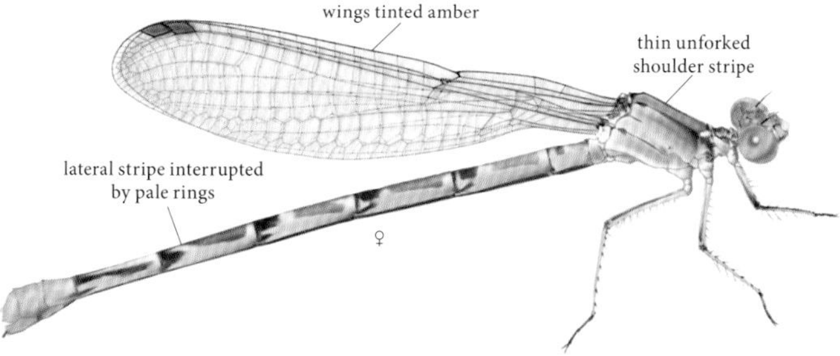

wings tinted amber

thin unforked shoulder stripe

lateral stripe interrupted by pale rings

♀

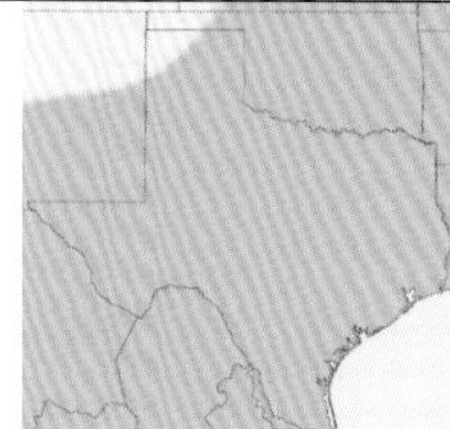

KEY FEATURES

♂—dark blue upper thorax contrasting with blue on abdomen; blue rings on S3–7

♀—wings tinted amber; thin unforked shoulder stripe; greenish brown thorax and abdomen

S5

Size
29–34 mm
(1.1-1.3 in)

IDENTIFICATION This is a small dark dancer with a dark blue thorax, a broad black middorsal stripe, and a broad shoulder stripe that is forked at its extreme upper end. The blue stripe between these black stripes is narrower than either of the dark stripes and darker than blue on lower thorax and abdomen. Abdomen is dark with blue rings on S3–7 and blue ventrolaterally, especially at middle on S3–6. S8–10 is blue with a ventrolateral stripe starting midway on S8 and running continuously to the end of S10. Female is tan with hint of green on the thorax and abdomen. Head has few or no dark markings. Middorsal dark stripe is black and not as wide as in males. Shoulder stripe is thin and dark brown. Legs are pale brown with dark stripes on the outer surfaces. Wings are usually tinted amber. Abdomen has dark brown rings on S3–6, sometimes confluent with lateral stripes. S8–10 and ovipositor are pale.

SIMILAR SPECIES Male Paiute Dancers have a deeply forked shoulder stripe, and the pale stripe above the shoulder stripe is wider and lighter blue. Paiute Dancers also have narrower, pale basal rings on S3–6. Male Seepage Dancers have wider pale abdominal rings. The dark middorsal stripe on S3–6 is divided by a pale area in Kiowas. Male Leonora's Dancers are bluer and have a different abdominal pattern. No other pond damsel has two different colors of blue on the thorax and abdomen. Female Golden-winged Dancers are larger, wings are a darker amber, and markings on the head are dark.

TEXAS STATUS Common. Widespread across state.

HABITAT Streams and rivers with gentle current and dense vegetation. Also occasionally found on ponds and lakes and can be found long distances from water on road and trail edges.

DISCUSSION This species is more prone to perching on vegetation, often in the shade, than most dancers. Pairs require 10–15 minutes to mate and egg laying occurs in tandem.

Jan
Feb
Mar
Apr
May
Jun
Jul
Aug
Sep
Oct
Nov
Dec

BLUE-FRONTED DANCER

Argia apicalis (AR-gē-ə ā-pi-CAL-iss)

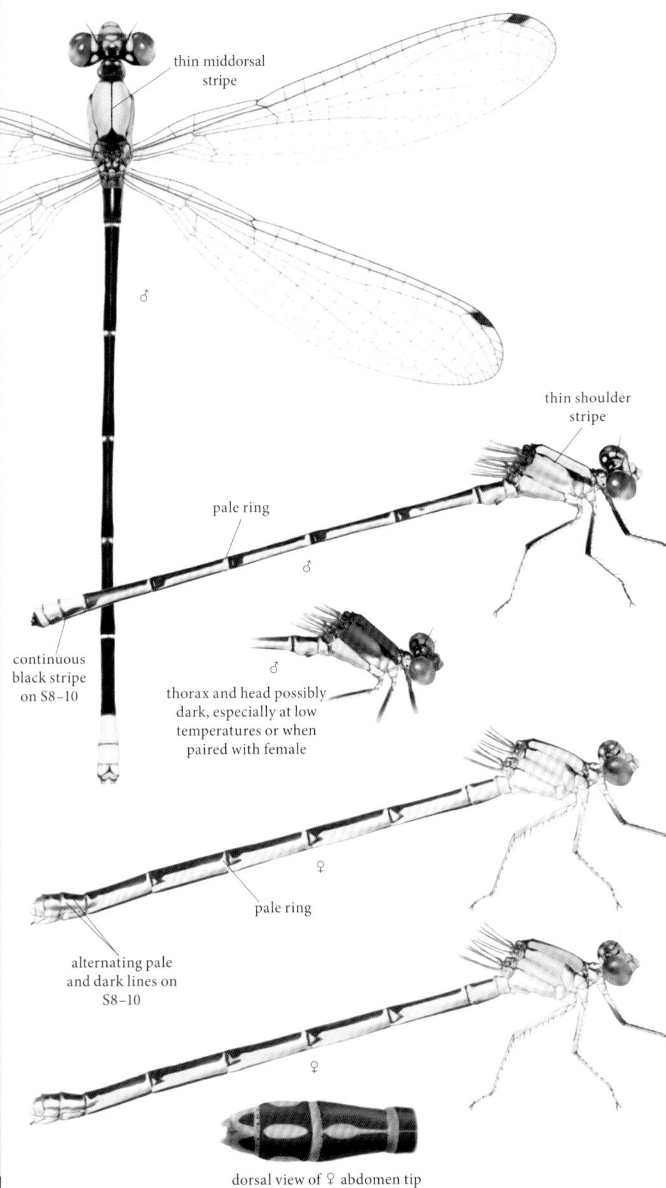

dorsal view of ♀ abdomen tip

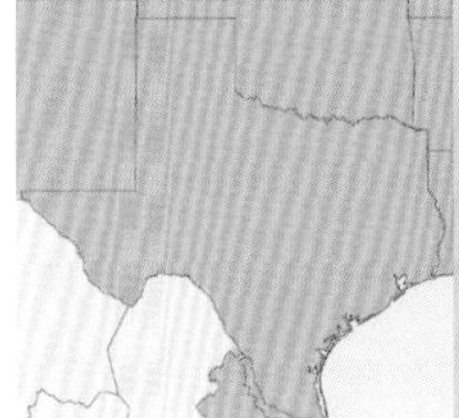

KEY FEATURES

♂—nearly all-blue thorax; abdomen dark; S8–10 blue with a continuous dark stripe laterally

♀—brown or blue with nearly all-pale thorax; dark abdomen; S8–10 with alternating pale and dark lines laterally

S5

Size
33–40 mm
(1.3–1.6 in)

Jan Feb Mar Apr May Jun Jul Aug Sep Oct Nov Dec

IDENTIFICATION Male has a blue eyes, face, and thorax. Thorax is largely unmarked, with only a hairline black middorsal and shoulder stripe. Distinctive broad dark spot at base of shoulder stripe. Sides of thorax pale, even white. Abdomen is largely black with blue on S8–10. These segments have a complete black stripe on their lower edges. The pale colors of males become much darker, nearly gray, when they are in tandem or exposed to cool temperatures. Female is either brown or blue, with a thin black middorsal stripe and usually a thin, incomplete dark shoulder stripe. Rarely, the shoulder stripe may be wider. Abdomen is brown or black, interrupted by pale rings. S8–10 has alternating dark and pale lines laterally.

SIMILAR SPECIES Female Powdered Dancers can be brown or blue and look very similar to Blue-fronted Dancers. Some Powdered Dancer females have heavier dark thoracic markings, but most do not. For those, the ventrolateral dark stripe on S8 does not continue on to S9, as it does in Blue-fronted females. Powdered females are also larger, but size can be difficult to compare if they are not side by side.

TEXAS STATUS Common statewide.

HABITAT Large rivers, including muddy ones, and occasionally streams, lakes, or ponds.

DISCUSSION Males and females reach reproductive age after a week. Peak activity occurs at noon. Males arrive at the water earlier than females and space themselves generally at 2-meter intervals. Mating lasts on average 15 minutes. Females may be gregarious, laying eggs either in tandem or alone. Males live more than a month and exhibit intra- and interspecific competition, flicking their wings as a warning to intruders within their territory. On hot days, they thermoregulate by obelisking, or pointing the abdomen toward the sun to minimize the surface area exposed to ultraviolet rays.

POWDERED DANCER

Argia moesta (AR-gē-ə mō-ES-tə)

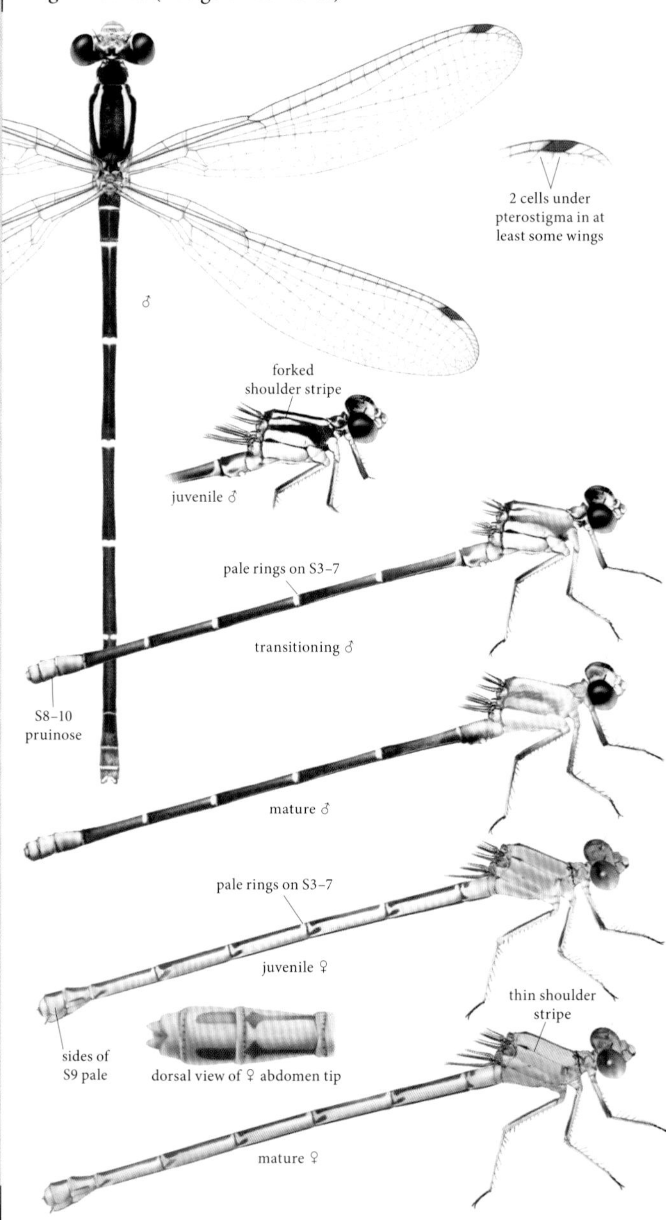

S5

KEY FEATURES

♂—powder white at maturity; pale rings on S3–7

♀—thin middorsal and shoulder stripes; pale rings on S3–7; sides of S9 pale

Size
37–42 mm
(1.5–1.7 in)

Jan Feb Mar Apr May Jun Jul Aug Sep Oct Nov Dec

IDENTIFICATION The most widespread and variable dancer in Texas. Males have dark eyes, a tan thorax, and a black middorsal stripe. Black shoulder stripe is either strongly forked or a single broad stripe. Legs are largely pale, but with some dark markings. Abdomen is black with pale rings. Males quickly develop a powder gray or white pruinosity that envelops the head and entire thorax, including legs, S1–2, and S9–10. Females are quite variable, starting off tan and becoming blue as they mature. They usually have a thin black middorsal stripe, but it may be thicker. Shoulder stripe is usually very thin, but may be thicker with a lower fork present. Legs are pale with few dark markings. Abdomen is generally dark with narrow pale rings visible, as in males. S8–9 has a lateral stripe. S8 also has a ventrolateral stripe, which is lacking on S9.

SIMILAR SPECIES Male Sooty Dancers are larger and darker, never turning white; Powdered Dancers are the only damselflies in Texas with a white thorax. Juvenile Sooty males have a broad dark middorsal stripe interrupted by a pale thin line on either side of the midline. In male Blue-fronted Dancers, S8–10 is blue. Female Blue-fronteds are very similar, but the dark thoracic markings are less extensive and S9 has a ventrolateral stripe. Female Dusky Dancers have a darker thorax and a ventrolateral stripe on S8–10.

TEXAS STATUS Common. Found statewide.

HABITAT Large rivers and streams, especially where rocks are available for perching. Often found some distance from water, along roadsides and trails.

DISCUSSION Mating and egg laying average 22 and 47 minutes, respectively, and many females turn dark while in tandem. Tandem pairs will aggregate in large numbers to lay eggs in roots, stems, debris, and algae, often submerging themselves more than a meter for periods up to an hour.

Argia lugens (AR-gē-ə LŪ-gins)

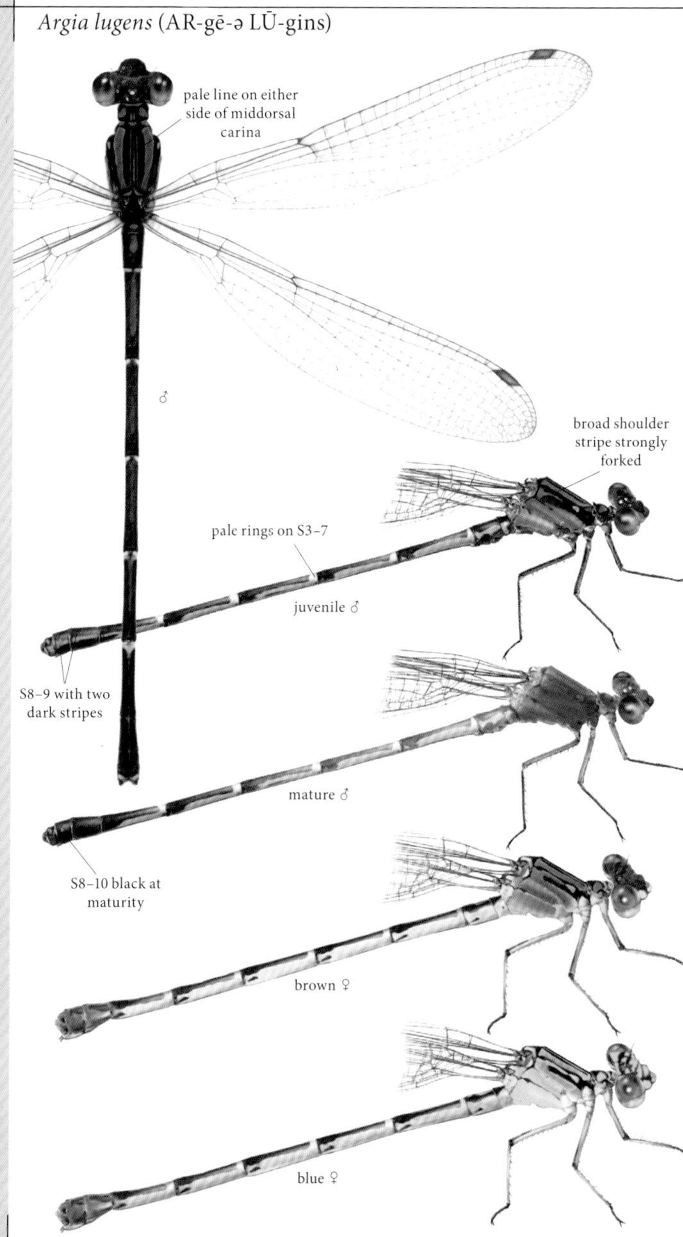

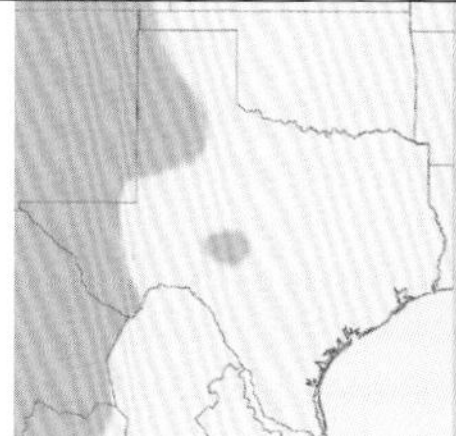

KEY FEATURES

♂—large and dark; thin pale line on either side of middorsal carina; pale rings on S3–7; thorax and head dark at maturity

♀—thin pale line on either side of middorsal stripe; deeply forked shoulder stripe

S4

Size
41–50 mm
(1.6–2.0 in)

Jan Feb Mar Apr May Jun Jul Aug Sep Oct Nov Dec

IDENTIFICATION The largest pond damsel in Texas. Juvenile males have dark eyes with brown thorax. There is a broad black middorsal stripe that is interrupted by a thin pale stripe on either side of the middorsal carina. Broad black shoulder stripe is strongly forked. Upper and lower forks are often connected, isolating a pale spot anteriorly. Legs are pale, but extensively marked with black. Abdomen is dark with a black lateral stripe on S1–7. There are pale rings on S3–7. S8–9 has 2 dark lateral stripes in juveniles. S10 is variously marked, becoming darker with age. Mature males develop dark pruinosity over the head, thorax, and legs, obscuring markings. S8–10 becomes nearly all black. Females are either brown or blue. Thoracic pattern is as in males, but doesn't develop heavy pruinosity. Legs are not as black. Abdomen resembles male's. Lateral stripe extends to S8–9. Ovipositor is pale.

SIMILAR SPECIES Powdered Dancers are smaller, and mature males are almost white rather than black. Females have thin middorsal and shoulder stripes. Dusky Dancers are smaller, males' shoulder stripes are not as deeply forked, and they have blue dorsally on S8–9.

TEXAS STATUS Common. May be locally abundant in the western parts of the state.

HABITAT Swift-flowing rocky desert rivers and streams of moderate size.

DISCUSSION This species may be the most abundant damselfly at certain desert streams, where it perches on emergent and marginal rocks—rarely on plants. Mating generally occurs in the afternoon, when pairs can be plentiful on a stream. Males remain active later in the day, moving to shaded areas, presumably to avoid the hot sun.

GOLDEN-WINGED DANCER

Argia rhoadsi (AR-gē-ə RŌDS-ī)

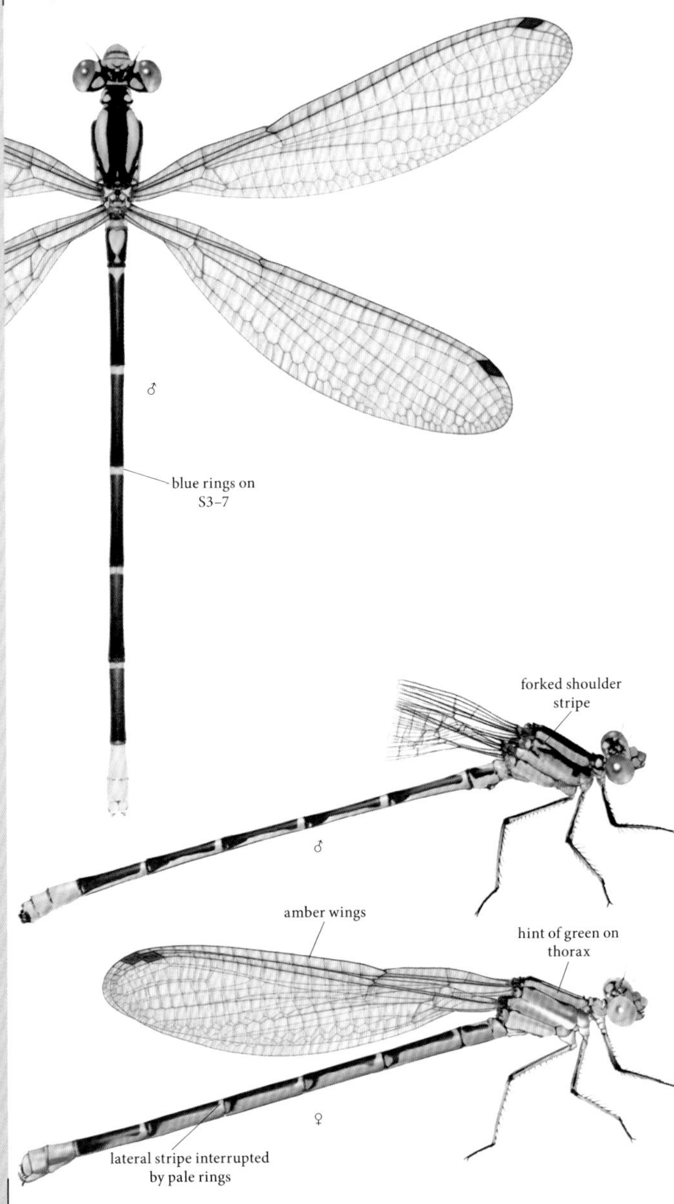

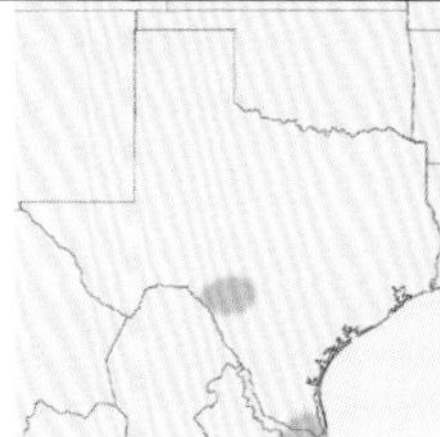

S3

KEY FEATURES

♂—deep amber wings; forked shoulder stripe; dark abdomen with blue rings; S8–10 blue

♀—deep amber wings; unforked shoulder stripe; green on thorax; lateral stripe on abdomen interrupted by pale rings

Size
34–35 mm
(1.3–1.4 in)

Jan Feb Mar Apr May Jun Jul Aug Sep Oct Nov Dec

IDENTIFICATION This is Texas's only bright blue pond damsel with amber wings. Males have blue eyes, face, and top of head. Thorax is blue with a black middorsal and a forked shoulder stripe. Legs are blue with a dark stripe on the upper leg. Wings are strongly tinted amber. Middle abdominal segments are mostly black with blue rings on S3–7. S8–10 is blue with no ventrolateral stripe. Females are brown, with hints of green on the thorax. The top of the head is tan with irregular black markings encompassing the eyespots and postoccipital bar. Legs are pale with black markings that are less extensive than males'. Wings are amber, but not as dark as in males. Abdomen is tan with a lateral brown stripe on S3–7, interrupted by pale ring. S8–10 and ovipositor are pale.

SIMILAR SPECIES The only other pond damsel with tinted wings is the smaller Blue-ringed Dancer. Males of that species have a darker thorax and a ventrolateral stripe on S8–10. Females lack the dark markings on the top of the head.

TEXAS STATUS Rare. Populations known in Cameron, Hidalgo, Kinney, and Val Verde counties.

HABITAT Lagoons and pools formed at the edges of streams and rivers. Often associated with springs. Also known from rain pools and resacas in South Texas.

DISCUSSION Nymphs have been found clinging to roots of a water hyacinth (Eichhornia sp.) at the edge of a lagoon. Laboratory emergences occur in the late morning. Males commonly perch in streamside vegetation. Seen more commonly later in the day, as they generally spend the cooler morning hours perched higher up in trees, away from the water's edge.

BLUE-TIPPED DANCER

Argia tibialis (AR-gē-ə tib-ē-AL-iss)

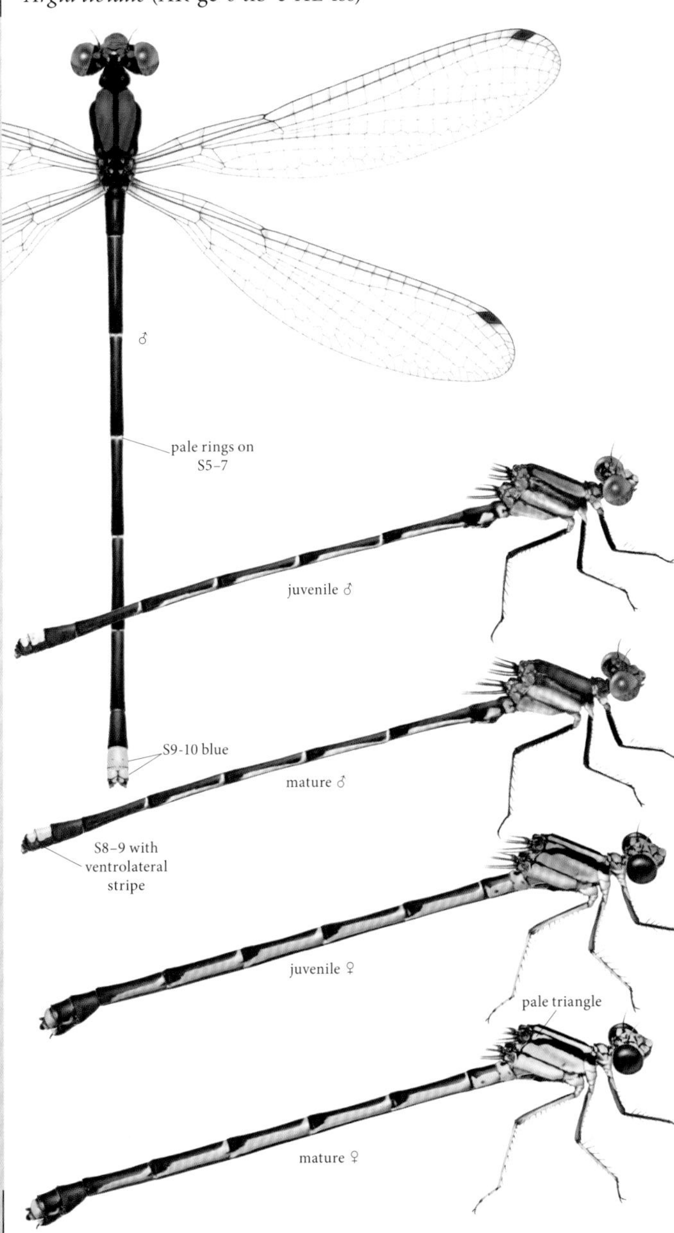

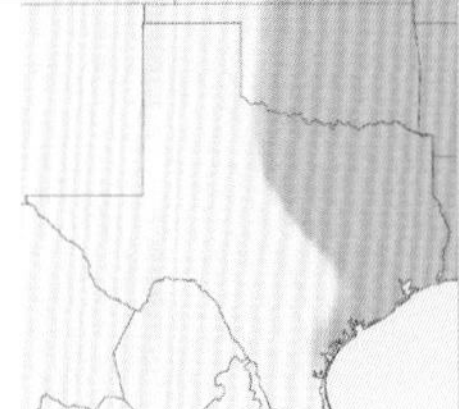

KEY FEATURES

♂—dark purple thorax; black abdomen with pale rings on at least S5–7; S9–10 blue

♀—tan or blue; forked shoulder stripe with triangle of color at upper end; abdomen black above

S5

Size
30–38 mm
(1.2–1.5 in)

IDENTIFICATION Face and upper thorax of male are dark purple. Eyes and top of head are dark. Purple eyespots, if present, are small. Thorax has a black middorsal stripe and an unforked broad shoulder stripe. Lower thorax is cream or white. Legs are dark with a thin pale stripe on the outer edge. Abdomen is black with thin pale rings on at least S5–7. S8 is black and S9–10 are blue with a continuous ventrolateral stripe. When in tandem or at low temperatures, males often show reddish violet on front of thorax. Females are either tan or blue. Middorsal thoracic stripe is thin. Black shoulder stripe is thick and forked at its upper end, encompassing a triangle of pale color. Legs are largely pale. Upper surface of abdomen is nearly all black; S10 is pale. Sometimes there are pale markings on S9 as well.

SIMILAR SPECIES Male Dusky Dancers have a darker thorax, a more strongly forked shoulder stripe, only a little blue on S8–9. Male Blue-tipped Dancers are the only dancer in Texas with a purple thorax and blue on S9–10. Female Dusky Dancers have more strongly forked shoulder stripe and dark and pale lateral stripes alternate on S8–10.

TEXAS STATUS Fairly common. Widespread in the eastern part of the state.

HABITAT Wooded, often sandy streams and rivers with a varying amount of flow. Also found at sloughs, ponds, and lakes.

DISCUSSION Usually perches on the ground, but does perch on vegetation and in shade more than most dancers. Egg laying occurs in tandem, and eggs are generally deposited in floating eel grass or debris, but sometimes in wet wood above the waterline. This species often occurs in large aggregations.

Jan
Feb
Mar
Apr
May
Jun
Jul
Aug
Sep
Oct
Nov
Dec

TEZPI DANCER

Argia tezpi (AR-gē-ə TEZ-pē)

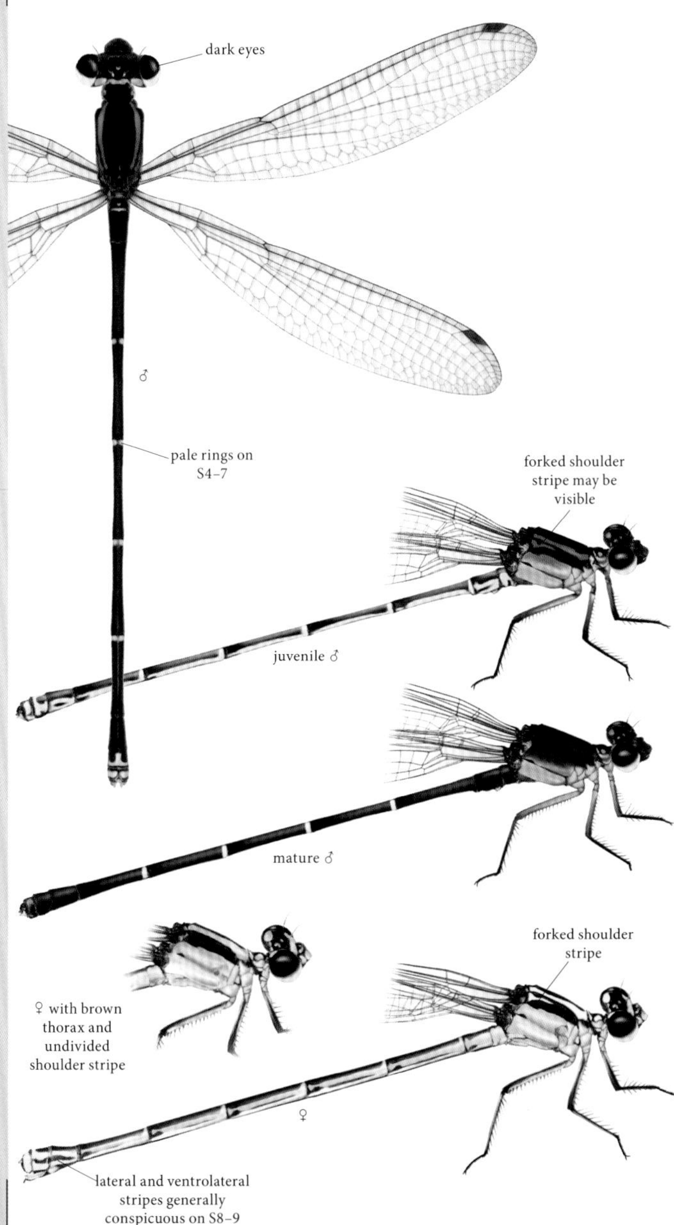

KEY FEATURES

♂—dark eyes; dark thorax; dark abdomen with pale rings; possible hint of amber on wings

♀—blue or brown thorax; shoulder stripe forked to undivided; dark eyes; S8–9 with lateral and ventrolateral stripe; S10 pale

S1

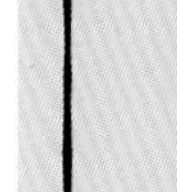

Size
32–42 mm
(1.3–1.7 in)

Jan Feb Mar Apr May Jun Jul Aug Sep Oct Nov Dec

IDENTIFICATION This is a dark dancer with black eyes. Some areas of face, eyespots, and postoccipital bar may be pale in juveniles. Broad middorsal thoracic stripe appears black with violet reflections. Shoulder stripe also has violet reflections and is forked at its upper end. Rest of thorax is pale. In older males, head and thorax become nearly all black, and pruinescence develops ventrolaterally on thorax. Legs are dark. Abdomen is nearly all black, with pale rings on S4–7. S8–10 is black; small blue areas are sometimes visible on S8–9. Females have either a brown or blue thorax and brown eyes. Thorax has a black shoulder stripe that ranges from unforked to deeply forked. Abdomen is generally black and similar to a juvenile male's. Pale rings are present on S3–7; some blue is visible on S8–9. Dark and pale lateral stripes alternate on S8–9. S10 is pale.

SIMILAR SPECIES The male Dusky Dancer is very similar, but its eyes are purple or blue, not black. Both Sooty Dancer and Powdered Dancer males are larger, generally with gray or white pruinosity, and have clear wings. Female Powdered Dancers lack a lateral stripe on S9. Male Blue-tipped Dancers are dark with purple eyes and S9–10 blue. The female Dusky Dancer has a shoulder stripe more deeply forked, and the dorsolateral stripe at the abdomen tip extends to S10.

TEXAS STATUS Rare. Known from only 1 locality.

HABITAT Open, rocky streams and rivers, generally with a lot of exposure to the sun and only moderate vegetation.

DISCUSSION This species has been found only once in Texas, at ZH Canyon in the Sierra Vieja. It may be more common and widely distributed in West Texas, but its similarity to the Dusky Dancer may result in it being overlooked. It is also known from New Mexico and Arizona. Males are commonly seen perching in the open on rocks.

DUSKY DANCER

Argia translata (AR-gē-ə trans-LA-tə)

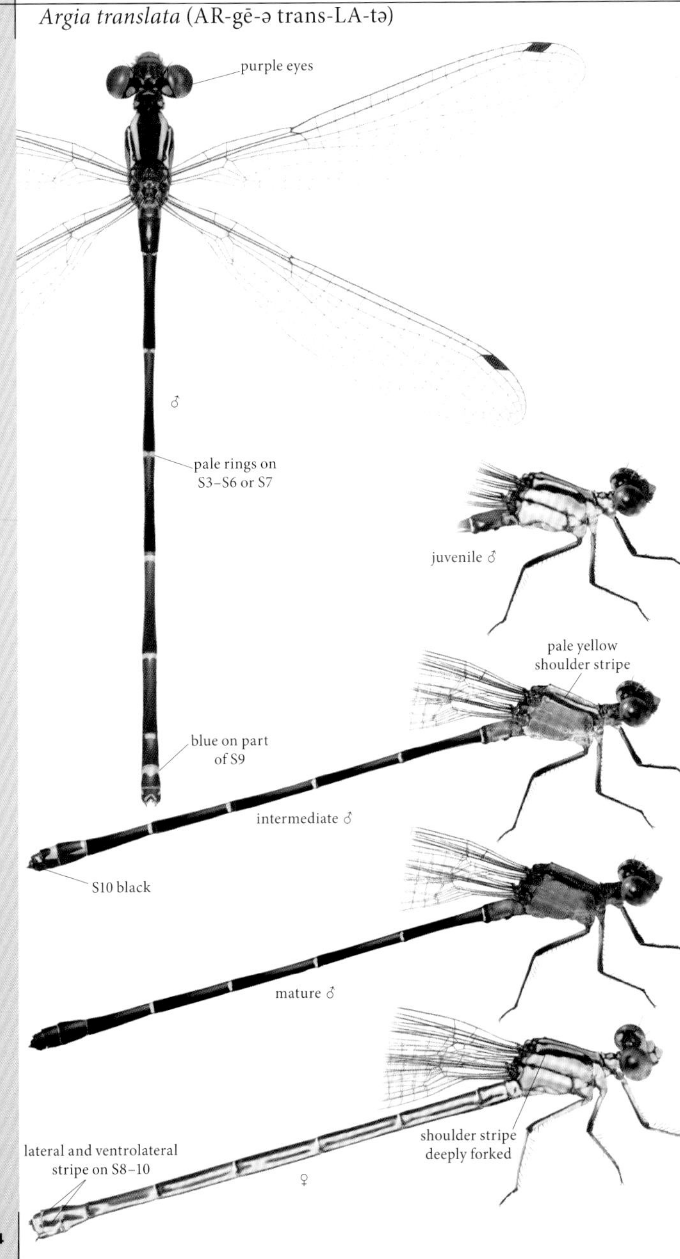

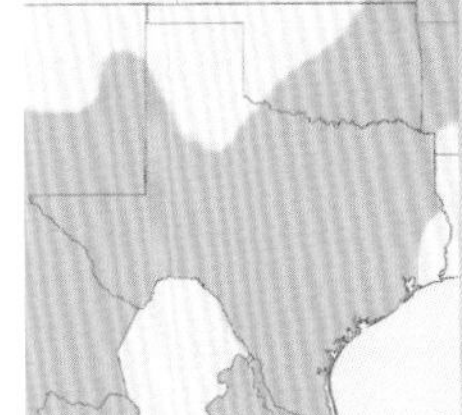

KEY FEATURES

♂—purple eyes; shoulder stripe divided full-length by yellow; dark abdomen with blue rings; S8–10 black with small blue marks on S8–9

♀—deeply forked shoulder stripe; alternating light and dark lateral stripes on S8–10

S5

Size
32–38 mm
(1.3–1.5 in)

Jan Feb Mar Apr May Jun Jul Aug Sep Oct Nov Dec

IDENTIFICATION This is a dark dancer with dark blue or purple eyes. Face, head, and thorax of male are very dark, sometimes all black. Small eyespots with a thin line between them are visible in juveniles. Middorsal stripe is broad and dark. Shoulder stripe is broad, but divided nearly its full length by a stripe of yellow. This becomes obscured in older males. Legs are dark. Abdomen is nearly all black with pale blue rings on S3–6 or S7. S8–10 is black; small blue areas are usually visible on S8–9. Females are generally tan with brown eyes, but may also be marked with blue on top of head and thorax. Dark middorsal thoracic stripe and deeply forked shoulder stripe, as in males. Legs are dark, but pale striping is visible. There is a dark lateral stripe on S2–10. Pale rings on S3–6 sometimes extend to S7. Dark and pale lateral stripes alternate on S8–10.

SIMILAR SPECIES The male Tezpi Dancer is very similar, but its eyes are black, not purple; also, it has amber in wings and lacks blue at tip of abdomen. Both Sooty Dancer and Powdered Dancer males are larger, generally have a gray or white pruinescence, and lack purple eyes. In female Tezpi Dancers the shoulder stripe is forked in only the upper half, and S10 is entirely pale. Female Powdered Dancers lack lateral stripes on S9–10. Male Blue-tipped Dancers are dark with purple eyes, but S9–10 is all blue.

TEXAS STATUS Common. Widespread statewide except for northern Panhandle.

HABITAT Streams and rivers, generally with a lot of exposure to the sun and only moderate vegetation.

DISCUSSION This species has the widest distribution of any dancer occurring in the United States. As an early adult, it is subject to a great deal of change, which is especially evident in the thoracic markings and on S8–10. Older males can be entirely black.

COMANCHE DANCER

Argia barretti (AR-gē-ə BEAR-it-ī)

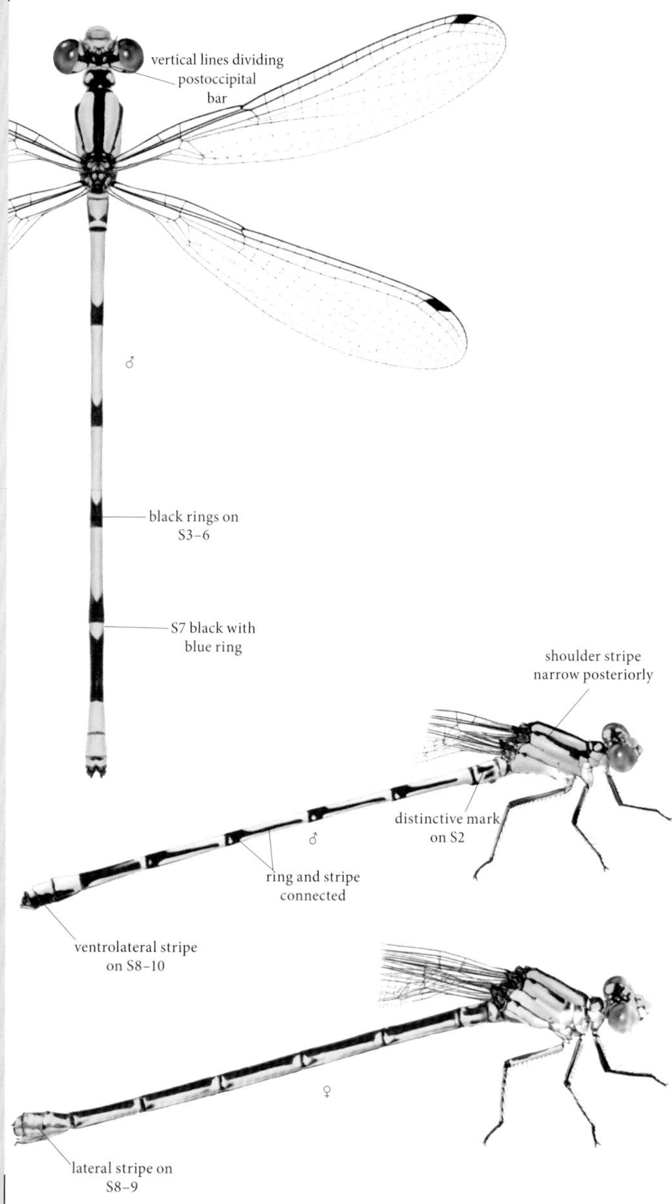

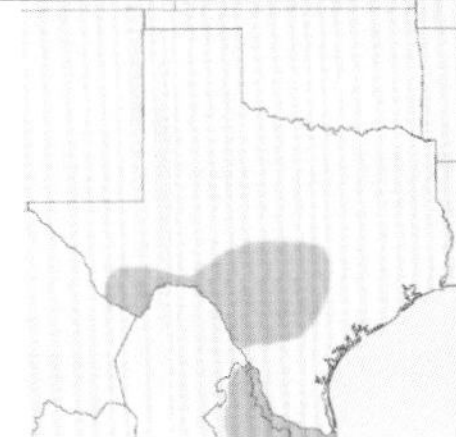

KEY FEATURES

♂—unforked shoulder stripe tapering posteriorly; S2–6 blue with black ring; S7 black with blue ring

♀—brown or blue; thin unforked shoulder stripe; lateral stripe on S8–9

S4

Size
38–43 mm
(1.5–1.7 in)

Jan Feb Mar Apr May Jun Jul Aug Sep Oct Nov Dec

IDENTIFICATION This is a large bright blue dancer. Male has blue eyes and face. Large blue eyespots are separated by a blue stripe that is divided by two vertical black lines. Thorax is blue with a black middorsal stripe. Black shoulder stripe narrows posteriorly. S1–6 is blue on top with a connected black ring and lateral stripe. S7 is black with a blue ring. S8–10 is blue with a continuous black ventrolateral stripe. Legs are variably dark, but outer surface of tibia is blue. Female is similar to male. Body may be tan or blue, and dark stripes are brown rather than black. Dark markings on legs are less extensive. There is a lateral stripe on S8–9. Ovipositor is pale.

SIMILAR SPECIES The Comanche Dancer is one of the largest and most easily recognized bright blue damselflies in the region. Blue-fronted Dancers are smaller, have very thin middorsal thoracic and shoulder stripes, and a dark abdomen. Springwater Dancers are similar, but with incomplete markings laterally on abdomen. Aztec Dancers are smaller and have rings with no stripes laterally on middle abdominal segments. Paiute Dancers are much smaller and have a strongly forked shoulder stripe. Big Bluets are the same size, but paler blue with black dorsal markings on the abdomen in the shape of spear points.

TEXAS STATUS Uncommon. May be locally abundant on Hill Country streams.

HABITAT Rocky rivers and streams.

DISCUSSION Females lay eggs in tandem on floating debris at the river's edge. Males often seen perching on rocks in the middle of a stream.

APACHE DANCER

Argia munda (AR-gē-ə MUN-də)

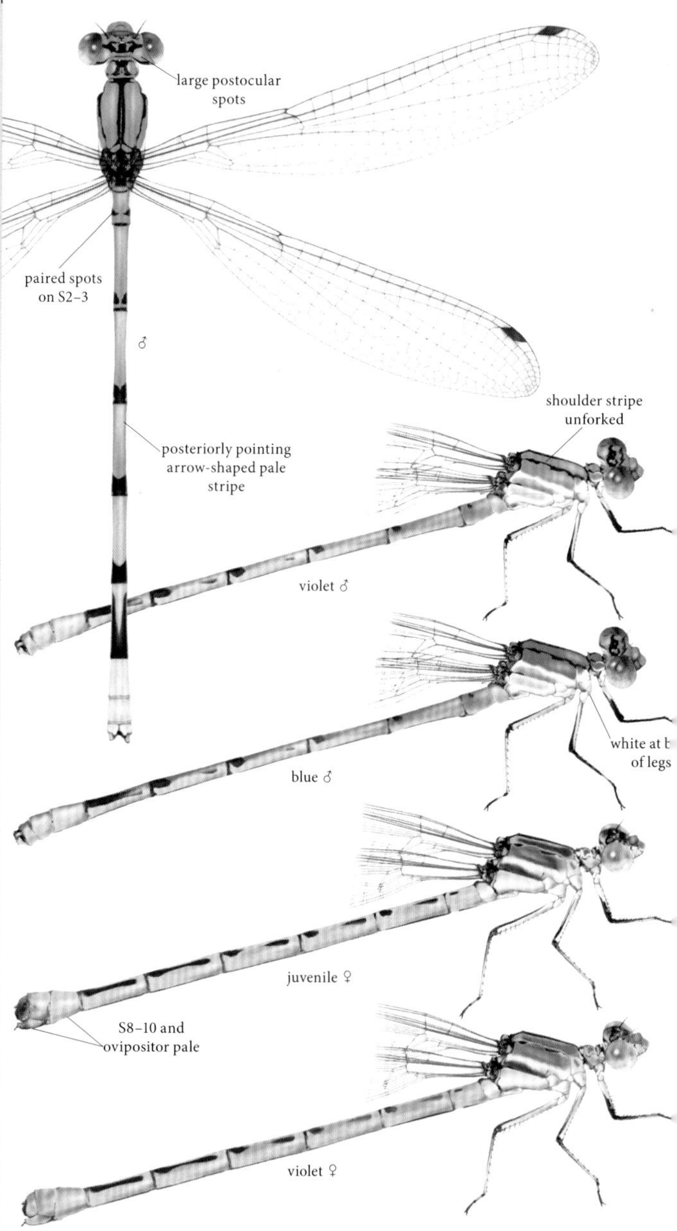

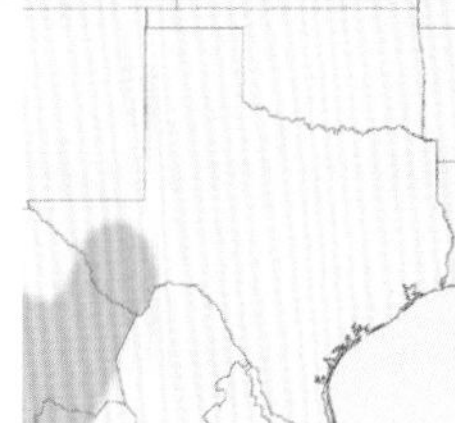

KEY FEATURES

♂—blue or purplish in color; unforked shoulder stripe; paired spots on upper surface of S2–3; S8–10 blue

♀—large eyespots confluent with postoccipital bar; unforked shoulder stripe; S8–10 pale

S3

Size
36–40 mm
(1.4–1.6 in)

Jan Feb Mar Apr May Jun Jul Aug Sep Oct Nov Dec

IDENTIFICATION This is a large western dancer. Male's face, eyes, and head are blue or violet. Postocular spots are large and connected by a pale occipital bar. Thorax is blue or violet with a thin black middorsal stripe and unforked shoulder stripe. Thorax becomes pale, almost white laterally. Legs are largely pale, but with a dark stripe on the femur. Abdomen is blue or violet with small paired spots on the upper surface of S2–3. S4–6 has apical black spots. S7 is mostly black with a pale anterior ring when viewed laterally and a posteriorly pointing arrow on its upper surface. S8–10 is blue, lacking a ventrolateral stripe. Female similarly patterned to male, but brown or violet. Eyespots are usually confluent with postoccipital bar. S8–10 and ovipositor are pale.

SIMILAR SPECIES Springwater Dancer males have a darker head, and their eyespots and occipital bar are not confluent. Middorsal thoracic stripe is thicker, and S2 has an elongated black lateral stripe. Female Springwater Dancers are very similar, but the head is generally darker, the middorsal thoracic stripe is broader, and there is usually a hint of black laterally on the distal part of S8 and/or apically on S9. Close, in-hand or microscopic examination of mesostigmal plates may be necessary to separate Springwater and Apache Dancer females. Comanche Dancers have a black ventrolateral stripe on S8–10.

TEXAS STATUS Uncommon.

HABITAT Primarily found at desert streams, including small, intermittent canyon streams.

DISCUSSION Males are often seen perching on emergent and streamside rocks in areas where water is pooled. Apache Dancers oviposit in tandem and, very unusually for dancers, may do so in the vegetation of dry streambeds before the monsoon rains.

SPRINGWATER DANCER

Argia plana (AR-gē-ə PLĀN-ə)

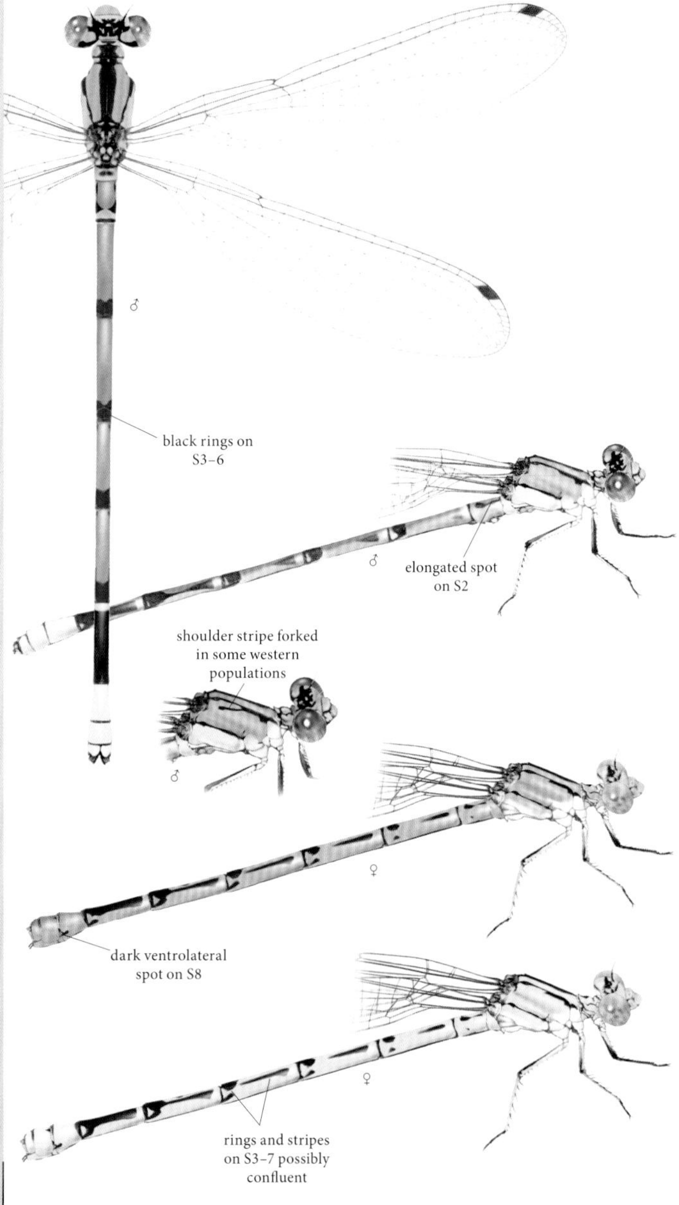

♂

black rings on S3–6

♂

elongated spot on S2

shoulder stripe forked in some western populations

♂

♀

dark ventrolateral spot on S8

♀

rings and stripes on S3–7 possibly confluent

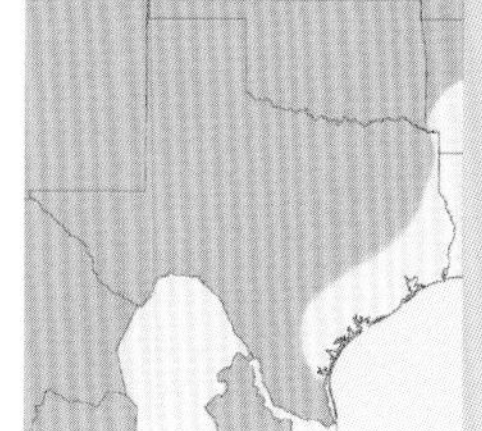

KEY FEATURES

♂—shoulder stripe generally unforked; black rings on S3–6 possibly confluent with lateral stripes; S8–10 blue

♀—tan or blue; shoulder stripe unforked; black rings and stripes on S3–7 confluent or nearly so

S5

Size
34–40 mm
(1.3–1.6 in)

Jan Feb Mar Apr May Jun Jul Aug Sep Oct Nov Dec

IDENTIFICATION Males have a blue face, head, and eyes. Individuals west of Texas are violet. Thorax is blue with a black middorsal stripe and a usually unforked shoulder stripe. Some populations in West Texas have forked shoulder stripes. Legs are blue with a black stripe on outer edge of femur. Abdomen is blue with a black stripe laterally on S2. On S3–6, black rings and the black lateral stripes anterior to them may become confluent, especially on S6. S7 is black with a blue ring. S8–10 is blue. Female is tan or blue with a head and thorax similar to the male's. Abdominal pattern closely approximates that of male, but with black markings more extensive. S8 has a black apical ventrolateral spot.

SIMILAR SPECIES Both Aztec and Variable Dancers are smaller and have forked shoulder stripes. Aztecs also lack black basal markings on S3–6. Lavender and Variable Dancer males have a black ventrolateral stripe on S8–10. Apache Dancer's legs are paler and the middorsal thoracic stripe is about the same width as the shoulder stripe. Comanche Dancers are larger with continuous black stripes laterally along abdomen.

TEXAS STATUS Common. Widespread except in the southeastern part of the state.

HABITAT Small, shallow, canopied or open spring seepages and small-to-medium streams. Often found along roadsides, away from water.

DISCUSSION Mating occurs, on average, 1.5 meters from the water's edge. Mating and egg laying last an average of 25 and 50 minutes, respectively. Females lay eggs just beneath or at the water surface in available vegetation and debris. Pairs separate quickly after oviposition. Males will space themselves out at about 1-meter intervals to avoid aggressive interactions.

SEEPAGE DANCER

Argia bipunctulata (AR-gē-ə bī-punk-chew-LA-tə)

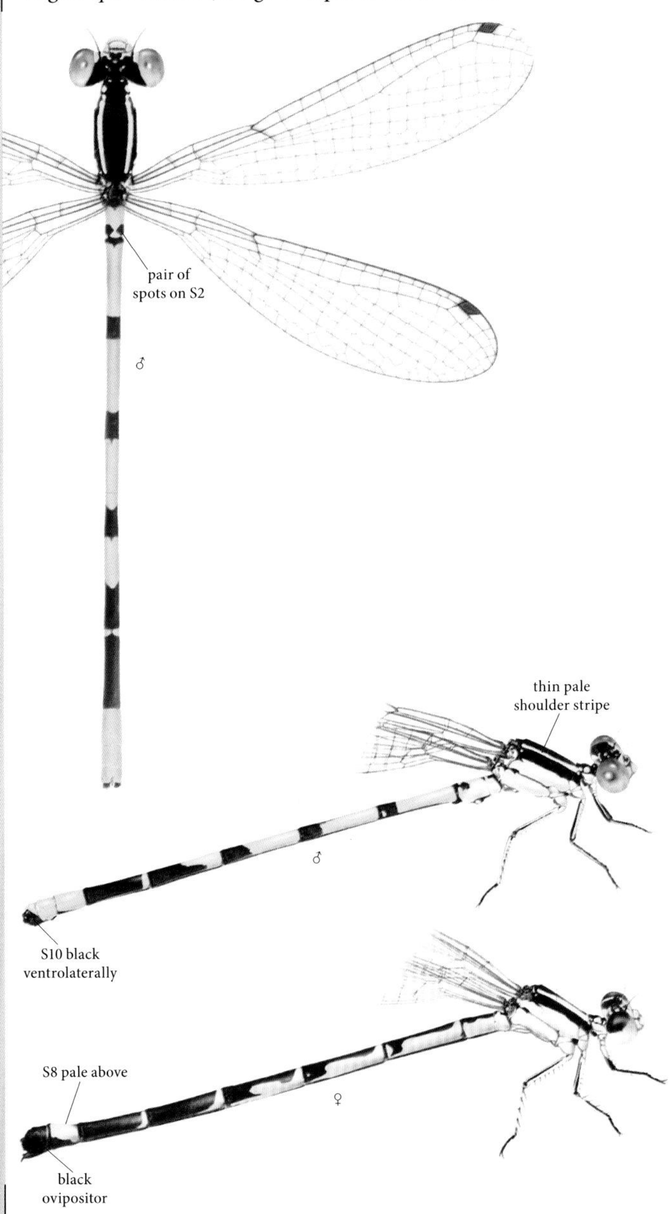

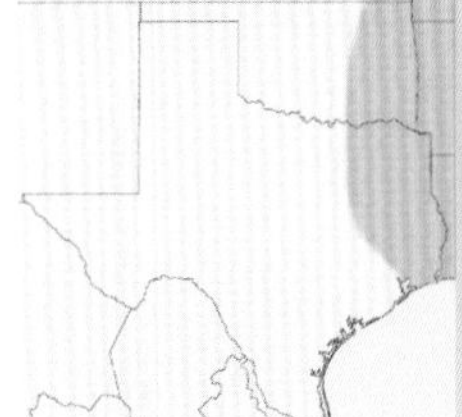

KEY FEATURES

♂—lacks eyespots; dark thorax with thin unforked shoulder stripe; abdomen blue with black rings

♀—lacks eyespots; dark abdomen with pale rings; S8 pale on upper surface

S3

Size
23–30 mm
(0.9–1.2 in)

Jan Feb Mar Apr May Jun Jul Aug Sep Oct Nov Dec

IDENTIFICATION This is Texas's smallest dancer. Male has a blue face and blue eyes, but lacks pale postocular spots on top of head. Thorax is mostly black dorsally with a thin blue shoulder stripe. Sides of thorax are pale blue. Legs blue with dark stripes. S2 has a dark spot laterally. S3–6 is blue with black rings, becoming larger posteriorly. S7 is black with a basal blue ring. S8–10 is blue with a black ventrolateral stripe on S10. Female either pale yellow or tan, sometimes with hint of blue on abdomen. Eyes and top of head are black, lacking pale eyespots. Legs are pale with dark stripes. Abdomen is largely black with pale rings on middle segments. Seepage females are the only dancers with S8 pale dorsally. Ovipositor is black.

SIMILAR SPECIES Most similar to the Aztec Dancer, but the Aztec has a broader pale shoulder stripe, and the top of the head is largely blue. Blue-ringed Dancer males have dark abdomens with only pale abdominal rings. Blue-form Blue-tipped females have an all-black abdomen. Because of their size and color, Seepage Dancers may be confused with bluets, but Texas bluets have pale eyespots, and most have wider pale shoulder stripes. Seepage Dancers also hold their wings above the abdomen, unlike bluets.

TEXAS STATUS Uncommon. Restricted to eastern part of the state.

HABITAT Associated with open, boggy sections of marshes and seepages of small lakes, ponds, and narrow streams.

DISCUSSION The Seepage Dancer often perches vertically on grass stems or other available perches in its habitat, only occasionally perching on the ground. Females are rarely seen except in tandem. The Seepage Dancer is generally not abundant where it is found.

Argia leonorae (AR-gē-ə lē-ō-NOR-ē)

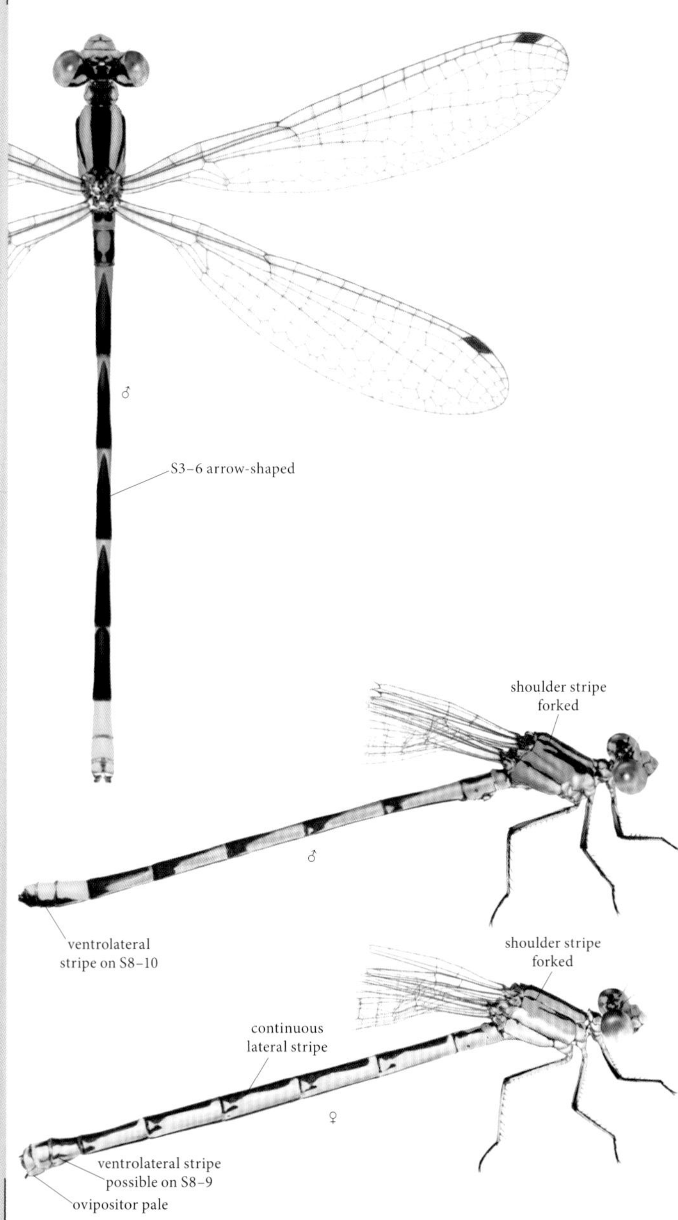

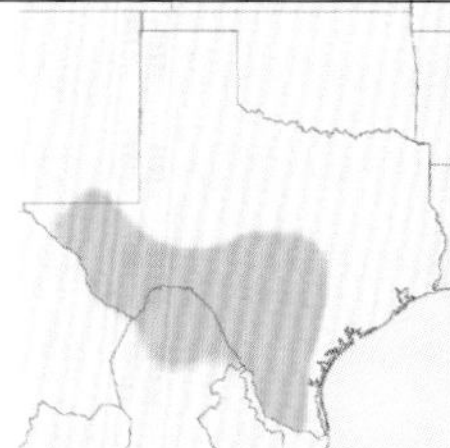

KEY FEATURES

♂—forked shoulder stripe; arrow-shaped marks on upper surface of abdomen; ventrolateral stripe on S8–10

♀—forked shoulder stripe; continuous, or nearly so, lateral stripe; ventrolateral stripe on S8–9

Size
28–32 mm
(1.1–1.3 in)

IDENTIFICATION This is a small blue dancer. Males have a blue thorax with a black middorsal stripe and a forked shoulder stripe. Legs are pale with dark stripes on femora. Abdomen is blue with black arrows pointing forward on upper surface and occupying at least half of S4–6. S7 is black with a blue ring. S8–10 is blue with a black ventrolateral stripe starting in the middle of S8. Female is generally brown, but may have a blue thorax. Shoulder stripe is forked, as in male. Legs have less extensive dark markings. Abdomen has a nearly continuous lateral black stripe on S2–9 interrupted only anteriorly on each segment, if at all. Lower ventrolateral stripe may be evident on S8–9.

SIMILAR SPECIES The Aztec Dancer is similar, but the dark rings on middle abdominal segments are truncate and don't taper to points. Female Aztecs have a black lateral stripe, but it is generally interrupted medially on each segment. The lower fork of the shoulder stripe in Aztec females is often faint. The Double-striped Bluet has a shoulder stripe divided by a thin pale line. Male Blue-ringed and Paiute Dancers have a darker thorax and a different abdominal pattern. Females of those species have interrupted lateral stripes on S3–6. Violet and Lavender females are similar. Black lateral stripes on S3–6 in Violet females tend to be interrupted in the middle. In Violet females, the dark ventrolateral stripes are often faint or absent on S8–9 and in Lavender females they only extend to midpoint of each segment. See comments about separating these females under Variable Dancer.

TEXAS STATUS Fairly Common. Found throughout the Trans-Pecos and Edwards Plateau southward.

HABITAT Small streams, seepages, and swales with abundant sedges for perching and oviposition.

DISCUSSION Females generally not found with males around water unless they are mating or laying eggs, which they do in tandem.

Jan Feb Mar Apr May Jun Jul Aug Sep Oct Nov Dec

AZTEC DANCER

Argia nahuana (AR-gē-ə na-WAN-ə)

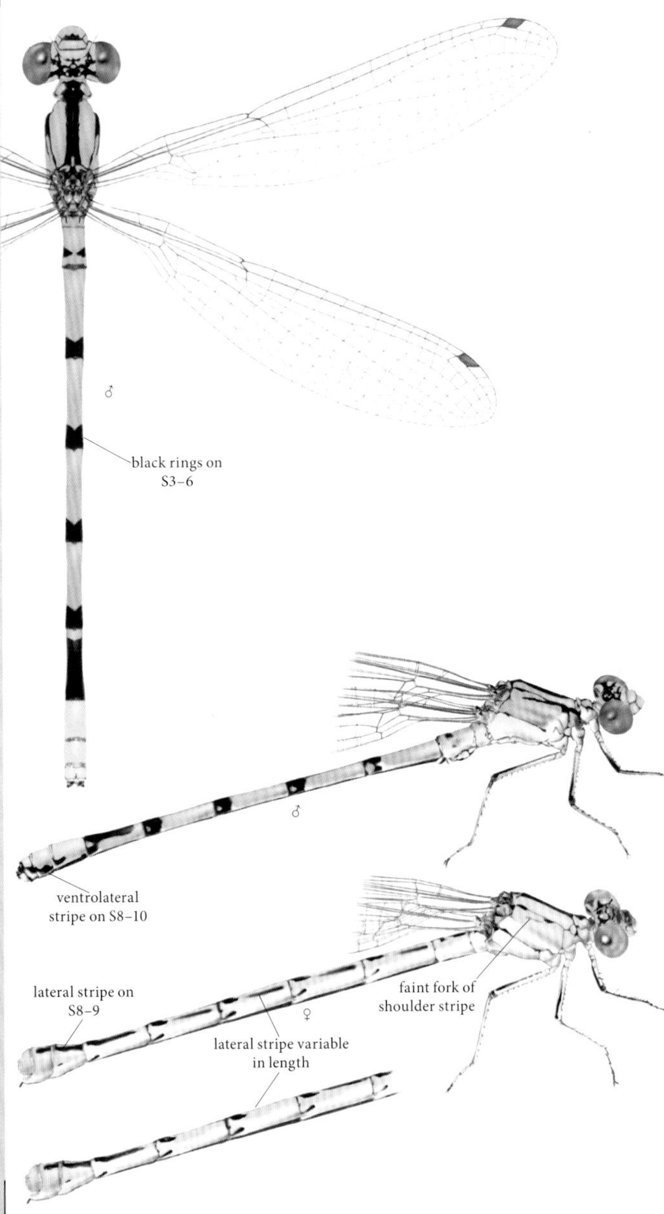

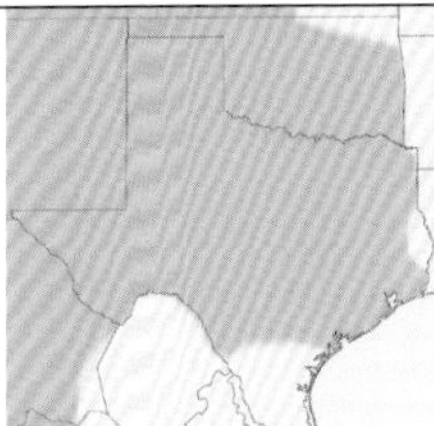

S5

KEY FEATURES

♂—forked shoulder stripe; black rings on S3–6; ventrolateral stripe on S8–10

♀—shoulder stripe possibly forked; rings or stripes on S3–6; lateral stripe on S8–9

Size
28–35 mm
(1.1–1.4 in)

Jan Feb Mar Apr May Jun Jul Aug Sep Oct Nov Dec

IDENTIFICATION This is a beautiful small, bright blue species. Thorax is blue with a dark middorsal stripe and a strongly forked shoulder stripe. Legs are pale with some black markings on outer surfaces of femora. Abdomen is blue with black rings on S3–6. S7 is black with a blue ring. S8–10 is blue with a black ventrolateral stripe on S8–9, which may be continuous. Female is similar to male, but tan or light blue in color. Black middorsal thoracic stripe is interrupted by a thin pale stripe. Lower fork of shoulder stripe is often faint and hard to see. Abdomen is largely pale with black rings on S3–6, as in the male, and a dark lateral stripe may be confluent with these rings. There is a black ventrolateral spot on S3–7 and sometimes S8.

SIMILAR SPECIES Male Leonora's Dancers have black arrow-shaped markings on the upper surface of the abdomen. Female Leonora's Dancers have a more prominently forked shoulder stripe, and the abdomen has a continuous lateral stripe. Male Violet Dancers and Lavender Dancers are violet and both have dark markings on S10. Female Violet and Lavender Dancers can also be violet, and have distinctly forked shoulder stripes. Springwater Dancers are larger and males have a prominent black stripe laterally on the middle segments.

TEXAS STATUS Common. Widespread except in the Lower Rio Grande Valley and extreme southeast Texas.

HABITAT Small, shallow clear-water streams, fully exposed to sunlight with only moderate marginal vegetation.

DISCUSSION Aztec Dancers can be far and away the dominant species at the streams they inhabit. Females lay eggs in tandem, generally in open sunlight where the water is only 1–2 inches deep. The female bends her abdomen at a sharp angle, and eggs are deposited in the leaves of plants just below the water surface. Pairs lay eggs in multiple plants, spending around 30 seconds at each plant.

VARIABLE DANCER

Argia fumipennis (AR-gē- ə fūm-i-PENN-iss)

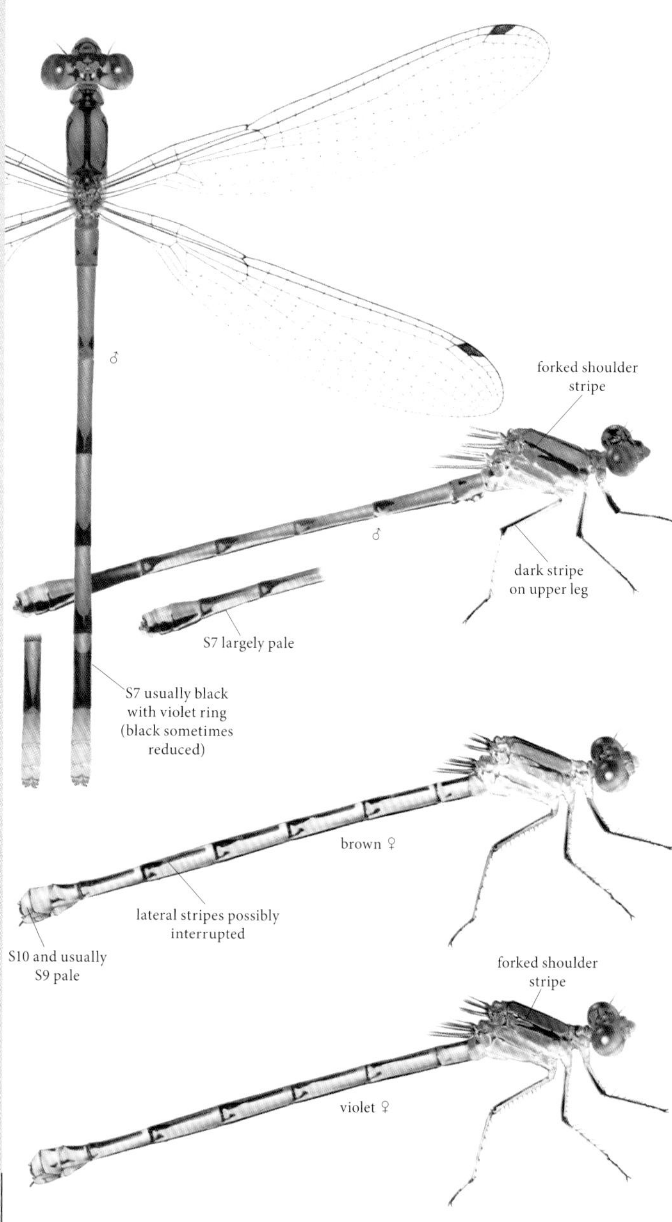

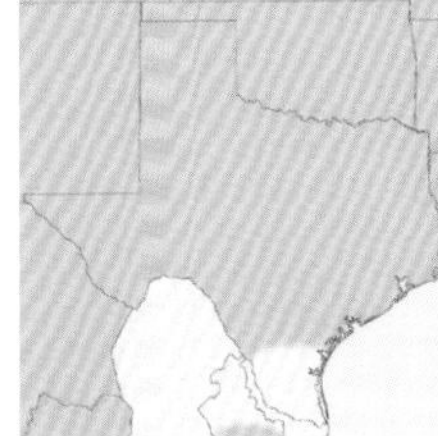

KEY FEATURES

♂—violet body; S8 violet; S9–10 blue; forked shoulder stripe; continuous lateral stripe on S8–10

♀—forked shoulder stripe; S10 and usually S9 pale; lateral abdominal stripes often interrupted in the middle

S5

Size
29–34 mm
(1.1–1.3 in)

Jan Feb Mar Apr May Jun Jul Aug Sep Oct Nov Dec

IDENTIFICATION This is the most common small violet damselfly in Texas. Thorax is violet with a black middorsal stripe and a strongly forked shoulder stripe. Legs are pale, but femora have a dark outer stripe. Abdomen is mostly violet with black rings on S3–6. S7 is usually black with a violet ring, but occasionally black limited to single band. S8–10 is blue, but S8 often has a strong hint of violet. There is a continuous black ventrolateral stripe on S8–10. Females are either brown or violet. Thorax is similar to male's, with a strongly forked shoulder stripe. S2–7 has black lateral stripes (may be interrupted) extending to S8 and rarely to S9. Ovipositor and S10 are pale.

SIMILAR SPECIES Male Blue-tipped Dancers have a nearly black abdomen. Blue-tipped and Dusky Dancer females have darker abdomens and a thicker shoulder stripe, which is forked differently. Male and female Amethyst Dancers have unforked shoulder stripes. Male Lavender Dancers appear more slender, and the ventrolateral stripe on S8–9 extends across half or less of each segment, never continuing to S10. Dark markings on the head and thorax of Lavender Dancers are also less extensive. Female Lavender and Leonora's Dancers are very similar, but lateral stripes on S3–6 tend to be wider and usually not disconnected in middle. Lateral stripe on S8–9 in female Lavender and Leonora's Dancers is usually more distinct. Where these 3 species occur together, microscopic examination is necessary to accurately separate females.

TEXAS STATUS Common. Absent from Lower Rio Grande Valley.

HABITAT Small shallow streams with exposed rocks. Often found on ponds and small lakes and perching along roadsides.

DISCUSSION *A. f. violacea*, known as the Violet Dancer, is the subspecies found in Texas. The 2 other subspecies, which are found in the southeastern United States, have darker wings. Egg laying usually takes place in pairs on submerged plants and debris.

LAVENDER DANCER

Argia hinei (AR-gē- ə HIN-ē-ī)

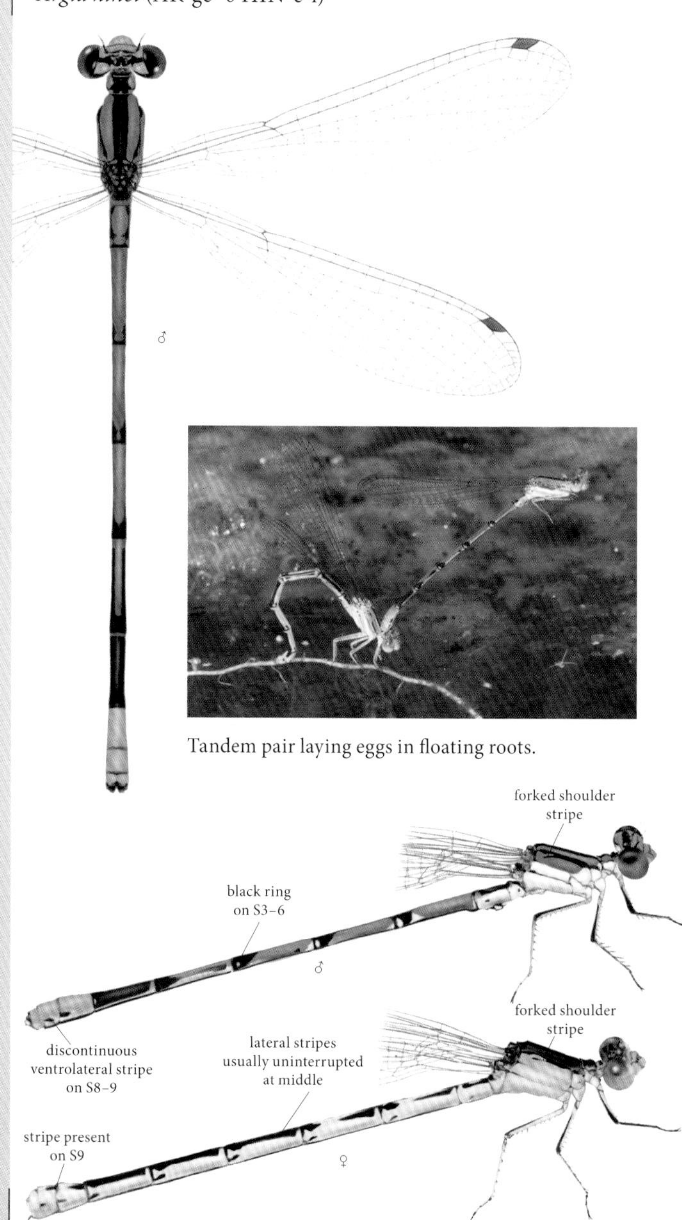

Tandem pair laying eggs in floating roots.

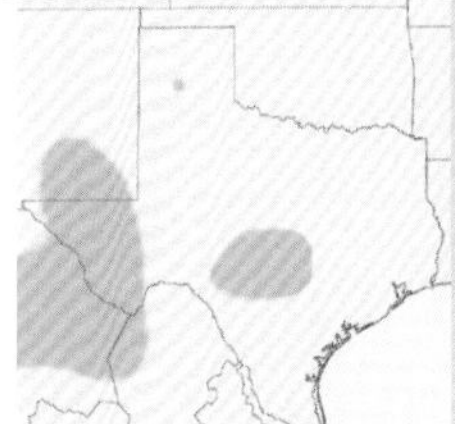

S4

KEY FEATURES

♂—violet; forked shoulder stripe; ventrolateral stripe on S8–9 not continuous

♀—forked shoulder stripe; S9 with dark stripe laterally; lateral abdominal stripes usually uninterrupted at middle on at least S5–6

Size
30–35 mm
(1.2–1.4 in)

IDENTIFICATION In this violet species, the male has a dark mid-dorsal stripe and a forked shoulder stripe. Sides of thorax are pale, often appearing distinctly white. Legs are pale with a dark outer stripe on the femur. Abdomen is violet with black rings on S3–5, more extensive markings on S6, and a nearly all black S7 with a pale ring. S8–10 is blue, sometimes with hint of violet on S8. A black ventrolateral stripe on S8–9 occupies no more than half of each segment. S10 and terminal appendages are pale. Female is brown, often with a reddish tinge. Thorax is brown, fading to cream or white on sides. Legs are pale with less extensive dark markings than male's. Black middorsal and shoulder stripes are as in males. Abdomen has black lateral stripes on S2–9, but these stripes don't extend the entire length of S8 and S9.

SIMILAR SPECIES Male Variable Dancers are similar, but are generally a brighter purple and appear stockier. Male Violets have a nearly complete black ventrolateral stripe on S8–10. Male and female Amethyst and Springwater Dancers have an unforked shoulder stripe. Male Leonora's Dancers are blue and have anteriorly pointing, arrow-shaped dark markings on S3–7. Female Violet and Leonora's Dancers are very similar. Black lateral stripes on S3–6 in Violet females tend to be interrupted in the middle. In Violet females, the dark ventrolateral stripes are often faint or absent on S8–9, and in Leonora's females they extend the entire length of the segments. See the Similar Species section for the Variable Dancer.

TEXAS STATUS Uncommon. May be locally abundant in the Hill Country and the western parts of the state.

HABITAT Creeks, streams, and rivers with abundant emergent vegetation. Often associated with springs.

DISCUSSION Males commonly seen perching on rocks in stream.

Jan
Feb
Mar
Apr
May
Jun
Jul
Aug
Sep
Oct
Nov
Dec

KIOWA DANCER

Argia immunda (AR-gē-ə i-MUN-də)

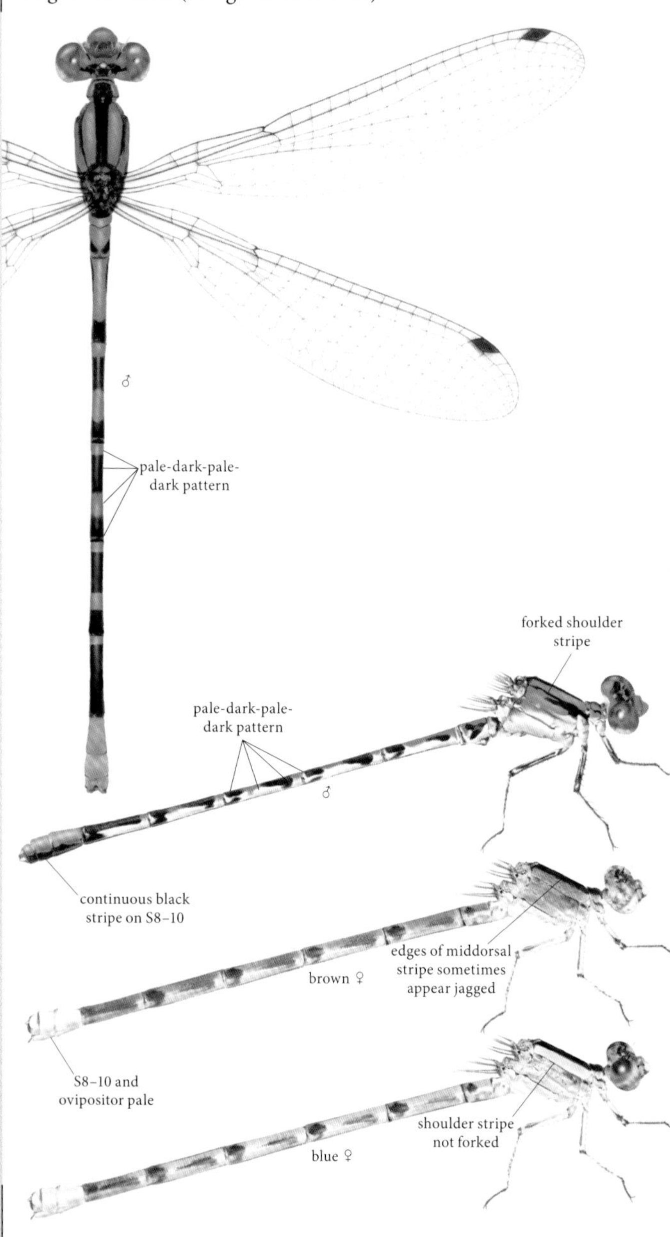

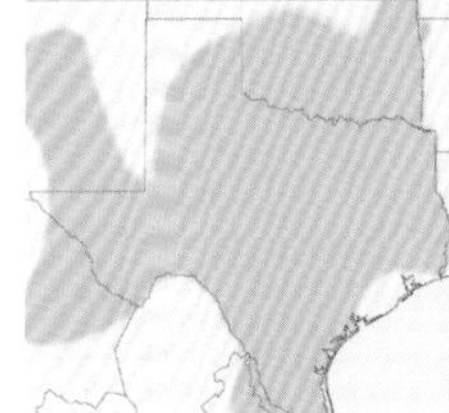

S5

KEY FEATURES

♂—dark purple; forked shoulder stripe; pale-dark-pale-dark pattern on S4–6; continuous black ventrolateral stripe on S8–10

♀—middorsal stripe with jagged edges; shoulder stripe generally not forked; S8–10 pale

Size
30–35 mm
(1.3–1.5 in)

Jan Feb Mar Apr May Jun Jul Aug Sep Oct Nov Dec

IDENTIFICATION Males can look violet or blue and are generally dark. Eyes are dark violet above and blue below. Head and thorax are dark violet or gray. Black middorsal and shoulder stripes are present. Shoulder stripe is forked about midlength; upper fork is very thin. Thorax is pale laterally. Legs are pale with a dark stripe on femur. Abdomen is violet or blue with 2 dark bands per segment on S4–6; from above, these segments form a pale-dark-pale-dark banding pattern. S3 is similar, but the anterior-most dark band is sometimes interrupted. S7 is nearly all black. S8-10 is blue with a continuous ventrolateral stripe. Female can be pale blue or brown. Black middorsal stripe often appears to have jagged edges. Shoulder stripe is thin and faint, sometimes appearing forked anteriorly and posteriorly. Legs are pale with less extensive dark markings than males. Abdomen is similarly patterned to males, but anterior dark bands on S4–6 are not connected, and posterior bands are connected narrowly in one spot. When viewed laterally, pattern appears light-dark-light-dark. S8–10 is blue, sometimes with a ventrolateral stripe on S8–9. Ovipositor is pale.

SIMILAR SPECIES No other damselfly in Texas has the same distinctive light-dark-light-dark abdominal pattern. Females may look superficially similar to those of other species, but the combination of abdominal pattern, unique middorsal stripe, and shoulder stripe distinguishes them.

TEXAS STATUS Common. Widespread across the state.

HABITAT Streams and rivers, but often found perching on the ground, rocks, or vegetation some distance from water. Especially common along roadsides and trails.

DISCUSSION Pairs may be abundant at stream riffles. Females are often perched on the ground away from water.

Argia pallens (AR-gē-ə PAL-ins)

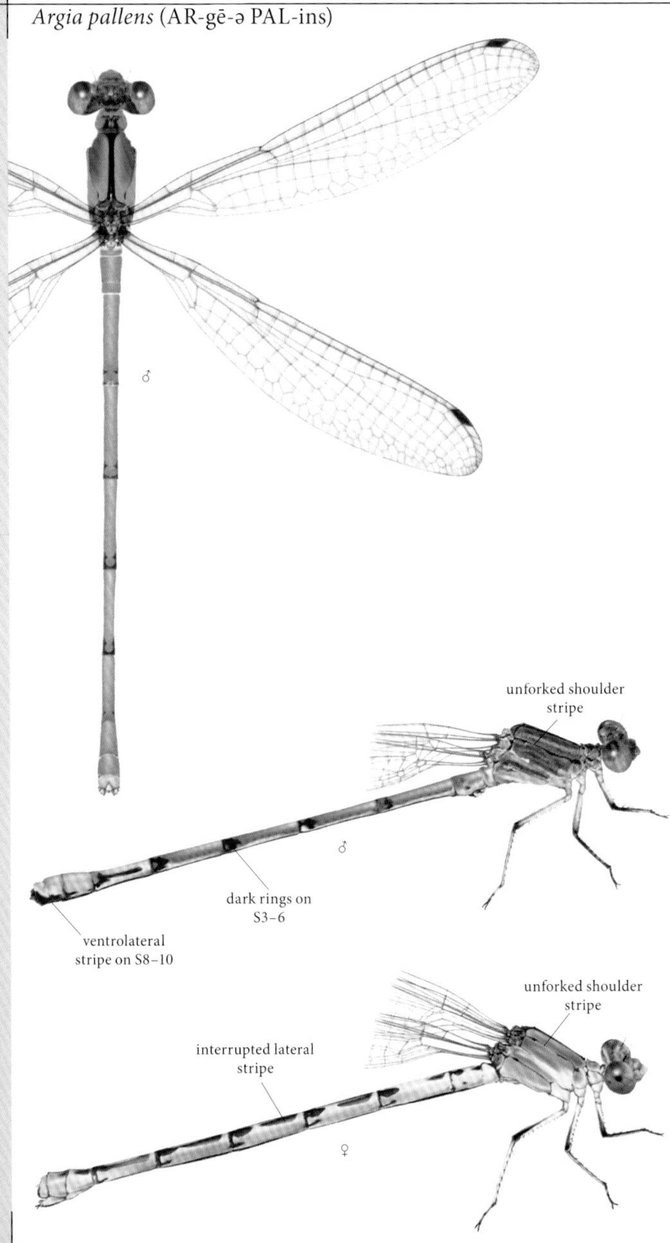

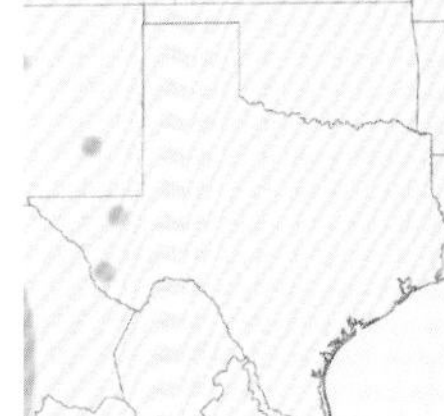

S2

KEY FEATURES

♂—red-violet species with few markings; unforked shoulder stripe; narrow rings on S3–6; S8–10 blue or violet

♀—unforked shoulder stripe; interrupted lateral stripe on S3–6; S9–10 and ovipositor pale

Size
32–35 mm
(1.3–1.4 in)

Jan Feb Mar Apr May Jun Jul Aug Sep Oct Nov Dec

IDENTIFICATION Males of this slender, pale, red-violet species have dark violet or brown eyes. Face, top of head, and thorax are violet. There is a thin black middorsal stripe and an unforked shoulder stripe. Thorax is white on sides. Legs are pale with a thin dark stripe on outer edge of femur. Abdomen is violet with black rings on S3–6. S1–2 is largely violet. S7 is violet with a black lateral stripe reaching nearly the full length of segment. S8–10 is bluish violet with a faint brown ventrolateral stripe that may be absent entirely, especially on S10. Female is similarly patterned to the male, but her overall color is tan. Abdomen has a lateral stripe, which is interrupted on S3–6. S9–10 lacks a ventrolateral stripe, which may be faint on S8.

SIMILAR SPECIES Male Violet and Amethyst Dancers are similar in color, but Violets have forked shoulder stripe and S8 is blue. Female Violet and Leonora's Dancers have forked shoulder stripes. Male Aztec Dancers are blue and have a forked shoulder stripe. Female Aztecs have a darker abdomen with ventrolateral spots on S3–7. Springwater Dancer males are generally blue, and S7 is black dorsally in both males and females.

TEXAS STATUS Rare. Two populations known in Texas.

HABITAT Open, rocky areas of shallow desert streams and occasionally in shade-covered pools.

DISCUSSION Males are often seen perching in the open on rocks. Females will oviposit alone or in tandem on emergent and floating vegetation. One location in Texas where they were found in 2004 has been dry ever since. Many possible habitats are often inaccessible to the public, and it is unclear how common or rare they may be in Texas.

COPPERY DANCER

Argia cuprea (AR-gē-ə CŪ-prē-ə)

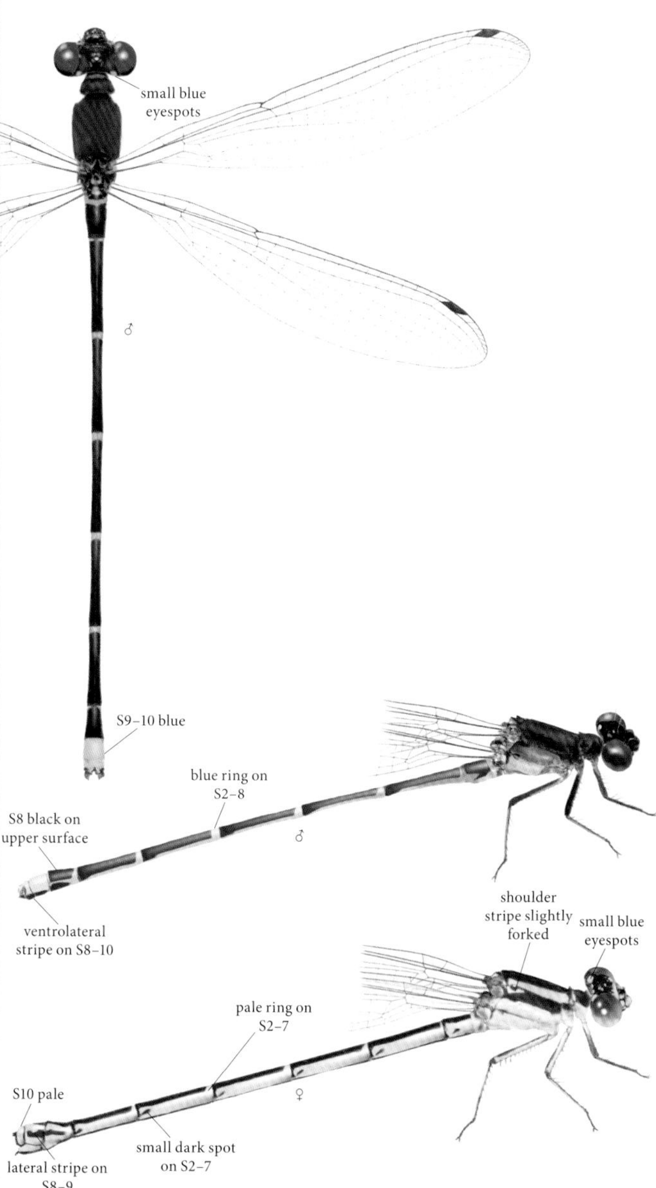

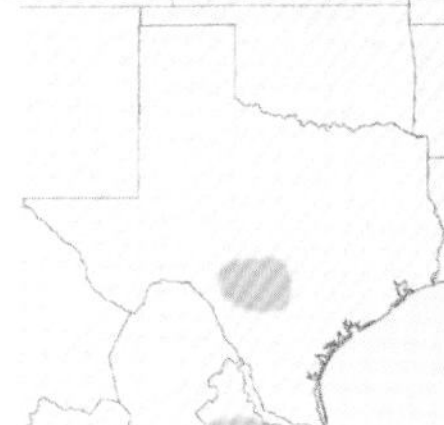

KEY FEATURES

♂—cherry red eyes; coppery red thorax; S8 black and S9–10 blue on upper surface

♀—small blue eyespots; slightly forked shoulder stripe; S2–7 with pale rings and dark ventrolateral spot

S3

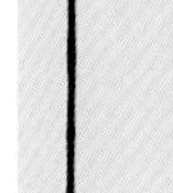

Size
39–42 mm
(1.5–1.7 in)

Jan Feb Mar Apr May Jun Jul Aug Sep Oct Nov Dec

IDENTIFICATION One of Texas's 2 red-eyed dancers. Male has eyes that are brilliant cherry red in front and black in back, fading to blue below. Face and head are coppery red with small circular blue eyespots. Thorax is coppery red, fading to blue on the sides and below. Legs are dark with pale stripe on outer edge. Abdomen is largely black with blue rings. S9–10 is blue, and S8 is black on top. There is a ventrolateral stripe on S8–10. Female is duller in color, but with coppery reflections. Two small blue circular eyespots present. Thorax is tan or bluish with coppery red middorsal and shoulder stripes. Shoulder stripe is broad, but may be forked at its extreme upper end. Sides of thorax are pale. Abdomen is black with pale rings and ventrolateral spots. S8–10 is pale with a dark lateral stripe on S8–9. S10 and ovipositor are nearly all pale.

SIMILAR SPECIES Male Fiery-eyed Dancer is the only other species with red eyes and a coppery red thorax, but that species has a paler abdomen and blue on the upper surface of S8. Female Fiery-eyed Dancers have a deeply forked shoulder stripe. Female Dusky Dancers have a pale postoccipital bar and a deeply forked shoulder stripe. Comanche Dancer females have a pale postoccipital bar and thin shoulder stripe.

TEXAS STATUS Uncommon. May be locally abundant in Hill Country streams.

HABITAT Shallow rivers and streams with floating or emergent vegetation.

DISCUSSION This species was not known from the United States until its discovery in Texas in 1985. It is known from the Nueces, Frio, West Frio, and Sabinal rivers of the Hill Country. Males perch on emergent and streamside rocks and vegetation. Pairs lay eggs in dead leaves and algae floating on water surface.

FIERY-EYED DANCER

Argia oenea (AR-gē-ə ē-NĒ-ə)

Pair laying eggs in tandem.

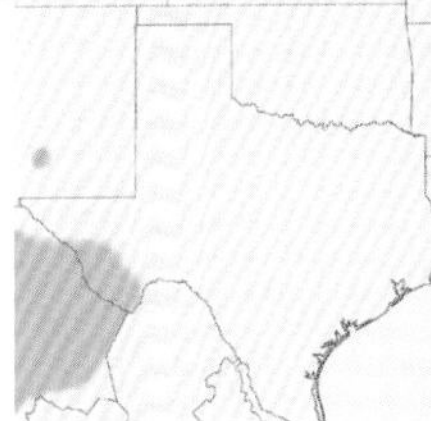

KEY FEATURES

♂—cherry red eyes; coppery red thorax; S8–10 violet with ventrolateral stripe

♀—small eyespots; strongly forked shoulder stripe; S2–7 with pale rings and dark ventrolateral spot

S2

Size
33-39 mm
(1.3-1.5 in)

Jan Feb Mar Apr May Jun Jul Aug Sep Oct Nov Dec

IDENTIFICATION This is another brilliantly colored red-eyed species. The head in males is coppery red with small circular well-separated blue eyespots. Thorax is coppery red, fading to blue or violet laterally and ventrally. Legs are dark with pale stripe on outer edge. Abdomen is violet or blue with black rings tapering anteriorly on S3–6. S7 is black with a pale ring. S8–10 is violet or blue with a continuous black ventrolateral stripe on S8–10. Female is duller in color, but with coppery reflections. Eyespots are as in male. Thorax is tan with a coppery red middorsal stripe. Shoulder stripe is coppery red and deeply forked. Sides of thorax are pale. Abdomen has a nearly continuous black lateral stripe, and S8–9 has a dark ventrolateral stripe.
SIMILAR SPECIES Male Coppery Dancer is the only other species with red eyes and a coppery red thorax, but that species has a largely black abdomen and S8 is black dorsally. Female Coppery Dancers have shoulder stripes barely if at all forked. Female Dusky Dancers have a pale postoccipital bar, and the middorsal thoracic stripe is black, not coppery red. Comanche Dancer females are larger, with a pale postoccipital bar and a thin shoulder stripe.
TEXAS STATUS Rare. Known from only a few localities in the Chinati Mountains and the Sierra Vieja of West Texas.
HABITAT Shallow rivers and streams with floating or emergent vegetation.
DISCUSSION Females lay eggs in tandem on vegetation floating or submerged just beneath the water. They will often completely submerge themselves while the male stays attached. Pairs may aggregate in large numbers when laying eggs.

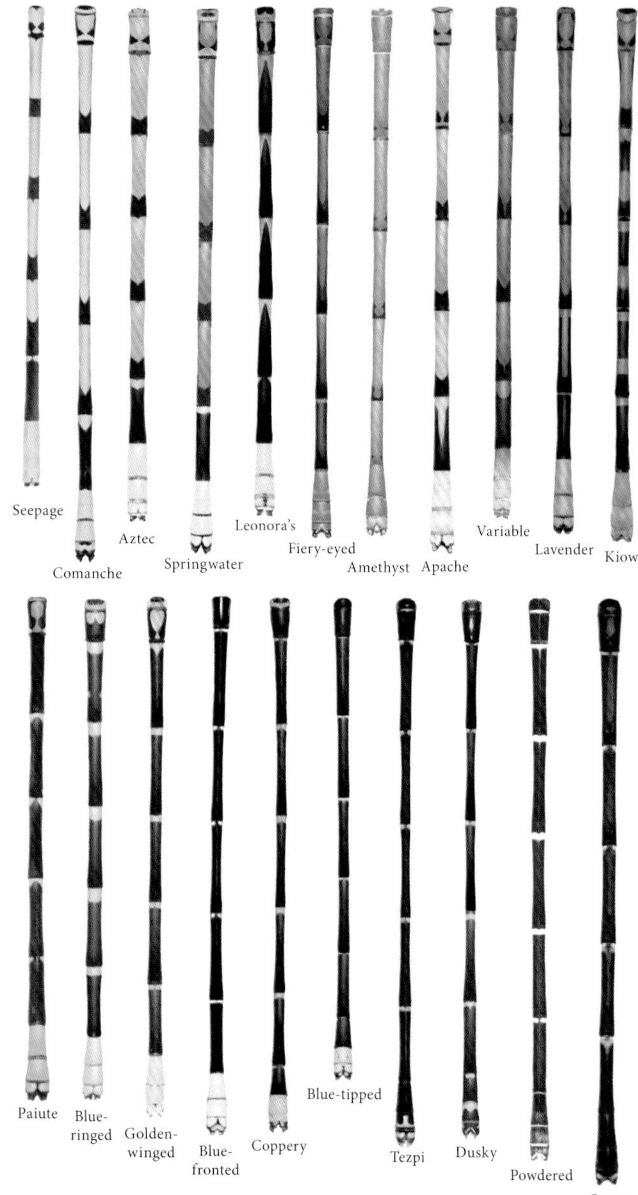
Seepage
Comanche
Aztec
Springwater
Leonora's
Fiery-eyed
Amethyst
Apache
Variable
Lavender
Kiowa
Paiute
Blue-ringed
Golden-winged
Blue-fronted
Coppery
Blue-tipped
Tezpi
Dusky
Powdered
Sooty

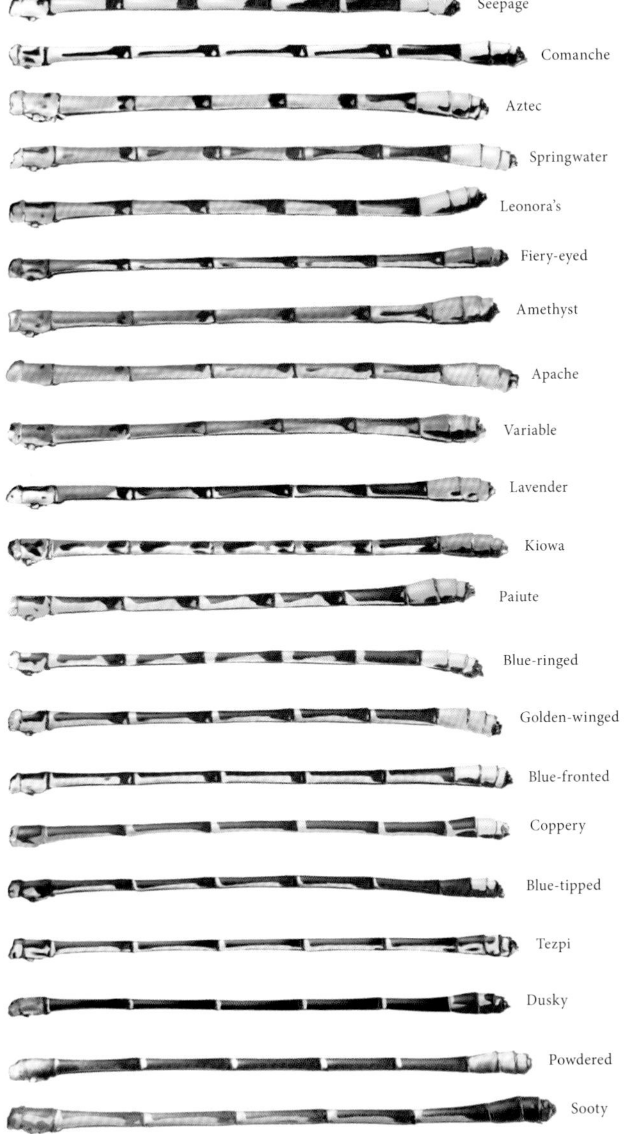
Seepage
Comanche
Aztec
Springwater
Leonora's
Fiery-eyed
Amethyst
Apache
Variable
Lavender
Kiowa
Paiute
Blue-ringed
Golden-winged
Blue-fronted
Coppery
Blue-tipped
Tezpi
Dusky
Powdered
Sooty

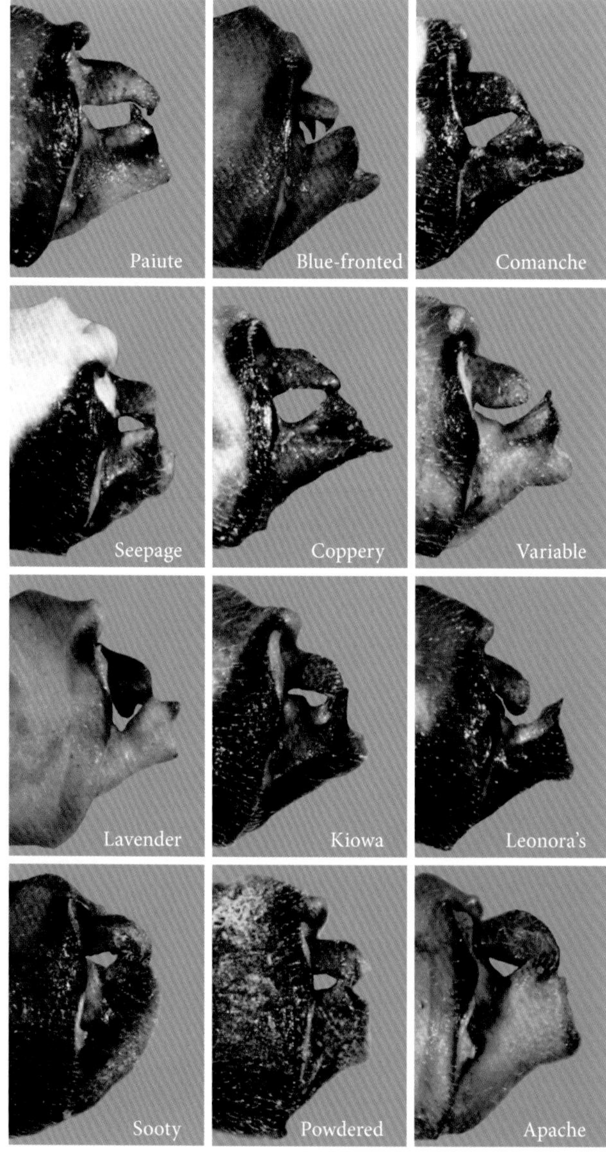
Paiute
Blue-fronted
Comanche
Seepage
Coppery
Variable
Lavender
Kiowa
Leonora's
Sooty
Powdered
Apache

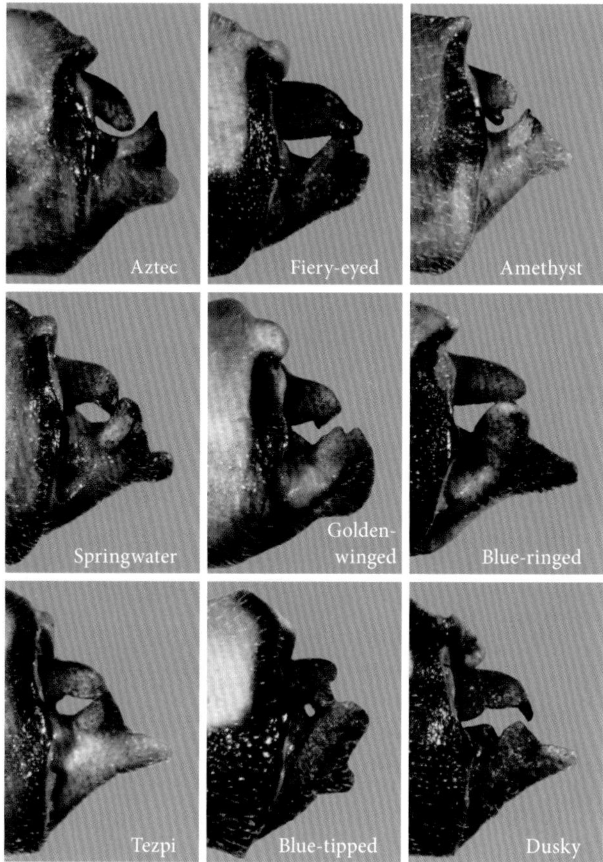
Aztec
Fiery-eyed
Amethyst
Springwater
Golden-
winged
Blue-ringed
Tezpi
Blue-tipped
Dusky

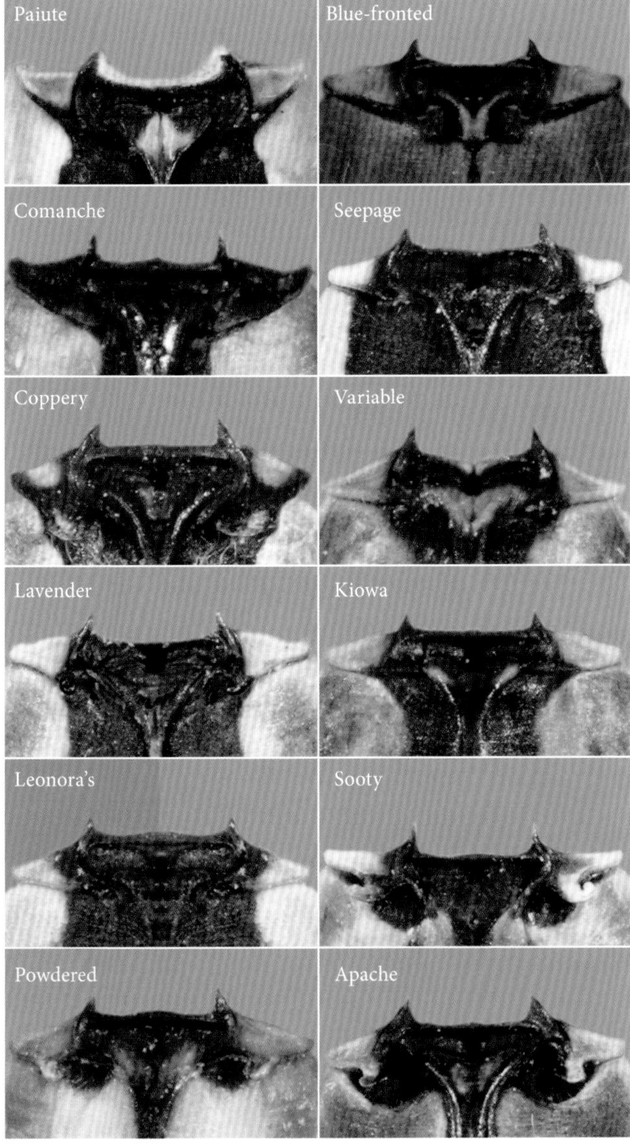
Paiute
Blue-fronted
Comanche
Seepage
Coppery
Variable
Lavender
Kiowa
Leonora's
Sooty
Powdered
Apache

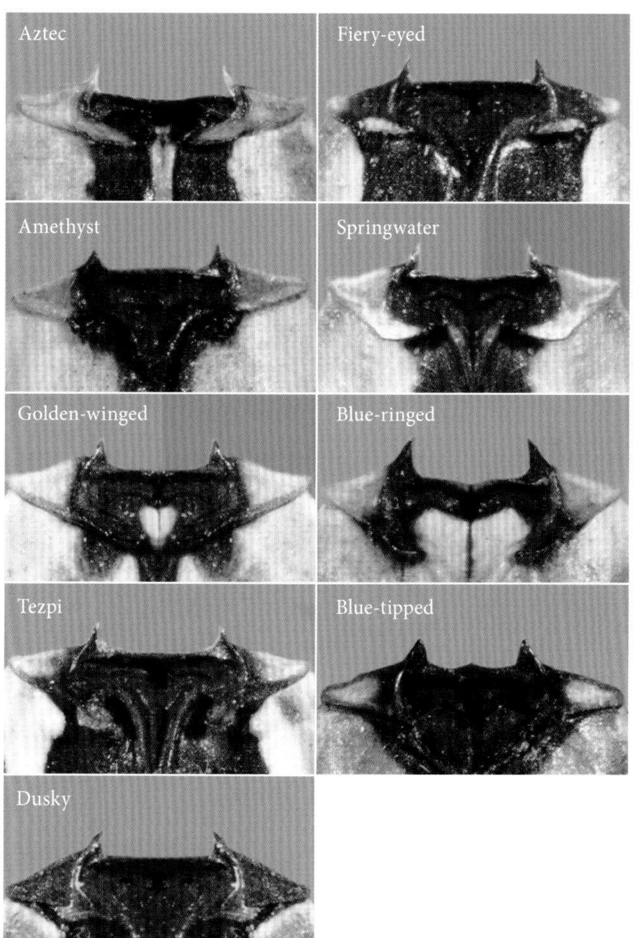
Aztec
Fiery-eyed
Amethyst
Springwater
Golden-winged
Blue-ringed
Tezpi
Blue-tipped
Dusky

BURGUNDY BLUET

Enallagma dubium (en-a-LAG-mə DEW-bē-um)

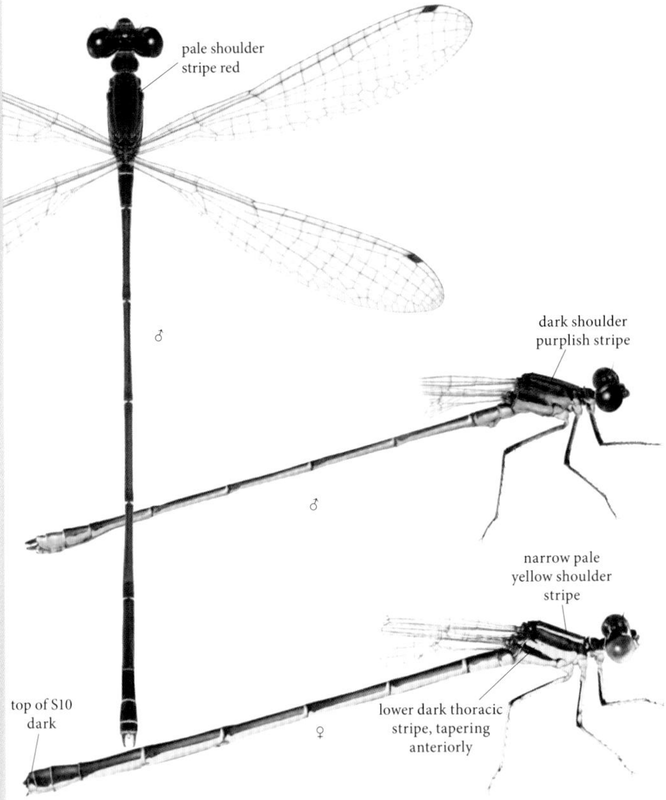

pale shoulder stripe red

♂

dark shoulder purplish stripe

♂

narrow pale yellow shoulder stripe

top of S10 dark

♀

lower dark thoracic stripe, tapering anteriorly

Pair laying eggs among lily pads.

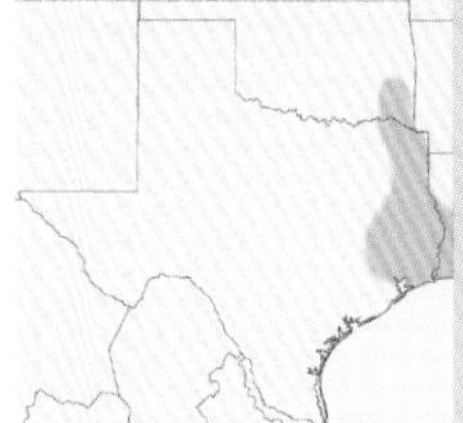

KEY FEATURES

♂—thin red eyespots and occipital bar; broad purple shoulder stripe; tapering stripe low on side of thorax

♀—narrow yellow pale shoulder stripe; tapering stripe low on side of thorax; S10 dark

S3

Size
25–30 mm
(1.0–1.2 in)

IDENTIFICATION This is the only red bluet in Texas. Male has deep red eyes and face. Top of head is black with metallic reflections. Eyespots and occipital bar form a continuous thin red line. Middorsal stripe is black with a metallic purple or blue-green luster. Broad black shoulder stripe, often revealing a metallic luster, is bordered above by a thin red pale shoulder stripe. Black stripe on lower thorax tapers anteriorly toward the legs. Lower thorax is red-orange. Legs are orange-red. Abdomen is largely black with orange-red on sides. Female is paler, more orange-yellow or tan, but otherwise similar in pattern to the male.

SIMILAR SPECIES The male Orange Bluet is larger, lacks a lower tapering thoracic stripe, and is more orange in color. Female Orange and Vesper Bluets are also larger, lack a tapering lower thoracic stripe, are generally greener, have a narrower dark shoulder stripe, and are pale on top of S10.

TEXAS STATUS Uncommon. May be found throughout East Texas.

HABITAT Heavily vegetated black-water ponds, lakes, oxbows, and sloughs, and the slow reaches of streams.

DISCUSSION Burgundy Bluets seem to be locally restricted from west of the Mississippi River to Caddo Lake, the southeastern Piney Woods, and the Big Thicket region of eastern Texas and southeastern Oklahoma. It is infrequently encountered in these areas, generally in areas where lily pads are abundant. These bluets can become amazingly inconspicuous, seemingly disappearing as they enter shaded areas while patrolling. Mating pairs can be seen from midday into the afternoon on floating vegetation. Pairs prefer to lay eggs through holes in water lily leaves, where the female may submerge her abdomen to deposit eggs in semicircular rows on the underside of the leaf, a process that can take up to 30 minutes.

Jan
Feb
Mar
Apr
May
Jun
Jul
Aug
Sep
Oct
Nov
Dec

ORANGE BLUET

Enallagma signatum (en-a-LAG-mə sig-NĀ-tum)

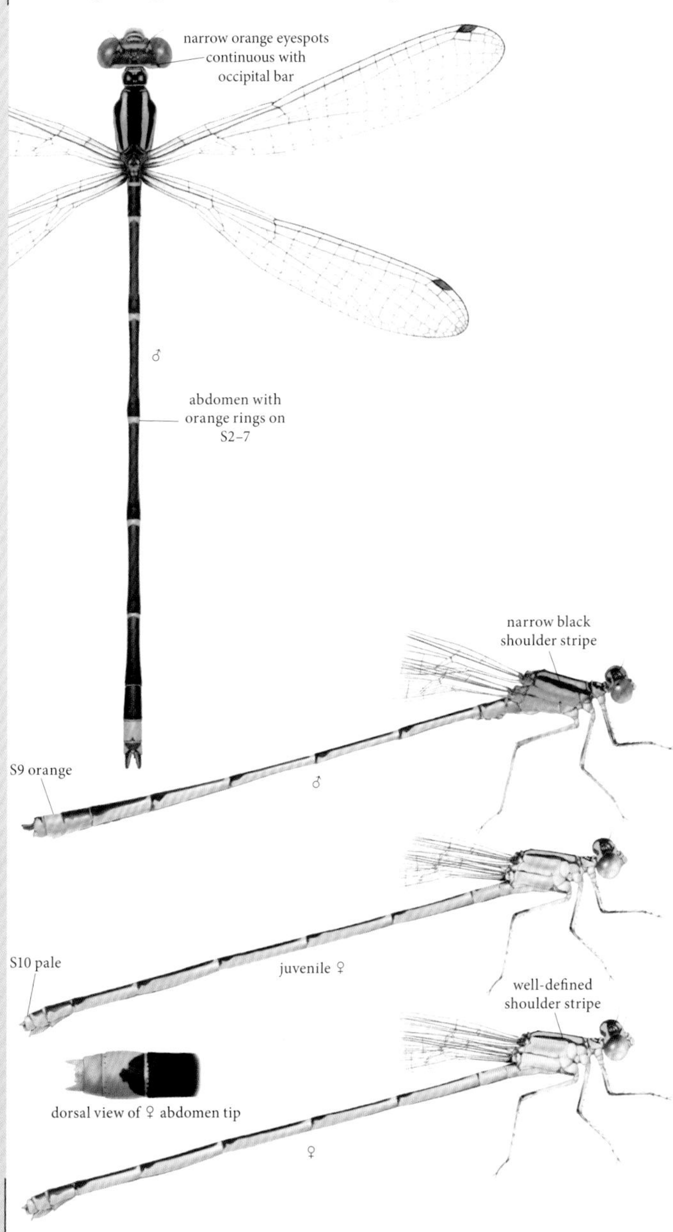

KEY FEATURES

♂—orange face and thorax; thin black shoulder stripe; abdomen black with orange rings; S9 orange

♀—green or blue; well-defined black shoulder stripe; abdomen black; S10 pale

Size
28–37 mm
(1.1–1.5 in)

Jan Feb Mar Apr May Jun Jul Aug Sep Oct Nov Dec

IDENTIFICATION This is the only orange bluet in Texas. Mature males are long and slender with orange eyes and face. Top of head is black with narrow orange eyespots connected by an occipital bar. Middorsal stripe is wide and black. Black shoulder stripe is narrower than the orange stripe above it. Rest of thorax is orange. Legs are orange with black stripe on outer surface. Abdomen is largely black with orange rings on S2–7. S8 is all black. S9–10 is orange with prominent black spot on top of S10. Caudal appendages of male are elongate and distinctive. Juvenile males are as above, but pale blue. Female is similarly patterned to male, and blue as juvenile, becoming yellow-green. S1–8 is generally as in male. S9 is black above, and S10 is pale.
SIMILAR SPECIES Burgundy Bluets are smaller and red. Vesper Bluets are similar, but males are yellow with blue abdominal segments distally. In that species, the shoulder stripe is very narrow in both sexes, often nearly absent in males and suffused with brown in females. Texas threadtail species are red or orange and are found alongside Orange Bluets, but have much longer and thinner abdomens (twice as long as the wings), and S9 is dark. Lilypad and Eastern Forktails are stockier and lack orange at abdomen tip. Juvenile Orange Bluet males appear similar to Stream Bluets, but that species has a narrower pale shoulder stripe.
TEXAS STATUS Common. Widespread, but lacking in Panhandle and western part of state.
HABITAT Ponds, lakes, and slow-moving streams and rivers.
DISCUSSION The Orange Bluet is unusual in that it is most active in the late afternoon. Females stay some distance from the water, and are not often encountered except in copula or tandem. Males are often seen hovering low above the water, occasionally perching on water lilies or other emergent vegetation. Females have been recorded laying eggs underwater for up to 20 minutes.

Enallagma vesperum (en-a-LAG-mə və-SPARE-um)

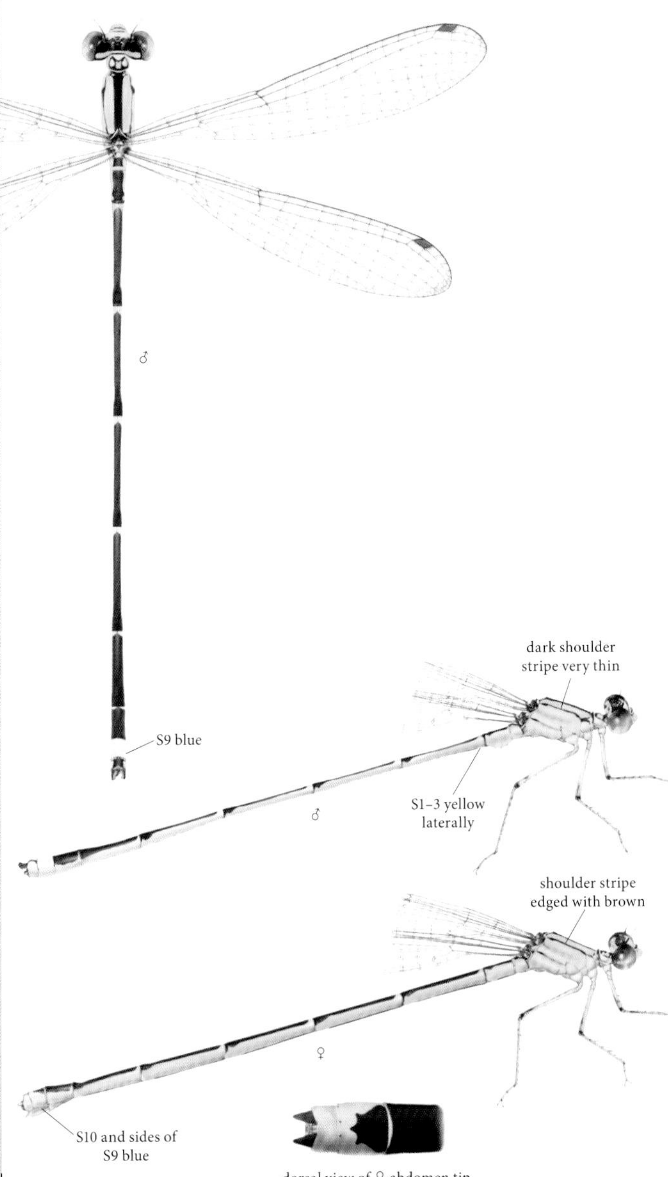

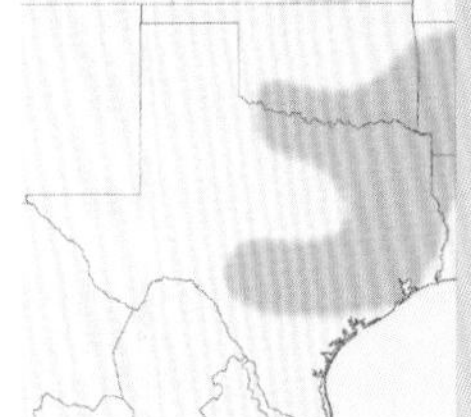

KEY FEATURES

♂—head and thorax yellow; thin shoulder stripe may be edged with brown; S9 blue

♀—yellow-green head and thorax; thin shoulder stripe edged with brown; S10 and sides of S9 pale

S5

Size
29–37 mm
(1.1–1.5 in)

IDENTIFICATION Males of this long, slender, bright yellow species have narrow eyespots connected by a yellow occipital bar. Middorsal stripe is black. Shoulder stripe is very thin, often nearly absent, and sometimes edged with brown. Legs are yellow. Abdomen is largely black, but S1–3 may show yellow on sides. S9 and sides of S10 are blue. Juvenile males are blue, not yellow. Female similar to male, but generally greener in color, and shoulder stripe more often has brown edges. Abdomen is largely black. S9 has a wide black triangular spot above. S10 is pale.
SIMILAR SPECIES The Vesper Bluet is the only yellow bluet in Texas. Juvenile Vesper males are blue and similar to juvenile male Orange Bluets, but Orange Bluets have a much more distinctive shoulder stripe. Female Vesper and Orange Bluets are also similar, but can be separated by the latter's more prominent shoulder stripe. The female Turquoise Bluet has a wider dark shoulder stripe divided by a thin stripe of brown. Juvenile male Stream Bluets have more blue on the side of S8 and a wider dark shoulder stripe. No forktail in Texas is yellow with S9–10 blue.
TEXAS STATUS Uncommon. Widespread in the eastern half of the state. Probably more common than records reveal because of its habit of flying only at dusk or after dark.
HABITAT Most commonly found in heavily vegetated ponds and lakes, but occasionally in slow reaches of streams.
DISCUSSION The Vesper Bluet is an unusual species in that it is most active in the late evening and often does not appear over water until sunset. They are sometimes attracted to lights at night. Their coloration and delicate shape allow them to easily take cover in vegetation during the day; however, they may be seen sneaking about in the morning hours as well. Pairs may leave the water, for up to 20 minutes, to mate. Egg laying occurs in tandem, occasionally after dark, in stems below the surface.

Jan
Feb
Mar
Apr
May
Jun
Jul
Aug
Sep
Oct
Nov
Dec

ALKALI BLUET

Enallagma clausum (en-a-LAG-mə KLAU-sum)

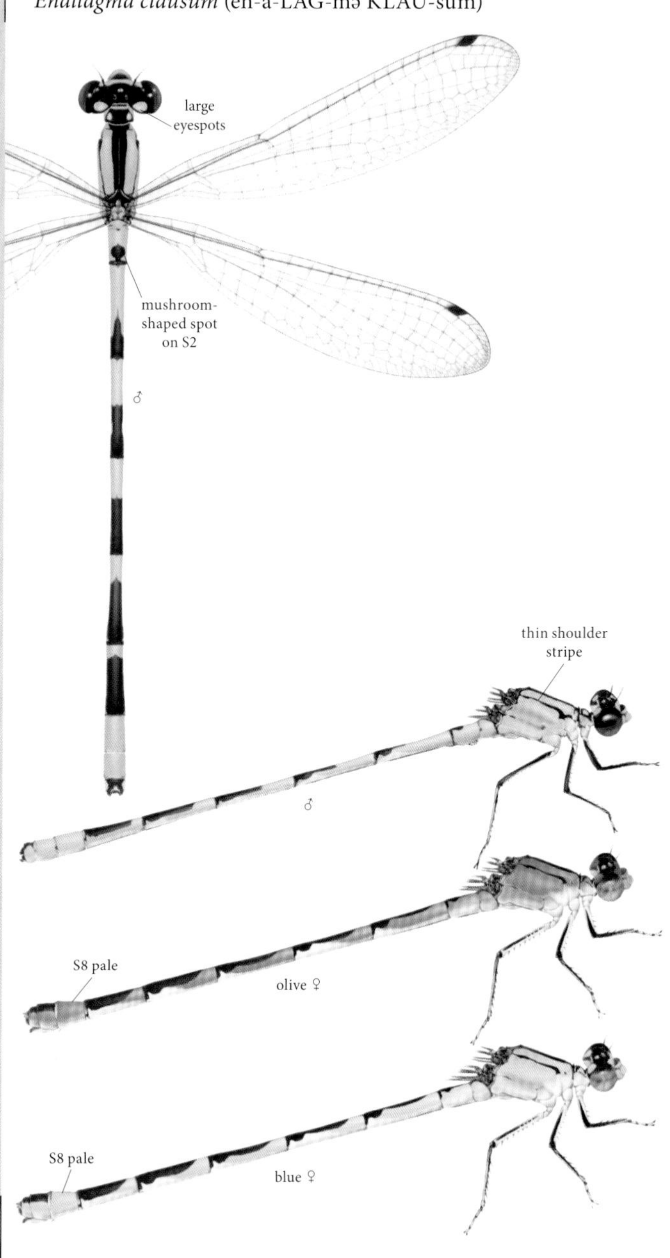

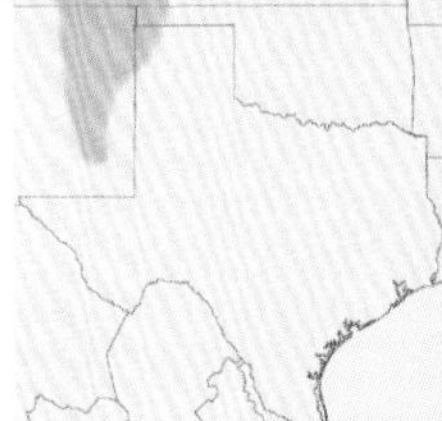

KEY FEATURES

♂—large eyespots; narrow shoulder stripe; black on S2–7 increases on each segment

♀—olive or blue; large eyespots; narrow shoulder stripe; S8 pale

S1

Size
28–35 mm
(1.1–1.4 in)

IDENTIFICATION Male has medium-to-large blue eyespots, generally separated by a thin blue occipital bar. Black middorsal thoracic stripe is divided by a thin blue line. Black shoulder stripe is narrow. Legs are blue or tan with black stripes. Abdomen is primarily blue. Top of S2 has a black mushroom-shaped spot. S3–5 has black rings occupying a third to half of each segment. S6 is black on three-fourths of the segment, and S7 is nearly all black. S8–9 is blue, and S10 is blue with black on upper surface. Female is olive or blue with the head and thorax similar to the male's, except the occipital bar is more apparent. Dark shoulder stripe is narrow, as in male. Abdomen is largely black, but S8 is entirely pale.

SIMILAR SPECIES Tule Bluets generally have more black on the abdomen and smaller eyespots. Familiar Bluets have smaller eyespots and more blue on abdomen. Big Bluets are larger, have a more distinctive blue middorsal carina, and arrow-shaped marks on the upper surface of S3–5. Females are very similar to a number of species, and close, in-hand, or microscopic examination may be required to reliably separate them. Female Alkali Bluets have a pair of pits on the prothorax, which may be visible with a hand lens.

TEXAS STATUS Rare. Known from a single location in Hartley Co. May show up in other localized areas of the Texas Panhandle.

HABITAT Ponds and lakes, especially those with saline or alkaline water.

DISCUSSION The Alkali Bluet gets its name because it is often the only damselfly inhabiting saline or alkaline lakes. It is not restricted to these bodies of water, however, and may be found on freshwater lakes and ponds. Males commonly perch on shoreline rocks and vegetation, but will also readily perch on the ground. Females oviposit in tandem or alone on algal mats.

Jan Feb Mar Apr May Jun Jul Aug Sep Oct Nov Dec

ARROYO BLUET

Enallagma praevarum (en-a-LAG-mə prē-VAR-um)

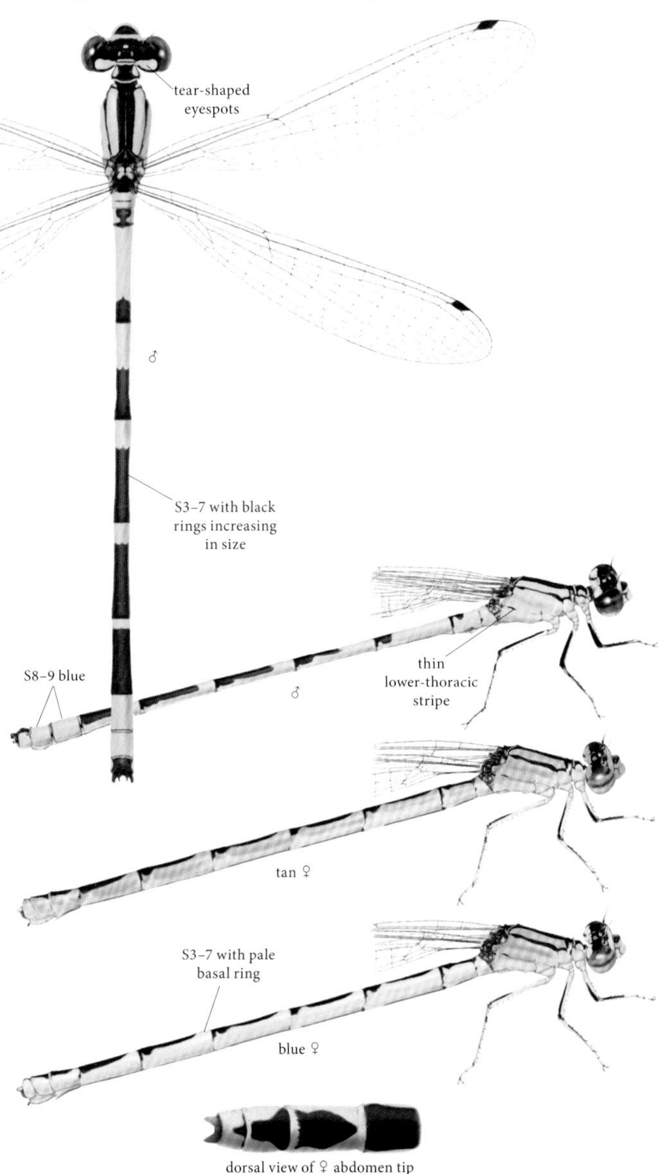

dorsal view of ♀ abdomen tip

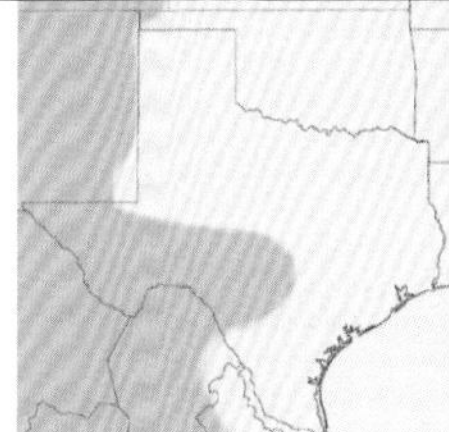

KEY FEATURES

♂—small blue tear-shaped eyespots; S3–7 with black rings getting wider posteriorly; S8–9 blue

♀—tan or blue; pale eyespots confluent with occipital bar; S8 with black triangle on top of segment; S9–10 with black stripe above

S5

Size
26–35 mm
(1.0–1.4 in)

Jan Feb Mar Apr May Jun Jul Aug Sep Oct Nov Dec

IDENTIFICATION This is a small blue western species. The male has tear-shaped blue eyespots separated by a blue occipital bar. Thorax is blue with a dark middorsal stripe generally divided by a pale blue line. Black shoulder stripe is thin and unforked. Evidence of a lower, thinner thoracic stripe may be visible. Abdomen is largely blue. S2 has a mushroom-shaped spot that generally covers entire length of segment. S3–7 has black rings that get progressively wider to nearly consume all of S7. S8–9 is blue. S10 is blue with large black spot on top. Female is similar to male, but may be either tan or blue. Eyespots are generally larger and confluent with occipital bar. Legs are paler than in male. Each segment of S3–7 has a broad black stripe above, interrupted anteriorly to reveal a blue ring from above. S8 has a black triangle above, and S9–10 has a black stripe above, usually narrowing at its middle on S10.

SIMILAR SPECIES The Familiar Bluet is similar, but black on the abdomen of the smaller Arroyo Bluet is generally more extensive, giving it an overall darker appearance. Other similar western bluets, like Alkalis and Tules, generally have less black on S2. Male forktails that may be found with Arroyo Bluets have a green thorax or a pale shoulder stripe divided into two pale dots.

TEXAS STATUS Common. Locally abundant in western portions of the state.

HABITAT Slow reaches of streams with emergent vegetation.

DISCUSSION Males may be common at streamside vegetation, but females are rarely seen except in pairs. Females oviposit in tandem in floating vegetation, but will also oviposit by moving headfirst down vegetation until submerged, when males release females and guard from above.

DOUBLE-STRIPED BLUET

Enallagma basidens (en-a-LAG-mə BAY-si-dens)

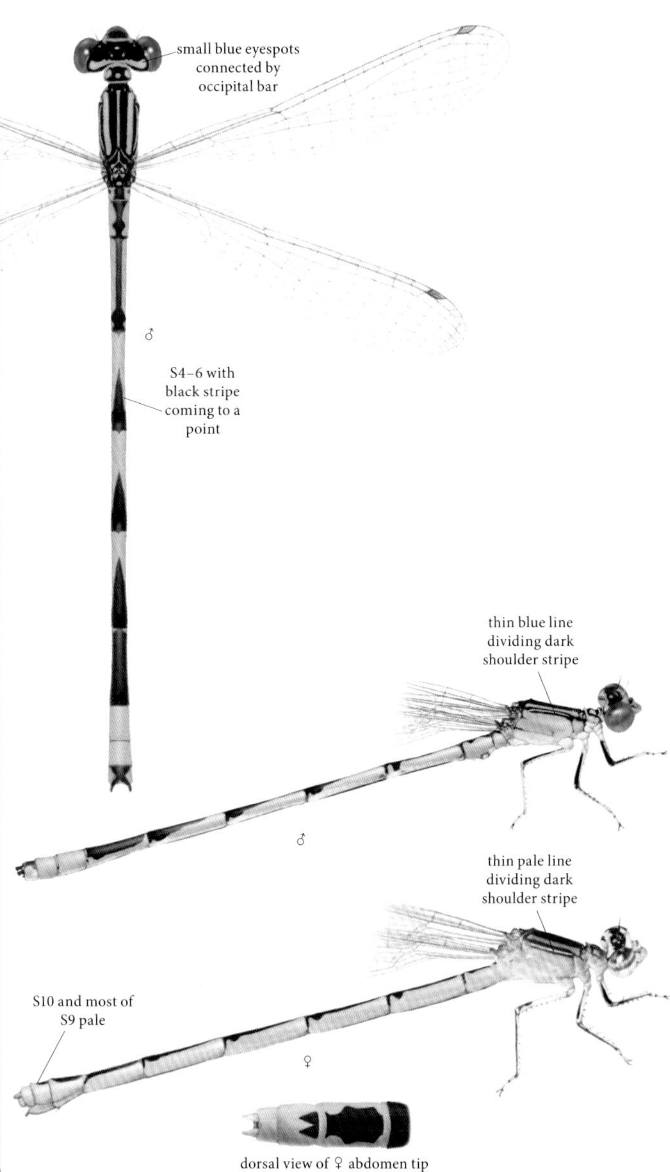

dorsal view of ♀ abdomen tip

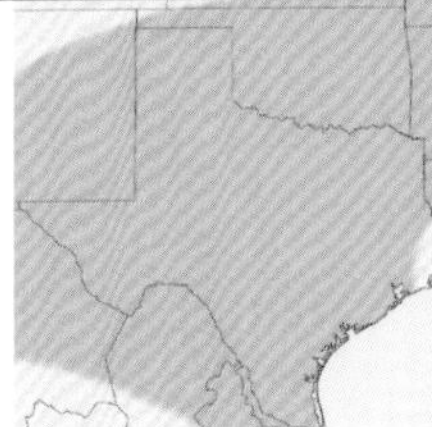

KEY FEATURES

♂—black shoulder stripe cleanly divided by thin blue stripe; S8–9 blue

♀—black shoulder stripe cleanly divided by thin blue stripe; most of S9 and all of S10 pale

S5

Size
21–28 mm
(0.8–1.1 in)

Jan Feb Mar Apr May Jun Jul Aug Sep Oct Nov Dec

IDENTIFICATION This is a small delicate blue damselfly. Top of male's head is largely black with a thin blue occipital bar connecting small blue eyespots. Black middorsal thoracic stripe is divided by a thin blue line. Black shoulder stripe is divided its entire length by a narrow blue stripe. Legs are pale blue or cream with dark stripe on outer surface of femur. Abdomen is largely blue. Top of S2 has a black medial stripe appearing like an hourglass. It connects to S3, where it abruptly expands to form a spot posteriorly. Top of S4–6 has black arrows pointing anteriorly and not reaching beyond middle of segment. S7 is all black. S8–9 is all blue, and S10 is black on top and blue on sides. Juvenile males may have the blue replaced with tan or brown. Head and thorax of female closely resemble male's, but with pale colors more extensive: light brown, green, or blue. As in the male, black shoulder stripe is divided its entire length by a thin pale line. S3–6 entirely black except for narrow pale ring. S8 is black on top. S9 is mostly pale with 2 dark black stripes on either side of the midline reaching posteriorly up to two-thirds of segment length. S10 is pale.
SIMILAR SPECIES The Double-striped Bluet is the smallest Texas bluet. No other damselfly has a thin pale stripe dividing both the dark shoulder stripe and the middorsal stripe for its entire length. Dorsal pattern on S9 of female is also unique.
TEXAS STATUS Common. Widespread throughout the state.
HABITAT Various permanent and semipermanent ponds, lakes, and reservoirs as well as slow reaches of streams and rivers.
DISCUSSION The Double-striped Bluet, originally described from Texas, has expanded its range considerably. This expansion is probably a result of extensive irrigation providing new suitable breeding habitats. Females are often observed around water only while in tandem. Egg laying occurs in tandem where floating masses of filamentous algae and other vegetation occur.

FAMILIAR BLUET

Enallagma civile (en-a-LAG-mə si-VILL-ē)

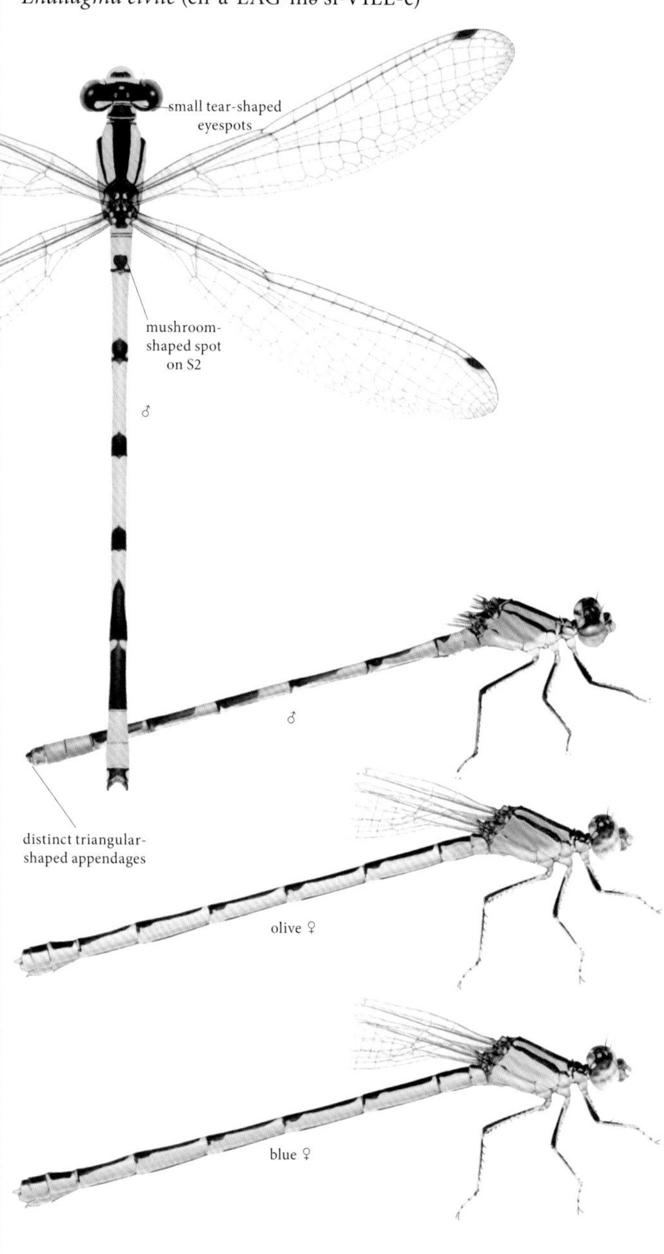

S5

KEY FEATURES

♂—small, tear-shaped eyespots; occipital bar thin; triangular-shaped caudal appendages as long as S10

♀—thin occipital bar generally present; black above all abdominal segments

Size
29–39 mm
(1.1–1.5 in)

Jan Feb Mar Apr May Jun Jul Aug Sep Oct Nov Dec

IDENTIFICATION Top of head is largely black except for 2 small blue tear-shaped eyespots. Occipital bar is generally present and connects eyepsots. Broad black middorsal thoracic stripe is at least twice as wide as black shoulder stripe. Legs are pale with a black stripe on outer surface. Abdomen largely blue, marked with black. S2 has large irregular black spot on top. S3–5 has similar but larger spots that become rings around abdomen and end in a point on top. These rings usually do not extend more than a fifth of each segment. Black stripe on S6–7 extends half to three-fourths the length of segment. S8–9 blue, and S10 is blue with black on top. Females may be blue, tan, or olive. Head and thorax are similarly marked to male's. Occipital bar is generally more pronounced than in males.

SIMILAR SPECIES S7 in male Azure Bluet is black. Generally, no more than a fourth of S2 is black in Alkali Bluets, and Arroyo Bluets are thinner and darker overall. Big Bluets are larger, have a dark middorsal thoracic stripe divided by blue, and have arrow-shaped marks on upper surface of S3–5. Atlantic and Tule Bluets are very similar. Tule Bluets have more black on abdomen. Atlantic Bluets generally have more pronounced occipital bar and larger eyespots, but in-hand examination is necessary to tell them apart.

TEXAS STATUS Common. Widespread throughout the state.

HABITAT Ephemeral or permanent ponds and lakes. Also, slow-flowing streams, regardless of salinity or vegetation.

DISCUSSION Peak activity is from midmorning into the afternoon. Mating averages 20 minutes. Egg laying occurs in tandem, with the male letting go to guard at a nearby perch before the female becomes completely submerged. Eggs are deposited in algae, roots, leaves, and upright stems at the surface of the water. Females usually remain submerged an average of 12 minutes, but may lay eggs for more than an hour below the surface, descending backward.

ATLANTIC BLUET

Enallagma doubledayi (en-a-LAG-mə DUB-el-dā-ī)

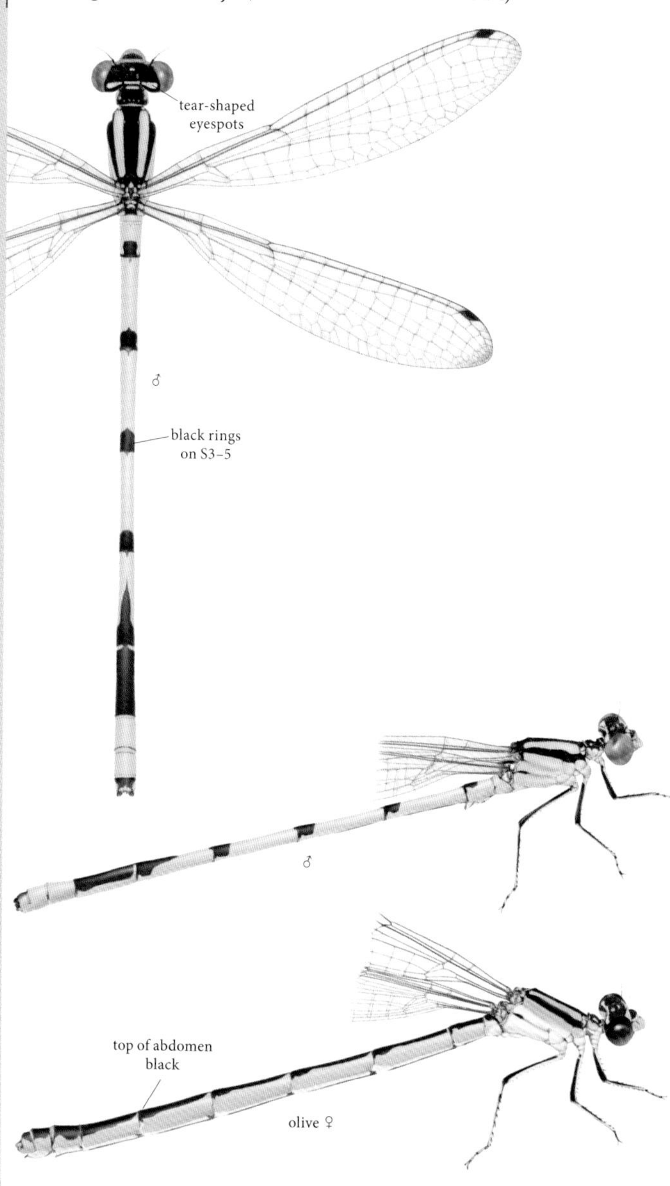

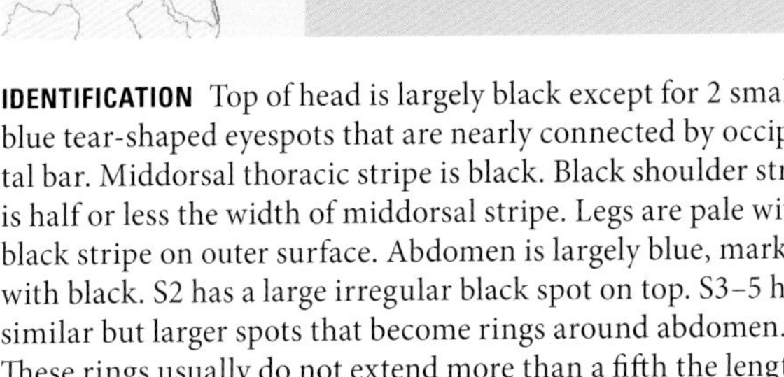

KEY FEATURES

♂—narrow tear-shaped eyespots; occipital bar present; abdomen with black rings; S8–9 blue

♀—tear-shaped eyespots and occipital bar present; S2–10 black on top

Size
28–37 mm
(1.1–1.5 in)

Jan Feb Mar Apr May Jun Jul Aug Sep Oct Nov Dec

IDENTIFICATION Top of head is largely black except for 2 small blue tear-shaped eyespots that are nearly connected by occipital bar. Middorsal thoracic stripe is black. Black shoulder stripe is half or less the width of middorsal stripe. Legs are pale with a black stripe on outer surface. Abdomen is largely blue, marked with black. S2 has a large irregular black spot on top. S3–5 has similar but larger spots that become rings around abdomen. These rings usually do not extend more than a fifth the length of the segment. Black stripe on S6–7 extends half to three-fourths length of segment. S8–9 is blue, and S10 is blue with black on top. Female's head and thorax are similarly marked to male's, but may be blue, tan, or olive.
SIMILAR SPECIES Atlantics may be easily confused with Familiar Bluets which generally have a narrower, shorter occipital bar and smaller eyespots. Males are easily distinguished in-hand by the larger superior appendages of Familiars. Male Big Bluets are similar, but usually much larger. The middorsal thoracic stripe of that species is also divided by a thin blue stripe medially. Females of Familiar, Big, and Atlantic Bluets are similar. The Familiar Bluet has a narrower, less extensive occipital bar, and the Big Bluet is usually much larger with a blue line bisecting the middorsal thoracic stripe. Careful in-hand examination is warranted to separate these 3.
TEXAS STATUS Rare. Known only from Anderson, Bastrop, and Collin counties.
HABITAT Newly formed or temporary shallow ponds and lakes.
DISCUSSION Males can generally be seen conspicuously perched on riparian vegetation at the water's edge. Pairs mate on emergent vegetation, and females lay eggs in tandem. The female remains underwater, laying eggs after pulling free from the male, for only a few minutes at a time. Males remain perched nearby, guarding the female. Leafhoppers are a common prey item.

BIG BLUET

Enallagma durum (en-a-LAG-mə DUR-um)

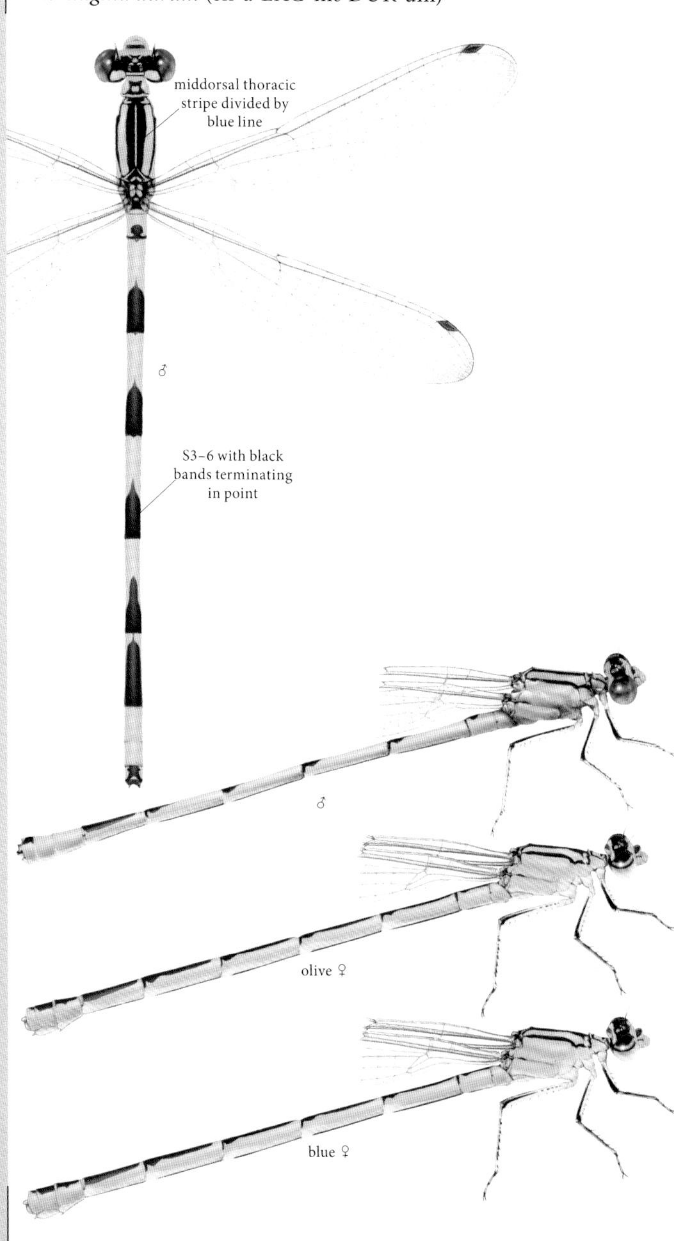

S3

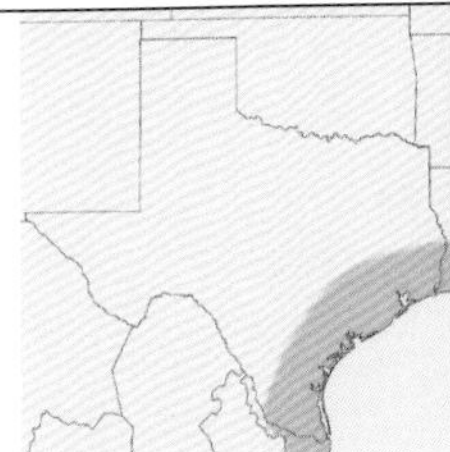

KEY FEATURES

♂—large; middorsal thoracic stripe divided by blue line; arrow-shaped markings on top of S3–6

♀—large; tan or olive; middorsal thoracic stripe divided by pale line

Size
34–44 mm
(1.3–1.7 in)

Jan Feb Mar Apr May Jun Jul Aug Sep Oct Nov Dec

IDENTIFICATION This is Texas's largest bluet. Face and eyes in male are blue. Narrow triangular eyespots are connected, or nearly so, by blue occipital bar. Middorsal thoracic stripe is bisected entire length by blue. Black shoulder stripe is slightly narrower than pale stripe above it. Legs are pale, either tan or blue, with black stripe on the outer surface. Abdomen is largely blue; arrow-shaped black marks on top of S3–6 come to a sharp point. S7 is nearly all black. S8–9 is blue, and S10 is blue with black spot on top. Female is blue, brown, or olive. Head and thorax are generally like those of males. Abdomen is largely black on top.

SIMILAR SPECIES Both sexes of Big Bluets can generally be recognized by their large size, but smaller individuals do occur and may be confused with Familiar and Atlantic Bluets. However, males of both those species lack the arrow-shaped markings on S3–6. If the overall size and appearance of eyespots are not conclusive, then in-hand examination will be necessary to separate females.

TEXAS STATUS Uncommon. Largely restricted to the coastline, where it may be locally abundant.

HABITAT Along the shores of large, often sandy lakes and estuaries, often with emergent vegetation.

DISCUSSION This species frequently inhabits brackish waters and seldom ventures far from the seacoast. It is considered one of the more primitive bluets because of its distinct venation and genitalia. Despite being the largest bluet in North America, little is known about its reproductive behavior. Females are known to lay eggs head-downward underwater while males guard from perching sites above. It has been suggested that the large size of Big Bluets may be an adaptation to high winds on open lakes and shorelines.

Enallagma carunculatum (en-a-LAG-mə ca-runc-ū-LOT-um)

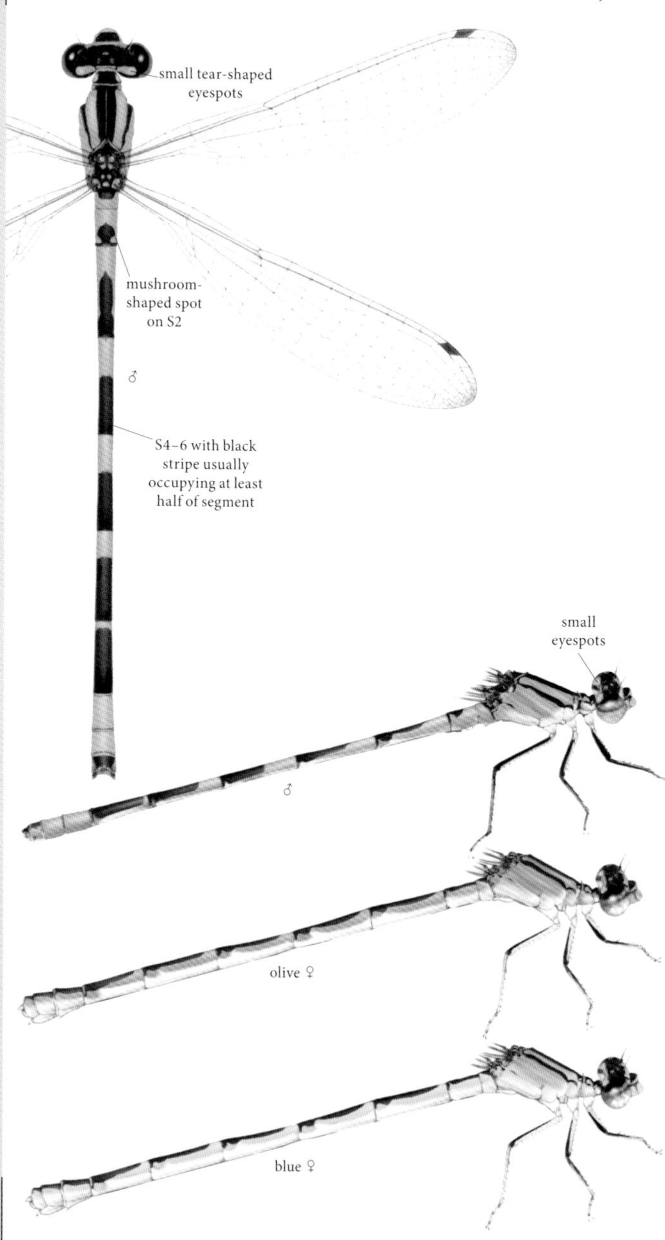

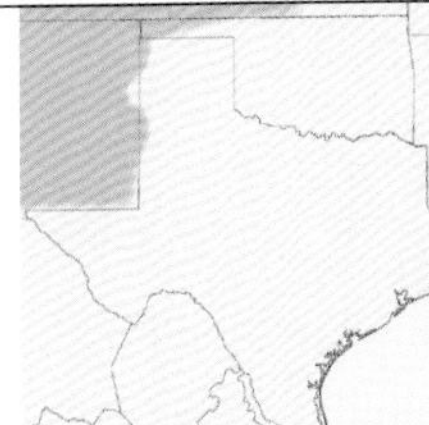

KEY FEATURES

♂—small tear-shaped eyespots; black on S4–6 usually occupying at least half of segment

♀—small tear-shaped eyespots; tan or blue; black on S3–6 tapers abruptly

S1

Size
26–37 mm
(1.0–1.5 in)

IDENTIFICATION The face of the male is blue, and the top of the head is black with blue tear-shaped eyespots separated by a thin occipital bar. Dark middorsal thoracic stripe is thinly divided by a blue line. Black shoulder stripe is narrower than blue area above it. Legs are blue or tan with black stripe on outer surface. Abdomen is mostly blue. There is a mushroom-shaped spot on S2. Top of each segment in S4–6 has a dark stripe extending at least half the length of segment. S7 is mostly black. S8–9 is blue, and S10 is blue with black spot on upper surface. Females can be pale blue or tan. Top of abdomen is largely black, including S8–10.

SIMILAR SPECIES Tule Bluets are generally recognizable by extensive black on S4–6. Atlantic and Familiar Bluets are very similar, but they have more blue than black on abdomen. Tules are variable in the amount of black, though, and it may be necessary to confirm this species by in-hand or microscopic examination of male terminal appendages and female mesostigmal plates. S7 in male Azure Bluets is all blue, or nearly so. Generally, no more than a fourth of S2 is black in Alkali Bluets, and Arroyo Bluets are thinner and darker overall. Big Bluets are larger, have middorsal thoracic stripe divided widely by blue stripe, and have arrow-shaped marks on upper surface of S3–5. Familiar and Doubleday Bluets are the only other bluets in Texas that have a tubercle on the male superior appendage; see photos of the appendages for differences.

TEXAS STATUS Rare. Known from only two counties in Texas (Bailey and Hartley). May turn up in other areas of the underexplored Texas Panhandle.

HABITAT Ponds, lakes, marshes, and slow reaches of streams.

DISCUSSION This species is known to tolerate waters with high salinity, though it is not found along the Gulf Coast. Females oviposit alone or in tandem in bullrushes and other vegetation.

Jan
Feb
Mar
Apr
May
Jun
Jul
Aug
Sep
Oct
Nov
Dec

Enallagma antennatum (en-a-LAG-mə an-tan-NĀT-um)

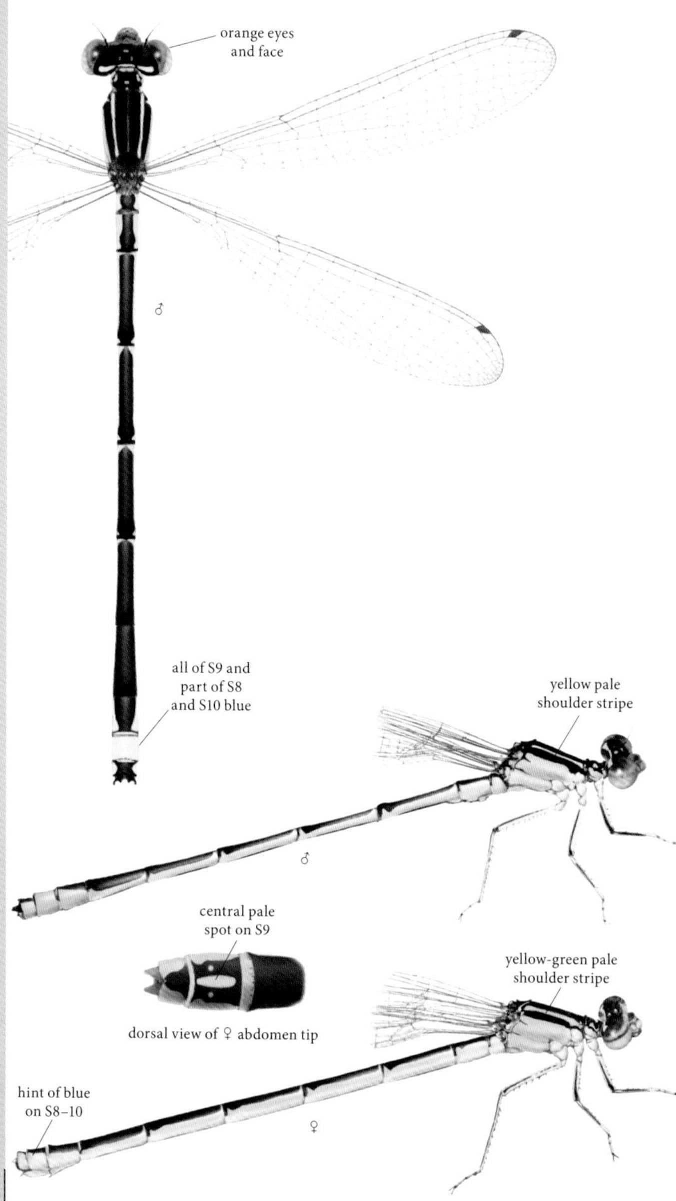

dorsal view of ♀ abdomen tip

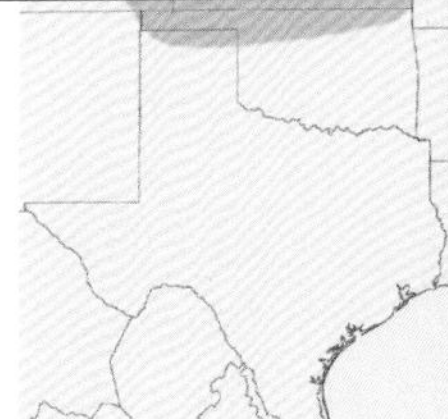

KEY FEATURES

♂—orange face and eyes; sides of thorax green; yellow pale shoulder stripe; S9 blue

♀—yellow-orange face; green eyes; yellow-green pale shoulder stripe; oblong blue spot on top of S9

S1

Size
27–33 mm
(1.0–1.3 in)

IDENTIFICATION This is Texas's most colorful bluet. Male has an orange face and eyes. Narrow blue eyespots are connected by a narrow interrupted line. Thorax is green with narrow yellow and wide black shoulder stripes. Legs are yellow with black stripes on femur. Abdomen is largely black on top with greenish blue laterally on S1–3; all of S9 and part of S8 and S10 are blue. Female is similar to male, though not as brightly colored. Pale shoulder stripe is more green-yellow. S7–8 has blue apical rings, and S8–10 is black on top with hints of blue. There is a narrow oblong blue spot on top of S9.

SIMILAR SPECIES The Rainbow is not likely to be confused with any other bluet, but its color is suggestive of a forktail. However, no forktail has the combination of an orange face, yellow pale shoulder stripe, and blue-tipped abdomen. Female Stream Bluets are similar, but not as yellow, and have more blue at abdomen tip.

TEXAS STATUS Rare. A single male has been collected in Palo Duro Creek in Hansford Co. This is the extreme southern edge of this species' range, but it may be discovered in additional areas of the northern Panhandle.

HABITAT Muddy-bottomed creeks and streams and in- and outflow areas of ponds and lakes, particularly where there is abundant vegetation.

DISCUSSION Adults are most often found in sunny areas that are not heavily vegetated. Females lay eggs in tandem with males in vegetation at the water surface, and are known to submerge themselves. This species is considered the most primitive of the bluets.

Jan
Feb
Mar
Apr
May
Jun
Jul
Aug
Sep
Oct
Nov
Dec

AZURE BLUET

Enallagma aspersum (en-a-LAG-mə as-PUR-sum)

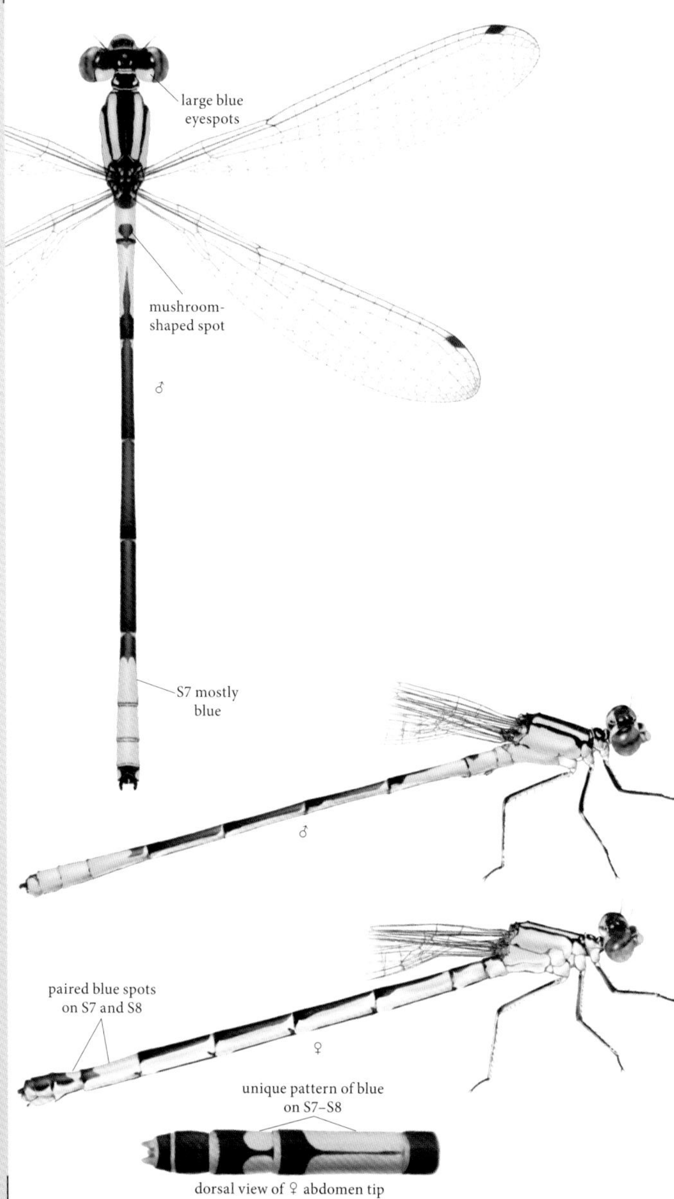

dorsal view of ♀ abdomen tip

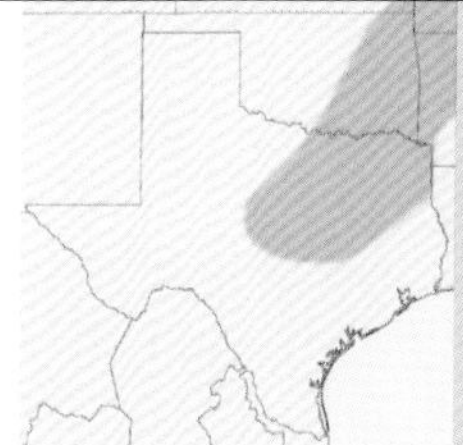

KEY FEATURES

♂—large blue eyepsots; mushroom-shaped spot on S2; black abdomen with mostly blue S7–S9

♀—black abdomen with paired blue spots on upper surface of S7 and S8

S3

Size

27–34 mm

(1.1–1.3 in)

Jan Feb Mar Apr May Jun Jul Aug Sep Oct Nov Dec

IDENTIFICATION This is a long thin bluet with blue eyes and body. Top of head is black with large blue eyespots. Middorsal stripe is black. Black shoulder stripe narrows slightly posteriorly. Legs are pale with dark stripe on sides. Middle segments of abdomen are black. S2 has a mushroom-shaped spot dorsally, and S3 has a narrow black stripe pointing anteriorly. S7 is mostly blue with an irregular black band anteriorly. S8–9 is blue, and S10 is black above with blue on the sides. Female is similar to male, but eyespots are significantly smaller. Abdomen is generally paler than male's, especially on sides. S7 and S8 are black with large blue paired spots on the upper surface. S9–10 is mostly black.

SIMILAR SPECIES The Azure is the only bluet with the combination of a predominantly black abdomen with most of S7 blue. The longer and more slender Attenuated Bluet is the only bluet with blue dorsally on about half of S7. Male Skimming Bluets have a black lower lateral stripe on S8–9, and S10 is black.

TEXAS STATUS Uncommon. Found in the north-central and eastern parts of the state, where it may be locally abundant.

HABITAT Predominately fishless lakes and ponds of all sizes. Also found in semipermanent ponds and bogs.

DISCUSSION Mating lasts an average of 14 minutes. Females most often lay eggs completely submerged and unaccompanied by males, but unlike most damselflies, female Azure Bluets do not begin laying eggs above the water and back down. Females determine an appropriate stem and immediately proceed down it headfirst. The male separates upon contact with the water and perches nearby. Females will submerge as low as 15 inches to lay eggs at the base of the plant, apparently as an adaptation to avoid summer drought. Egg laying generally lasts no more than 25 minutes.

ATTENUATED BLUET

Enallagma daeckii (en-a-LAG-mə DECK-ē-ī)

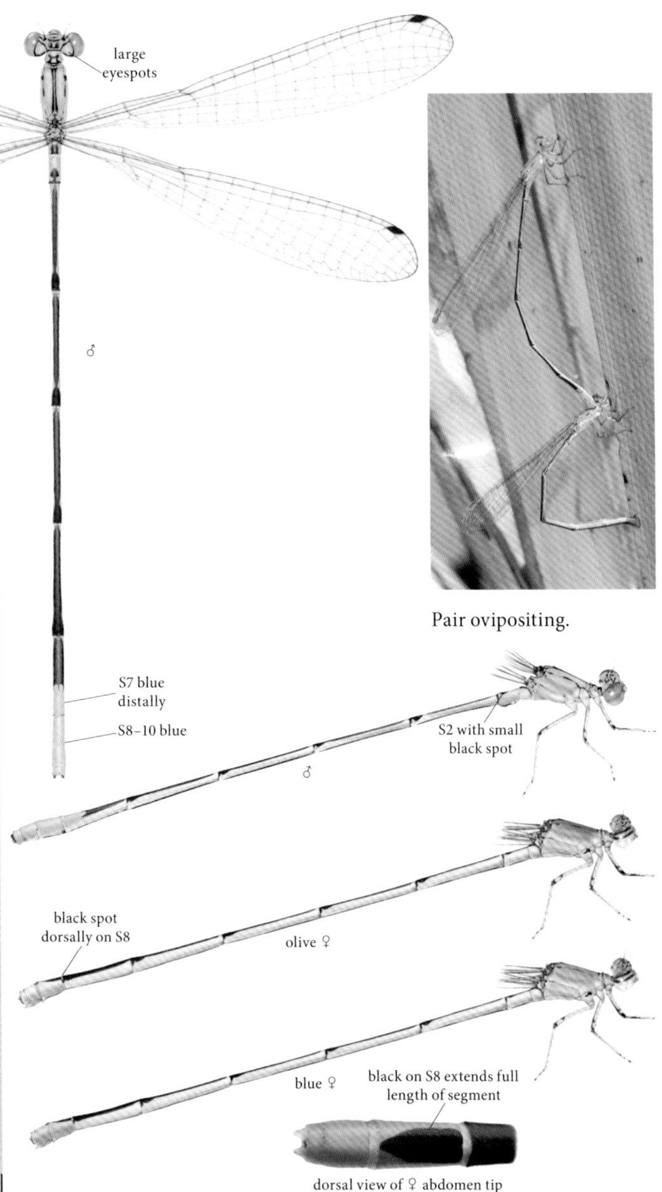

Pair ovipositing.

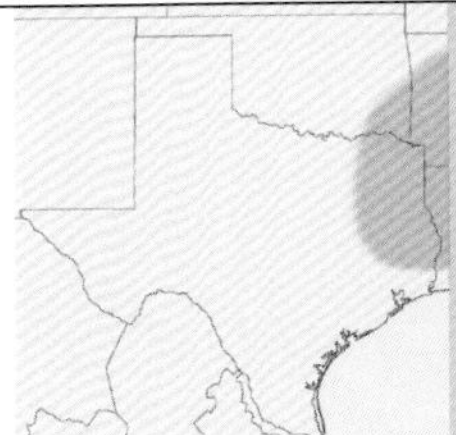

KEY FEATURES

♂—head and thorax pale blue with few black markings; long thin abdomen; posterior third of S7 and all of S8–10 blue

♀—head and thorax pale blue with few black marks; long, thin abdomen; S8 black dorsally

S3

Size
35–47 mm
(1.4–1.9 in)

Jan Feb Mar Apr May Jun Jul Aug Sep Oct Nov Dec

IDENTIFICATION Head and thorax of male are pale, with a few dark markings. Pale blue eyespots are large. Thorax is nearly all pale blue with a narrow black middorsal stripe reduced to a thin line on either side of a pale middorsal carina. Shoulder stripe is very thin, especially at the middle. Legs are largely pale. S1–2 is pale blue with a black spot on upper surface of S2. S3–6 is dark. S7 is black with blue on the posterior third of segment. S8–10 is all blue. Females are pale blue, green, or tan, with head and thorax similar to males'. S7 and S8 have a black stripe extending the full length of the upper surface. S9–10 is pale.

SIMILAR SPECIES The Attenuated Bluet is easily recognizable in the field because of its long slender body. It has the longest body of any pond damsel in North America. Slender Bluets are smaller and darker. Furtive Forktails are smaller and have black on the tip of the abdomen and front of the thorax.

TEXAS STATUS Uncommon. Known from scattered localities in East Texas.

HABITAT Margins of shady, often heavily vegetated ponds, lakes, and stream backwaters.

DISCUSSION The Attenuated Bluet is described as fluttering in the shade like a ghost among the tangled vegetation of its habitat, making it difficult to spot. Males tend to perch and fly higher than other bluets. Pairs searching for oviposition sites also fly higher than typical bluets until suitable vegetation is spotted. Pairs drop down to oviposit, and the female backs down vegetation, often submerging herself while the male stands guard above.

Enallagma divagans (en-a-LAG-mə DIV-a-gans)

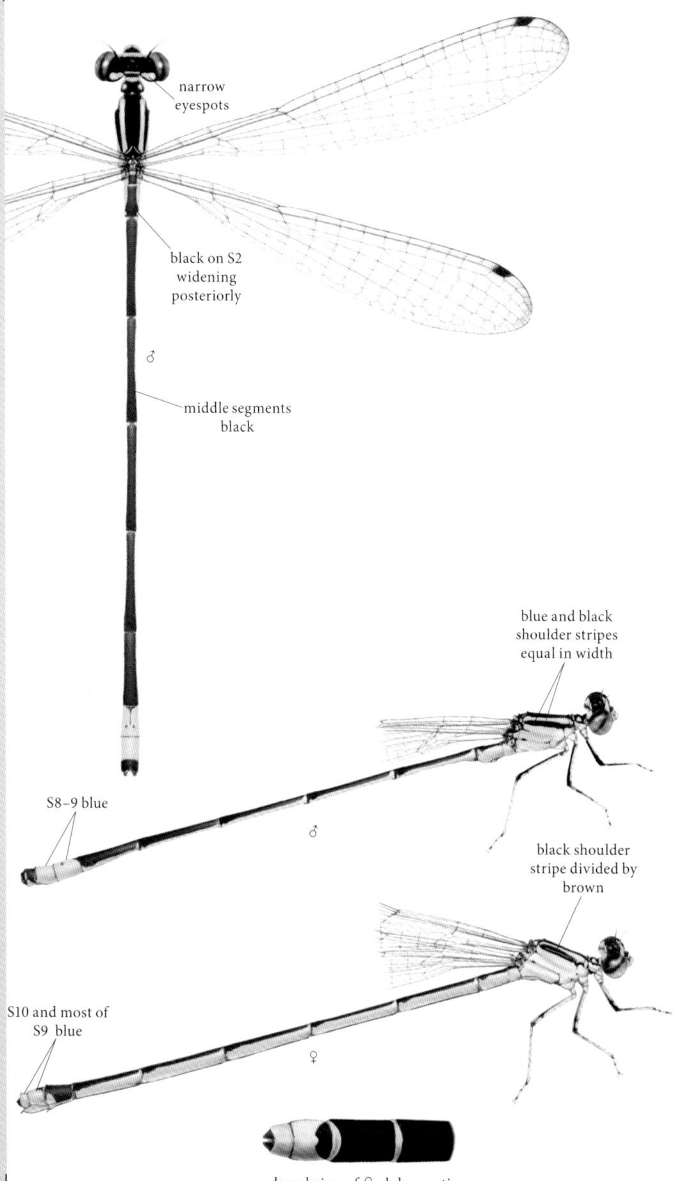

dorsal view of ♀ abdomen tip

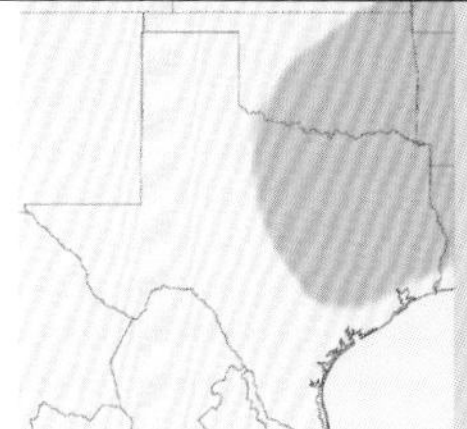

KEY FEATURES

♂—narrow blue eyespots and occipital bar; abdomen black except for blue S8–9

♀—narrow blue eyespots and occipital bar; black shoulder stripe divided by brown; S10 and most of 9 blue

S4

Size
26–36 mm
(1.0–1.4 in)

Jan Feb Mar Apr May Jun Jul Aug Sep Oct Nov Dec

IDENTIFICATION Males are dark with narrow blue eyespots. Blue occipital bar is present, but does not touch eyespots. Middorsal stripe is black. Black and blue shoulder stripes are equal in width. Legs are blue or tan with black stripes on outer surface. Abdomen is largely black. The black stripe on top of S2 widens abruptly posteriorly. S3–7 and S10 are black. S8–9 is blue. Female is generally paler than male. Dark shoulder stripe is often divided by brown for its entire length, sometimes nearly replacing the black. S3–7 is black, as in male. S8 is black with variable amount of blue on posterior edge. S9 is mostly blue with variable black on anterior edge. S10 is blue.

SIMILAR SPECIES S7 of both sexes in Azure Bluets is mostly blue. Male Stream Bluets have S8 black. Male Skimming Bluets generally lack occipital bar, have black laterally on S2, and a black stripe laterally on S8-9. Slender Bluets have larger eyespots, a thinner shoulder stripe, and blue rings on S3–6. Female Stream Bluets are generally greenish rather than blue. Female Orange and Vesper Bluets are similar, but have black on top of S9.

TEXAS STATUS Common. Locally abundant at certain localities throughout East Texas.

HABITAT Shaded sluggish creeks and streams, sloughs, or lakes.

DISCUSSION Male and female Turquoise Bluets rarely stray far from water. Their flight is deliberate and slow, with males often hovering a few inches above the water. Females lay eggs in tandem on submergent vegetation at the surface or work their way down vegetation, where they may remain submerged for up to 30 minutes while males guard from perches above.

STREAM BLUET

Enallagma exsulans (en-a-LAG-mə EX-sul-ans)

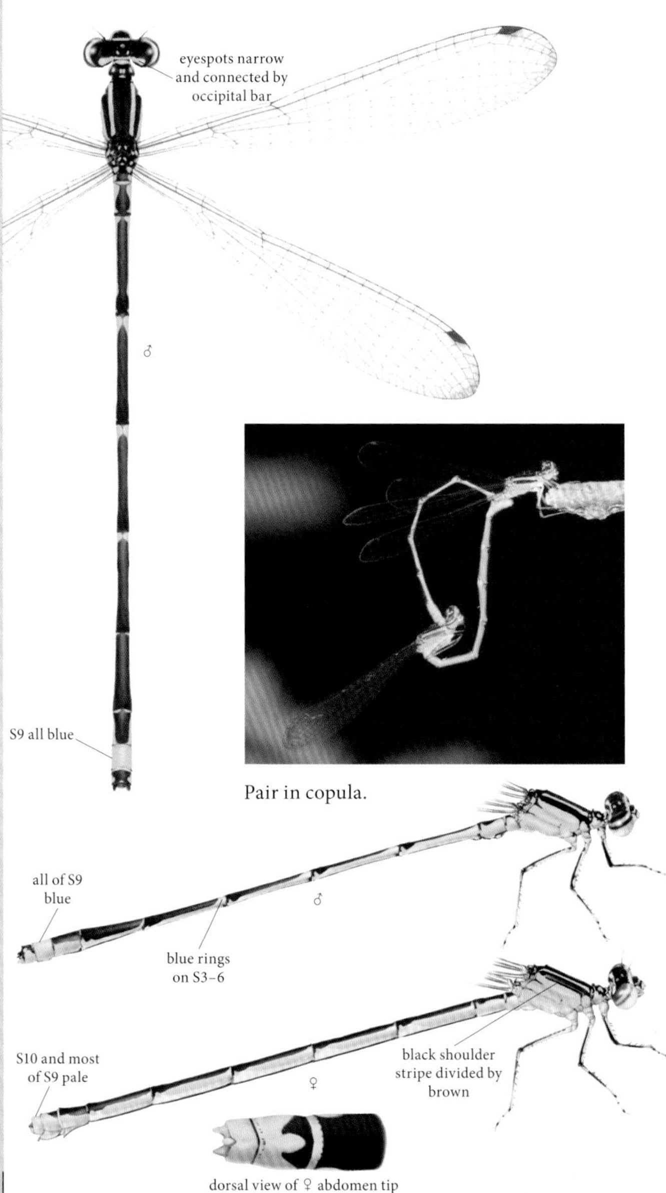

Pair in copula.

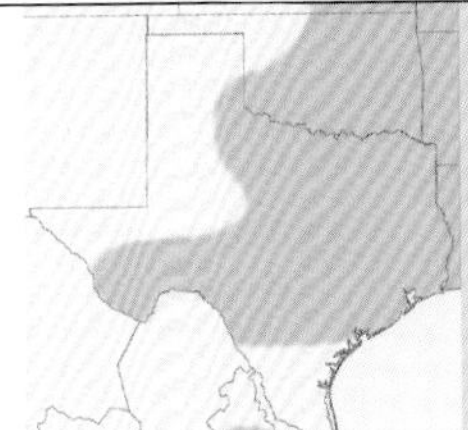

KEY FEATURES

♂—blue tear-shaped eyespots connected by occipital bar; blue rings on S3–6; S9 blue

♀—black middorsal and shoulder stripes edged by brown; S9 with W pattern above

S5

Size
31–37 mm
(1.2–1.5 in)

Jan Feb Mar Apr May Jun Jul Aug Sep Oct Nov Dec

IDENTIFICATION Blue tear-shaped eyespots in males connected by blue occipital bar. Middorsal thoracic stripe is black. Black shoulder stripe is broad; pale blue shoulder stripe above is narrow. Rest of thorax is blue. Legs are pale, occasionally with interrupted black stripe on outer surface. Abdomen is black with blue rings on S3–6. S7–8 is mostly black on top. S9–10 is blue with black spot on upper surface of S10. Female generally more green than blue. Head pattern like that of male. Dark shoulder stripe is divided lengthwise by brown. Abdominal pattern is similar to male's, but S8 generally has narrow pale ring. S9 has black W-shaped mark on top. S10 is entirely pale or occasionally has small black triangle visible above.
SIMILAR SPECIES Male Turquoise, Slender, and Skimming Bluets have blue dorsally on S8–9. S7 is blue in male Azure Bluets. Female Vesper Bluets have narrower dark shoulder stripe. Other female bluets with blue at abdomen tip also have blue on thorax. Juvenile Orange Bluet males are paler and have wider dark shoulder stripes. Juvenile male Vesper Bluets have less blue on S8 and a narrower dark shoulder stripe. Female Mexican Wedgetails are similar, but the eyespots are larger, more circular, and lacking an occipital bar.
TEXAS STATUS Common. Widespread throughout the central and eastern parts of the state.
HABITAT Common along shores of slow-moving streams and rivers, and occasionally lakes.
DISCUSSION They are often sparse in the early parts of the day, but seem to become more numerous in the late afternoon. Mating lasts an average of 76 minutes, but may take 2 hours. Females submerge themselves to lay eggs, sometimes while still in tandem with males and other times with the male breaking away after contact with the water.

Enallagma geminatum (en-a-LAG-mə gem-i-NĀTE-um)

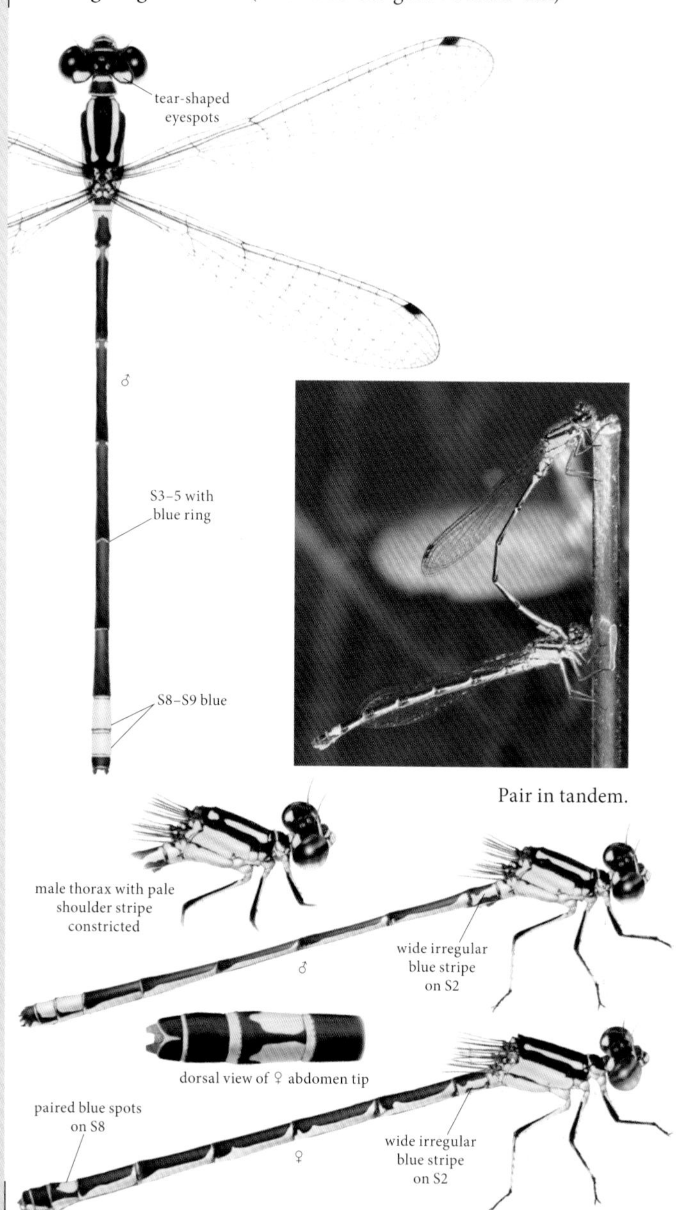

Pair in tandem.

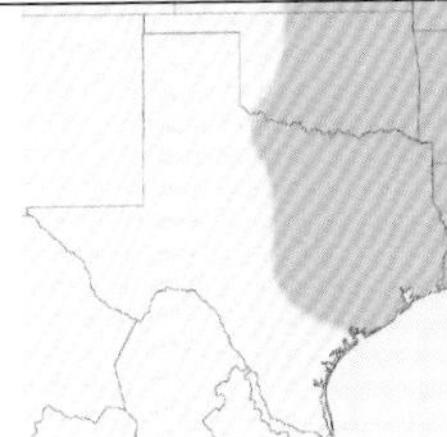

KEY FEATURES

♂—tear-shaped eyespots; irregular blue stripe on side of S2; S8–9 blue

♀—tear-shaped eyespots; irregular blue stripe on side of S2; S8 with paired spots

S5

Size
19–29 mm
(0.7–1.1 in)

Jan Feb Mar Apr May Jun Jul Aug Sep Oct Nov Dec

IDENTIFICATION Head of male is black with moderate-size blue tear-shaped eyespots. Occipital bar is usually absent, and middle of pronotum lacks pale markings. Black shoulder stripe widens posteriorly; blue shoulder stripe above it appears constricted. This blue stripe is sometimes completely broken, looking like an exclamation mark. Blue and black shoulder stripes are subequal in width. Thin black stripe is present lower on side of thorax. Abdomen is largely black and more robust than in other bluets. Sides of S2 have distinctive, broad, irregular blue stripe. S3–5 and sometimes S6 have a blue ring. S8–9 is blue; S10 is black. Head and thorax of female similar to male's. Abdomen has irregular blue stripe on S2, but largely lacks pale rings on subsequent segments. S8 has a pair of large oblong spots on top that may be fused at points. Some females appear green.
SIMILAR SPECIES Turquoise and Slender Bluets are both longer, have narrower eyespots connected by an occipital bar, and lack the irregular blue stripe on side of S2 and blue rings on S3–5. Most of S7 is blue in both sexes of Azure Bluets. S8 is black in both sexes of Stream Bluets. Male Lilypad Forktails have larger eyespots, a blue ring on S2, and blue on S7. Female Seepage Dancers lack eyespots, and S8 is all blue.
TEXAS STATUS Uncommon. Widespread in eastern half of state.
HABITAT Prefers open, muddy, heavily vegetated ponds and lakes with fish; seen more rarely on slow-moving streams and swamps.
DISCUSSION Skimming Bluets may be restricted to breeding in ponds and lakes containing fish in an effort to avoid predation by abundant dragonfly nymphs in fishless lakes. They are most active in the morning, flying out over the water and perching on algae and other vegetation. Mating pairs aggregate on riparian branches and stems. The female lays eggs, unaccompanied by the male, in algae and floating debris.

SLENDER BLUET

Enallagma traviatum (en-a-LAG-mə trav-ē-A-tum)

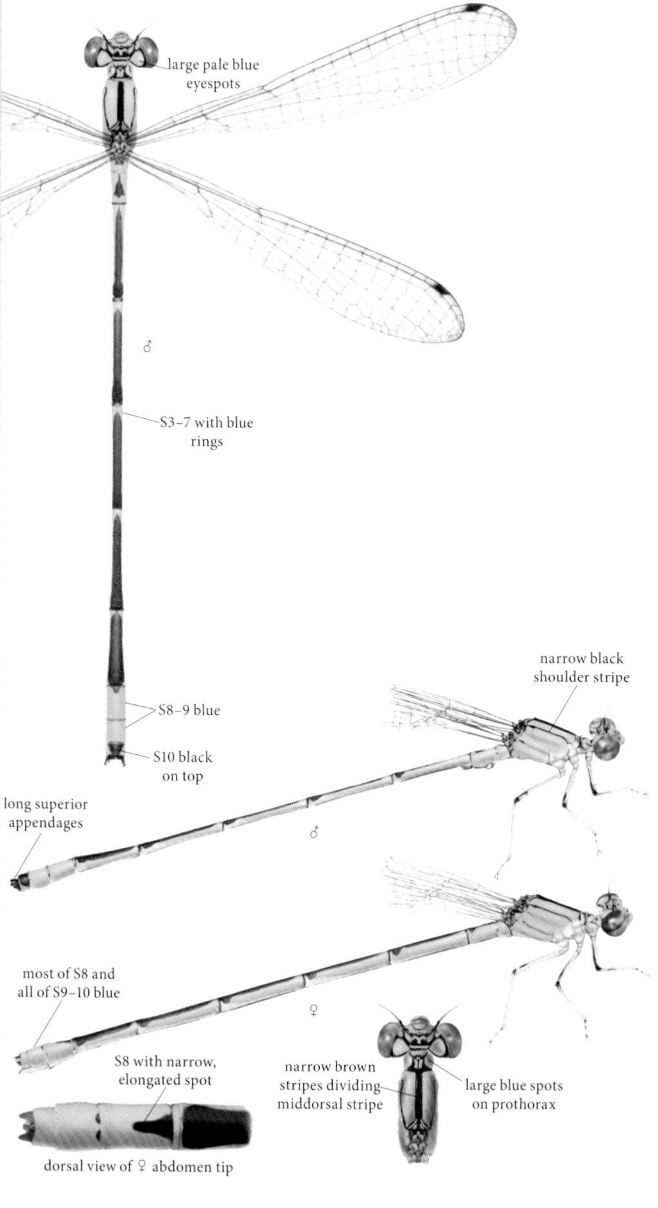

large pale blue eyespots

♂

S3–7 with blue rings

S8–9 blue

S10 black on top

narrow black shoulder stripe

long superior appendages

♂

most of S8 and all of S9–10 blue

♀

S8 with narrow, elongated spot

narrow brown stripes dividing middorsal stripe

large blue spots on prothorax

dorsal view of ♀ abdomen tip

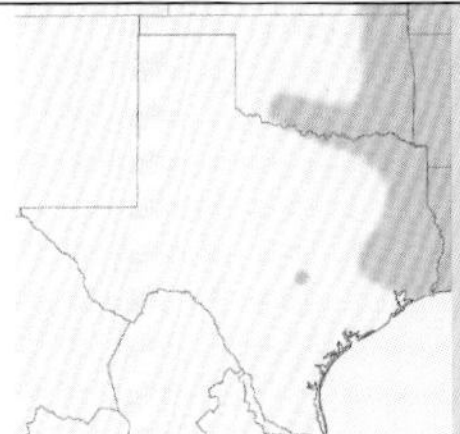

KEY FEATURES

♂—large pale blue eyespots; pale head and thorax; blue rings on S3–7; S8–9 blue; S10 black above

♀—large pale blue eyespots; overall pale in color; S8–10 blue with narrow, elongated black spot on top of S8

S2

Size
29–32 mm
(1.1–1.3 in)

IDENTIFICATION In this long, thin pale species, males have large blue eyespots separated by a thin occipital bar. Middorsal stripe is black. Shoulder stripe is narrow, especially at posterior end. Abdomen is largely black on upper surface with blue rings on S3–7. S8–9 is largely blue. Upper surface of S10 is black. Female is similar to male, but dark thoracic stripes are less well defined. Top of thorax in female has a thin brown stripe on either side of midline. S8–10 is blue, and S8 has an elongated dark spot on top.

SIMILAR SPECIES Only Attenuated Bluets are as pale. Male Attenuated Bluets are similar, but larger, and S7 is partially blue. Females have a large black spot extending the length of S8. Skimming Bluet males are smaller and have black on sides of S2. Turquoise Bluets lack pale abdominal rings and have smaller eyespots. Male Azure Bluets have more black on head, wider dark shoulder stripes and blue at tip of abdomen. Female Azure Bluets are similar but have a wider dark shoulder stripe.

TEXAS STATUS Rare. Only a few populations known, including a disjunct one in Bastrop County.

HABITAT Permanent ponds and lakes with sparse-to-abundant emergent vegetation.

DISCUSSION Males and pairs commonly seen perched on shoreline vegetation or hovering over the water. Females will oviposit in tandem or alone, sometimes submerging themselves. Slender Bluets are widespread throughout the eastern United States. The subspecies found in Texas, *E. t. westfalli,* was described by Donnelly (1964) from a pond in East Texas, near Cleveland, based on the relatively more robust posterodorsal arm of the male cerci. This subspecies and the nominate form are apparently geographically separated by the Appalachian Mountains.

Jan
Feb
Mar
Apr
May
Jun
Jul
Aug
Sep
Oct
Nov
Dec

Enallagma novaehispaniae (en-a-LAG-mə nō-vi-his-PAN-ē)

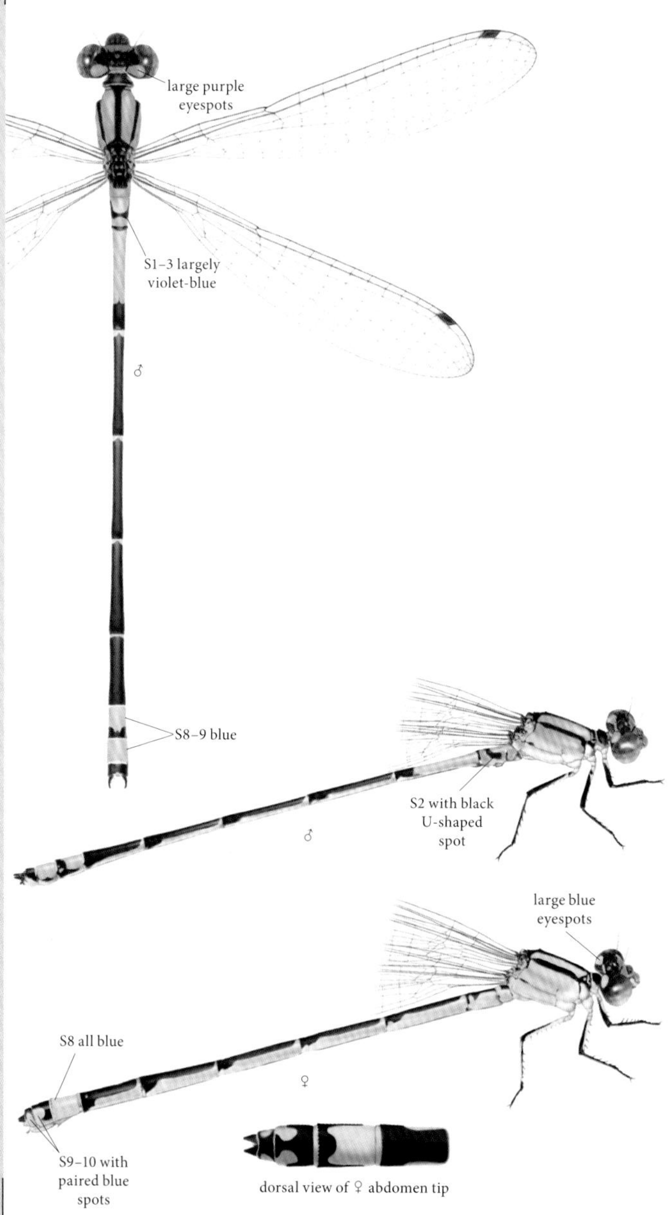

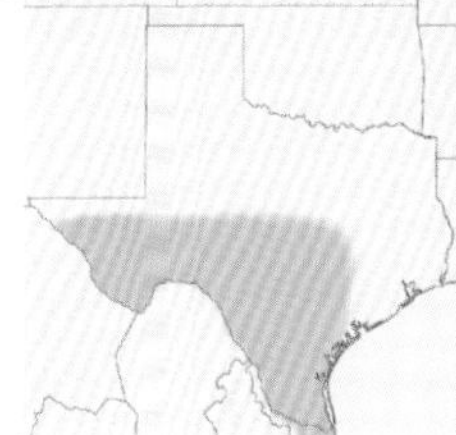

KEY FEATURES

♂—dark purple head and thorax; large oval eyespots; S1–3 violet-blue; S2 with black U-shaped spot; S8–9 blue

♀—large oval, blue eyespots; S8 all blue and S9–10 with blue spots on top

S5

Size
29–35 mm
(1.1–1.4 in)

IDENTIFICATION This is a dark purple and blue species. Male has large oval purple or blue eyespots that are usually nearly confluent with the occipital bar. Thorax is blue-purple with narrow black middorsal and unforked shoulder stripes. Legs are largely dark. The abdomen is largely pale on S1–3, with a distinct U-shaped spot on S2. S4–7 is dark. S8 is blue with a dark posterior ring. S9 is blue; S10, black. Female is similar to male, but often bluer. Dark thoracic stripes are generally wider. Abdomen is largely black above, but S8 is blue. S9 and S10 have paired prominent blue spots on top. Blue is visible on the sides of S2–7.
SIMILAR SPECIES Female Skimming Bluets are similar, but with S9 all black. In Dusky Dancers, middorsal and shoulder stripes are broader, and S8–10 is striped. All violet-colored dancers have mostly violet abdomens, and S8–10 is blue.
TEXAS STATUS Common. Abundant in Hill Country streams.
HABITAT Pools of slow, clear streams and rivers.
DISCUSSION Males perch at tips of overhanging vegetation. Pairs oviposit in emergent vegetation.

Jan
Feb
Mar
Apr
May
Jun
Jul
Aug
Sep
Oct
Nov
Dec

Male feeding on another male.

CARIBBEAN YELLOWFACE

Neoerythromma cultellatum (nē-ō-eh-ri-THRŌ-ma cull-te-LAT-um)

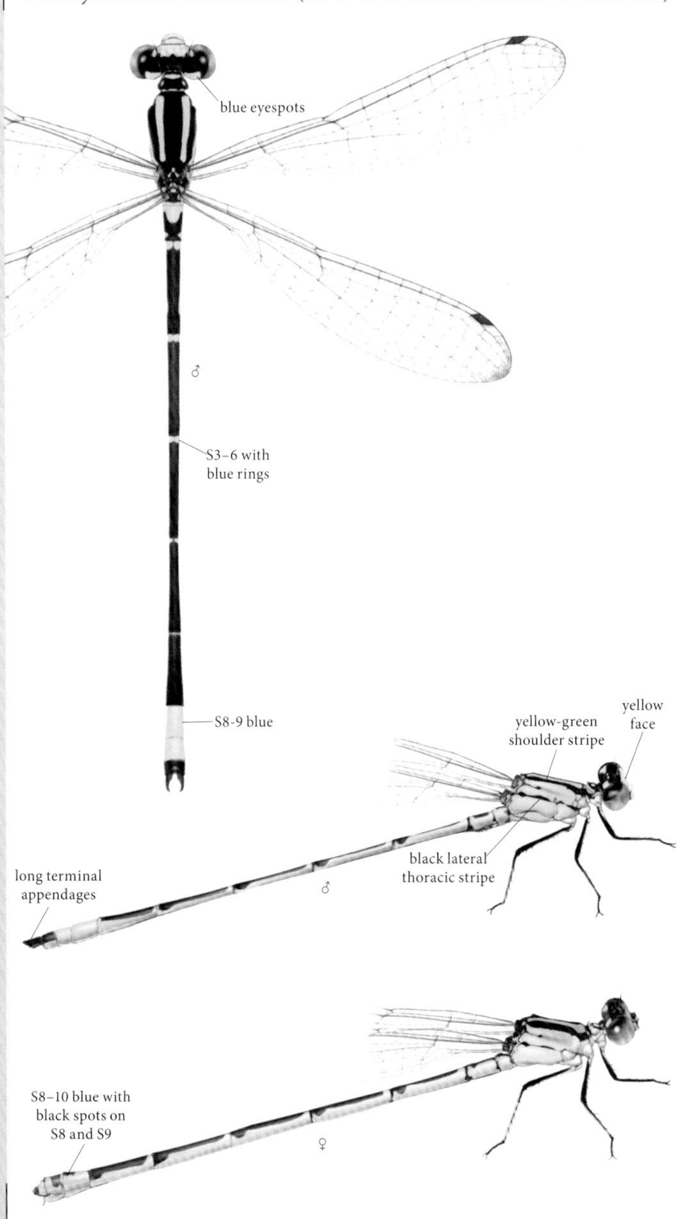

S3

KEY FEATURES

♂—yellow face; yellowish-green pale shoulder stripe; blue on sides of thorax and abdomen; S8–9 blue; long terminal appendages

♀—small blue eyespots; blue or yellow-green shoulder stripe; S8–10 blue with spots on S8–9

Size
27–31 mm
(1.1–1.2 in)

IDENTIFICATION Males are instantly recognizable by the bright yellow face and greenish eyes on an otherwise blue body. Eyespots are blue and tear-shaped. Thorax has a black middorsal stripe and a dark shoulder stripe. Pale shoulder stripe is blue, and an infusion of yellow makes it look yellowish green. Sides of thorax are blue with a dark stripe. Legs are dark. Abdomen is blue with a dark stripe above. S8–9 is blue; S10 is black. Superior appendage is long and prominent. Female is similarly colored to male, but with yellow on the face and thorax replaced by blue-green. Eyespots are rounder. S8–9 is mostly blue with a black spot on top that is more extensive on S9. S10 is nearly all blue.

SIMILAR SPECIES Males are unmistakable from the combination of a yellow face and blue body. Females evoke the overall appearance of a bluet, but the black stripe on the sides of their thoraxes and the pattern of black spots on S8–9 are unique.

TEXAS STATUS Uncommon. Restricted to the Lower Rio Grande Valley, where it may be locally abundant.

HABITAT Ponds, canals, and the slow reaches of streams or rivers with abundant floating debris.

DISCUSSION Recently emerged individuals mature in forests, some distance from the water. Males fly very low over the water, often some distance from shore, making them difficult to spot at times despite their contrasting colors. They are often seen perching horizontally on water lilies, but will also perch on vegetation stems. Females oviposit in floating debris or vegetation either alone or in tandem.

Jan Feb Mar Apr May Jun Jul Aug Sep Oct Nov Dec

MEXICAN WEDGETAIL

Acanthagrion quadratum (ā-can-THAG-rē-on qua-DRA-tum)

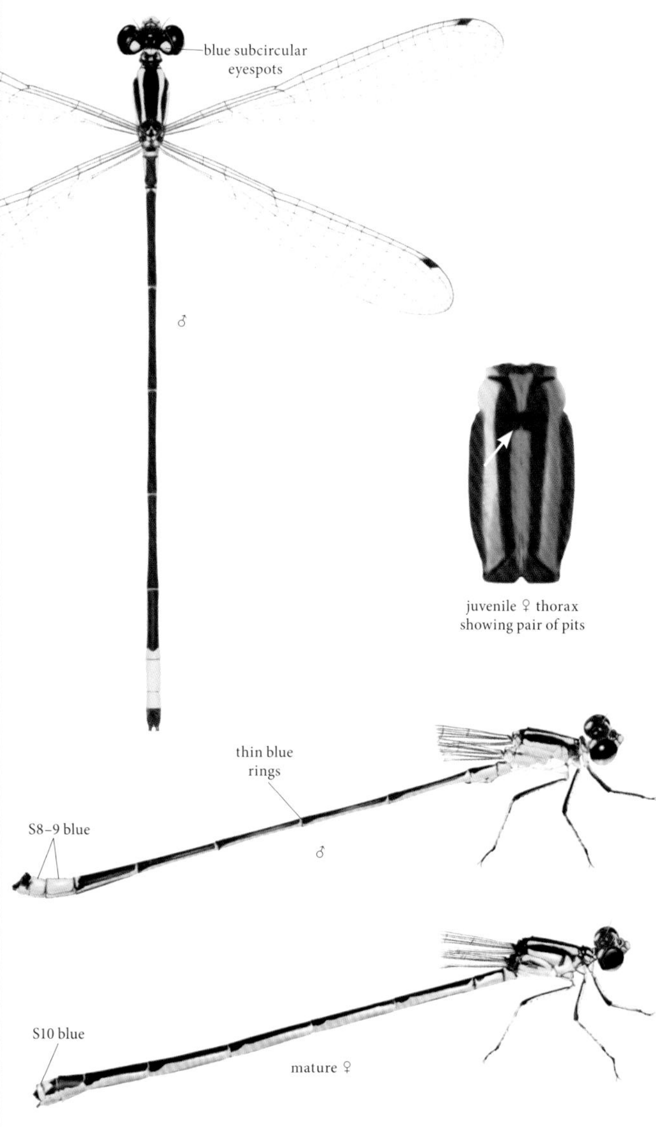

KEY FEATURES

♂—large blue subcircular eyespots; S8–9 all blue; distinctive 45°–60° downward slant to S10

♀—large blue subcircular eyespots; S9 mostly blue; S10 all blue

Size
29–33 mm
(1.1–1.3 in)

Jan Feb Mar Apr May Jun Jul Aug Sep Oct Nov Dec

IDENTIFICATION Males' eyes are black on top, fading to white or green below. Large distinctive blue eyespots present. Thorax is blue with black middorsal and shoulder stripes. Lower part of thorax is pale. Pale legs have incomplete black stripes. Abdomen is black with very thin pale rings on S4–7. S1–3 and posterior margin of S7 have some blue, and S8–9 is all blue. S10 is black on upper surface and blue on sides. It is distinctly slanted downward at a 45°–60° angle. Female is similar, but has brown eyes on top that become pale below. Top of thorax has a pair of pits that are touching the middorsal carina, which is pale above these pits. Legs are paler than male's. S8 is blue on posterior margin. S9 is blue except for black pattern anteriorly; S10 is all blue.

SIMILAR SPECIES Wedgetails resemble many bluets, but males have strongly slanted S10. Male Stream Bluets have black on S8, and blue rings on S3–6 are wider. In female Stream Bluets, elongated eyespots are connected by a blue bar; the pale middorsal carina is parallel its entire length (not interrupted by pair of dark pits); the abdomen shows blue laterally along its entire length; and the shoulder stripe is often divided lengthwise by pale color.

TEXAS STATUS Rare. Populations known from the Devils River in West Texas and in the Lower Rio Grande Valley.

HABITAT Weedy ponds, slow backwaters, and marshes.

DISCUSSION This species has been reported in the state from only a few localities in southern Texas and an apparently isolated population in the Devils River. It is a common species throughout most of its range, and I anticipate additional localities will be revealed in Texas. Males compete for territories by facing off and rising with the abdominal tip raised.

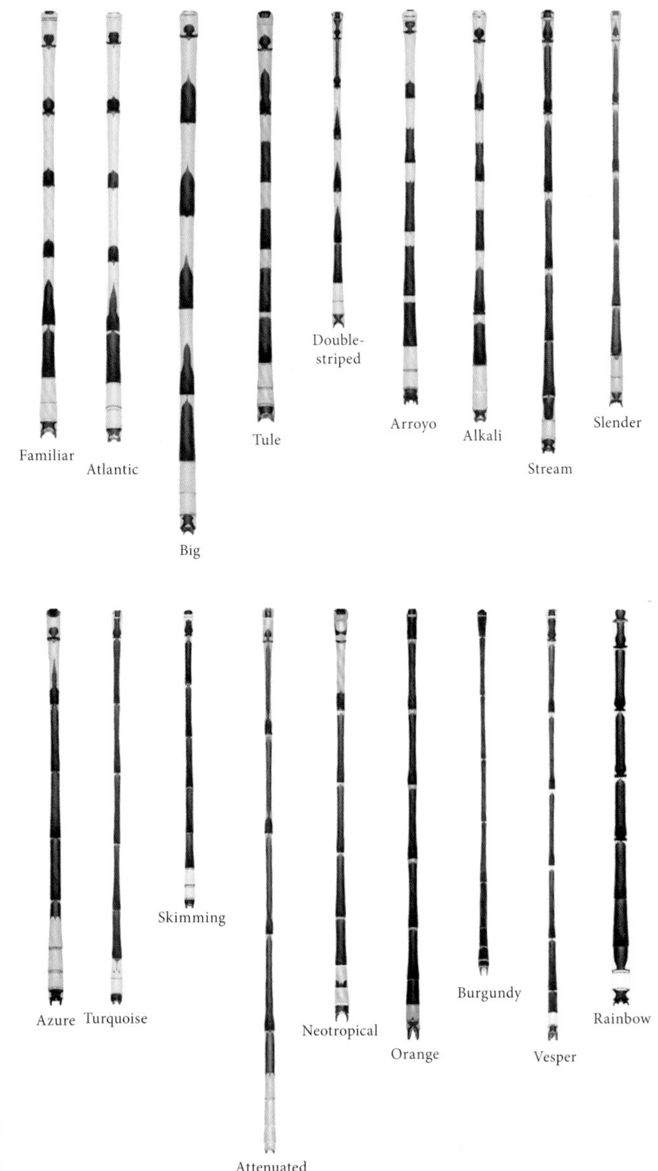
Familiar
Atlantic
Big
Tule
Double-
striped
Arroyo
Alkali
Stream
Slender
Azure
Turquoise
Skimming
Attenuated
Neotropical
Orange
Burgundy
Vesper
Rainbow

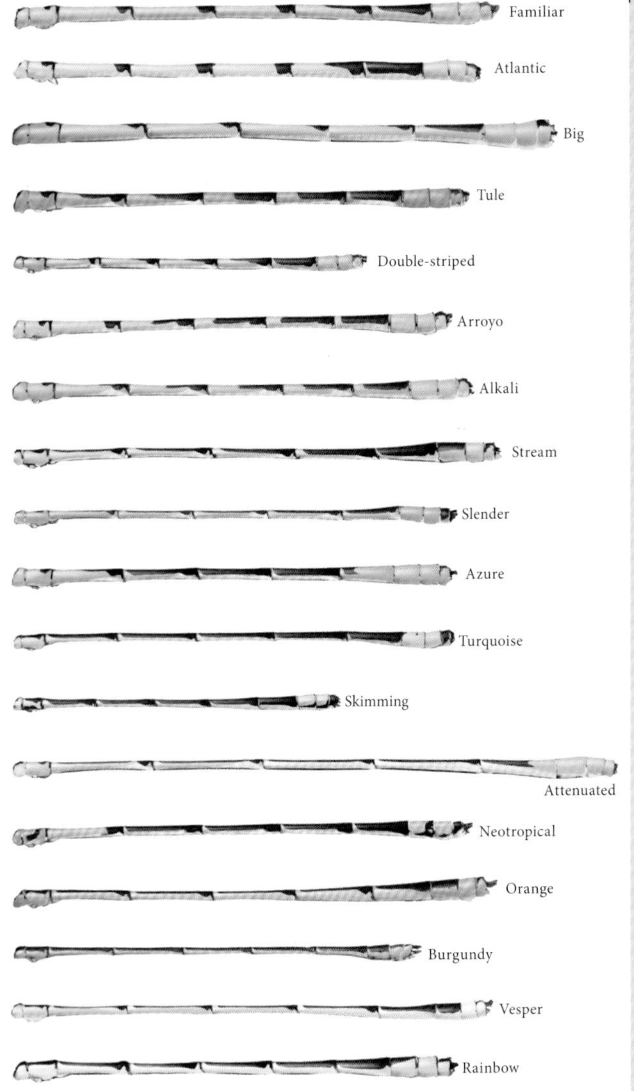
Familiar
Atlantic
Big
Tule
Double-striped
Arroyo
Alkali
Stream
Slender
Azure
Turquoise
Skimming
Attenuated
Neotropical
Orange
Burgundy
Vesper
Rainbow

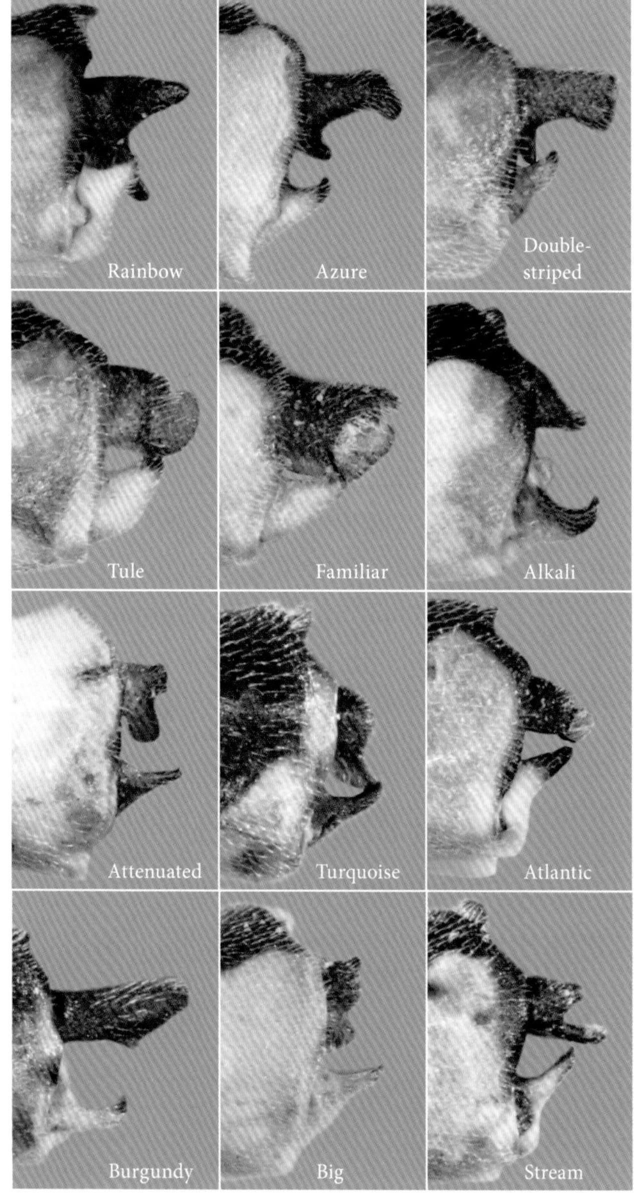
Rainbow
Azure
Double-striped
Tule
Familiar
Alkali
Attenuated
Turquoise
Atlantic
Burgundy
Big
Stream

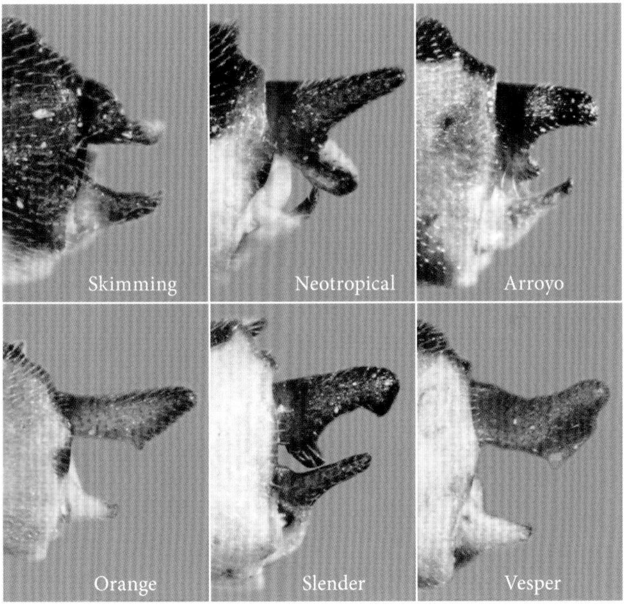

Skimming Neotropical Arroyo

Orange Slender Vesper

CARIBBEAN YELLOWFACE—MALE APPENDAGES

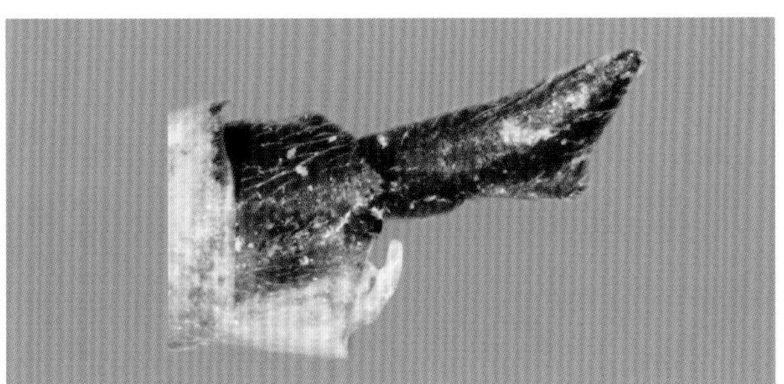

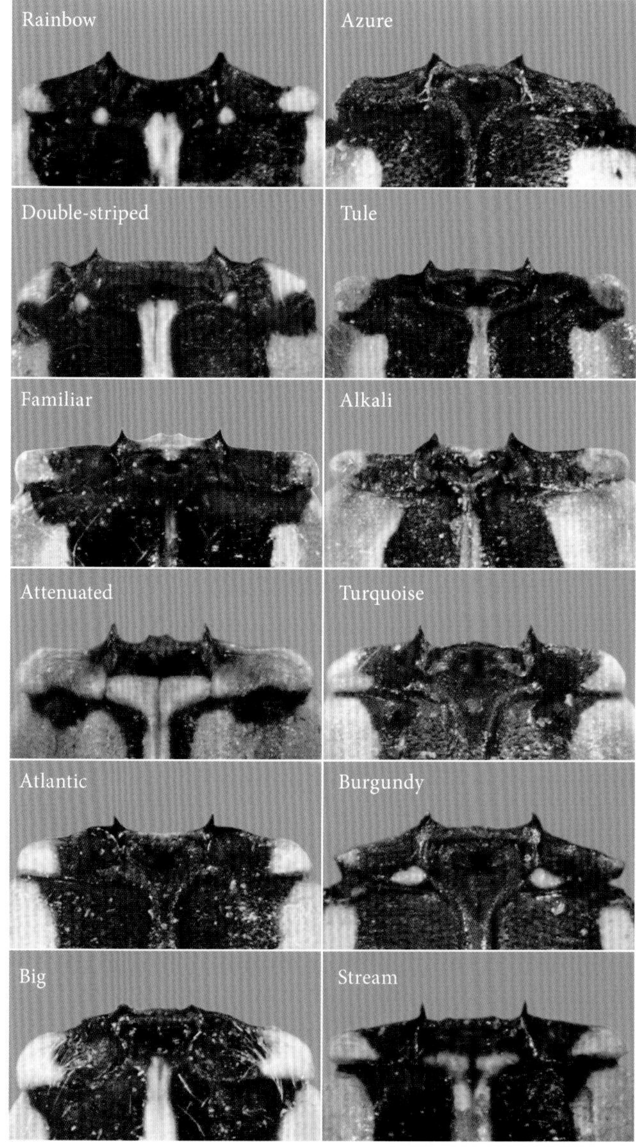
Rainbow
Azure
Double-striped
Tule
Familiar
Alkali
Attenuated
Turquoise
Atlantic
Burgundy
Big
Stream

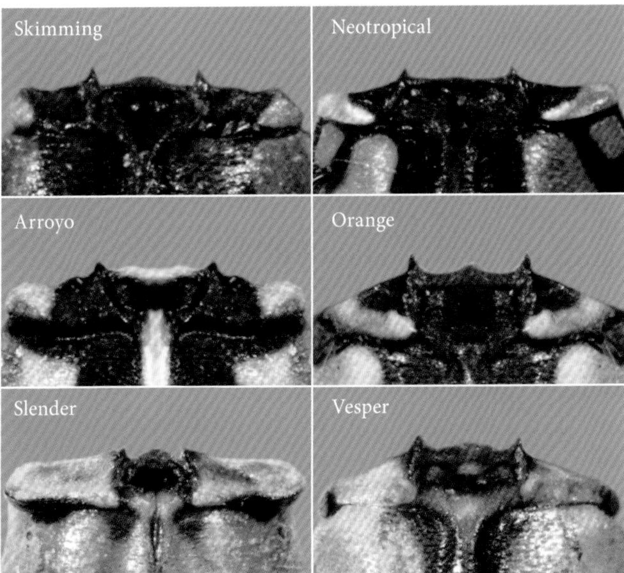

CARIBBEAN YELLOWFACE—MESOSTIGMAL PLATES

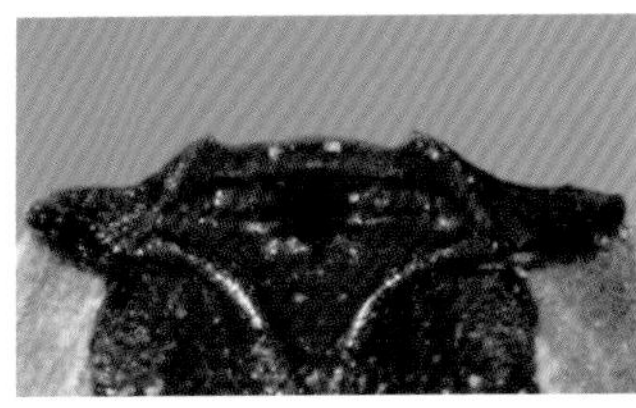

MEXICAN WEDGETAIL—MESOSTIGMAL PLATES

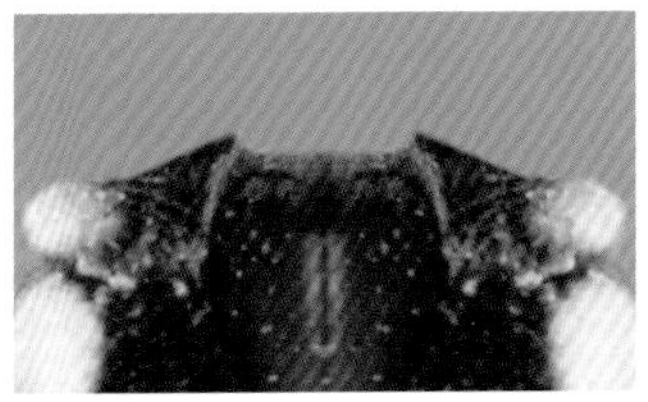

Hesperagrion heterodoxum (hes-pur-AG-rē-on he-tur-ō-DOX-um)

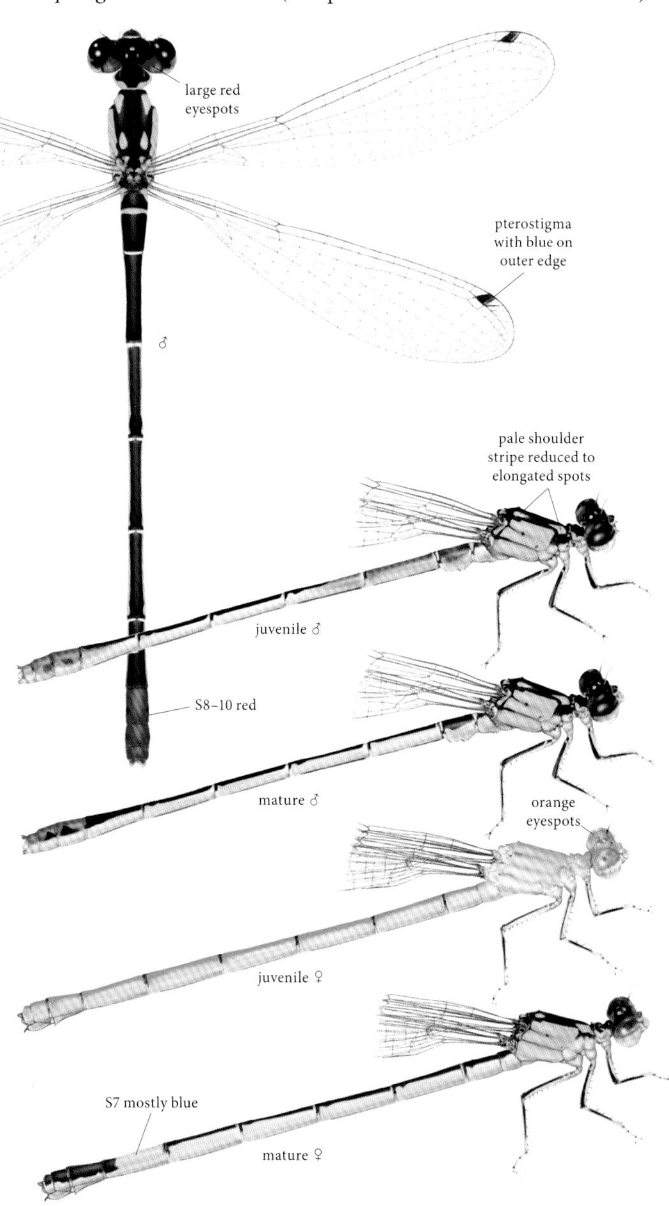

KEY FEATURES

♂—large red eyespots; pale shoulder stripe reduced to elongated spots; tip of abdomen red

♀—may be entirely orange including eyespots; similar to male but with S7 blue

Size
28–35 mm
(1.1–1.4 in)

Jan Feb Mar Apr May Jun Jul Aug Sep Oct Nov Dec

IDENTIFICATION Head of male is mostly black with 2 large bright red eyespots. Top of thorax is black with a blue shoulder stripe reduced to distinctive elongated spots. Rest of thorax is blue, fading below. Pterostigma is black bordered by blue at distal end. Abdomen is largely black dorsally and blue-green laterally. Tip of S7 and the majority of S8–10 are bright red. Females are similarly marked, but without red eyespots. The first three-fourths of S7 is bright blue. Juveniles of both sexes are orange. Juveniles go through a number of intermediate color stages that may occur at different rates on the head, thorax, and abdomen. Distinctive orange eyespots are visible in juveniles of both sexes.

SIMILAR SPECIES Painted Damsels are distinctively colored among Texas damselflies. The Plains Forktail has a black thorax with a pale shoulder stripe reduced to 2 spots, but these spots are smaller; also, it lacks bright red eyespots. Juvenile individuals are orange, not red like firetails.

TEXAS STATUS Common. Widespread and abundant west of the Pecos River.

HABITAT Permanent and ephemeral slow-flowing creeks and streams with moderate emergent vegetation.

DISCUSSION Both sexes may be common perching in grasses and other emergent vegetation streamside. Males can be seen mating with females of all ages. Mating pairs generally fly up into shoreline vegetation, including trees. Females oviposit alone or in tandem, though older females tend to oviposit alone in stems of emergent vegetation. It has been reported as an inhabitant of permanent streams, but it occurs along several streams in the Davis Mountains that dry up in the summer.

RAMBUR'S FORKTAIL

Ischnura ramburii (ish-NUR-a RAM-bur-ē-ī)

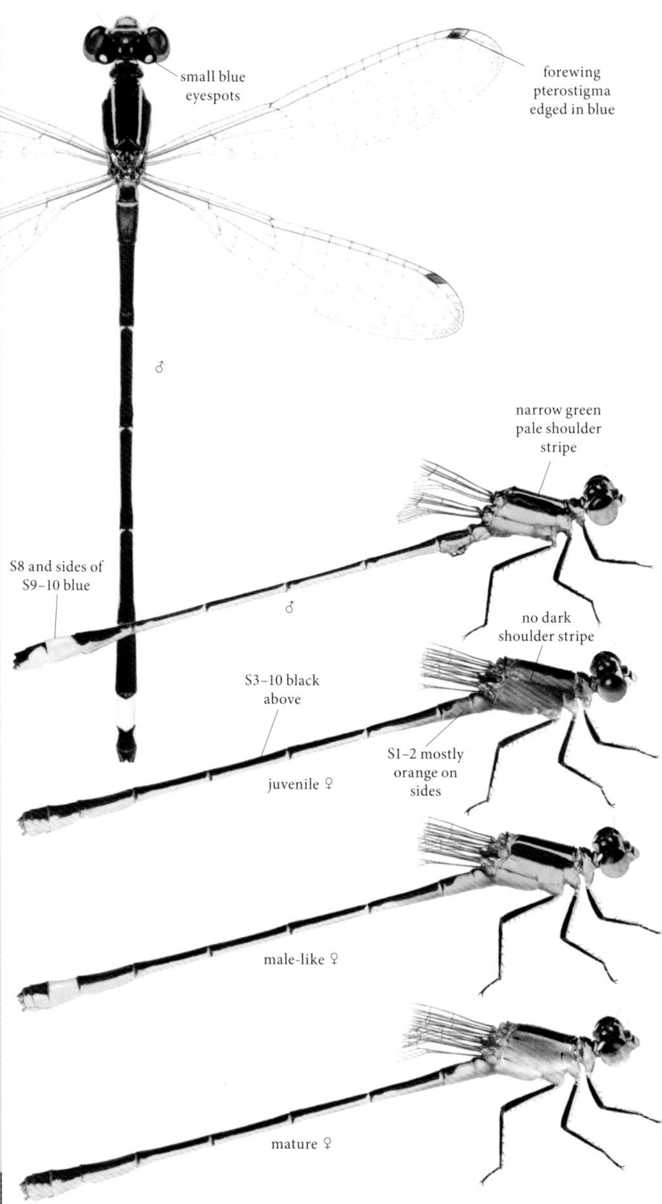

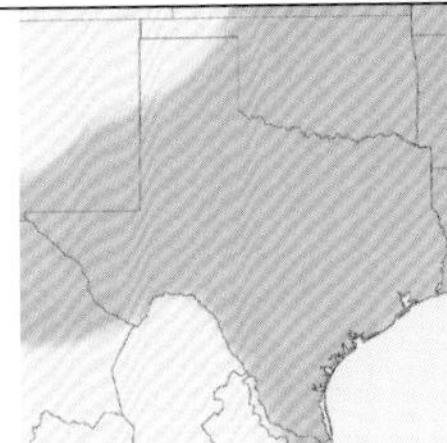

S5

KEY FEATURES

♂—small blue eyespots; green thorax; dark abdomen with yellow lower sides; S8 blue; S9–10 blue laterally

♀—colored like male, or else orange; orange form lacks shoulder stripe; S3–10 black above

Size
27–36 mm
(1.2–1.5 in)

IDENTIFICATION Males have dark head with small blue eyespots. Thorax is green or blue with broad black middorsal and dark shoulder stripes. Pale shoulder stripe is narrow and green. Legs are dark. Forewing pterostigma is edged in blue. Abdomen is black above on S1–7. S8 is blue. S9–10 is blue on sides with black above. Male-like females are nearly identical to males. Immature non-male-like females are orange with a broad middorsal thoracic stripe, but lack a dark shoulder stripe. S1 and part of S2 are orange. Rest of abdomen is black above and pale below on sides. Mature females are olive green, often with brown along shoulder line and base of abdomen.

SIMILAR SPECIES In male Desert Forktails, tear-shaped eyespots are connected by an occipital bar, the pale shoulder stripe is broader, and all of S9 is blue. Female Desert Forktails lack a broad black middorsal thoracic stripe. Only S9 is blue in male Furtive Forktails, and only S1–2, never S3–4, is pale in juvenile female Citrine and Furtive Forktails. Male Eastern Forktails are smaller, top of S8–9 is blue, eyespots are green, and there is no yellow on sides of abdomen. Immature female Eastern Forktails have a dark shoulder stripe.

TEXAS STATUS Common. Widespread and locally abundant throughout the state.

HABITAT Heavily vegetated ponds, lakes, marshes, and slow reaches of streams exposed to sunlight, including brackish waters.

DISCUSSION Males often do not release females from the wheel position for several hours, sometimes as many as 7, to secure their genetic contribution. Orange females will sometimes attack males, but will more often curl their abdomens downward while fluttering their wings in a refusal display. Females often lay eggs late in the afternoon, unattended by males, on the underside of floating vegetation or debris, by curling their abdomens.

Jan
Feb
Mar
Apr
May
Jun
Jul
Aug
Sep
Oct
Nov
Dec

Ischnura barberi (ish-NUR-a BAR-bur-ī)

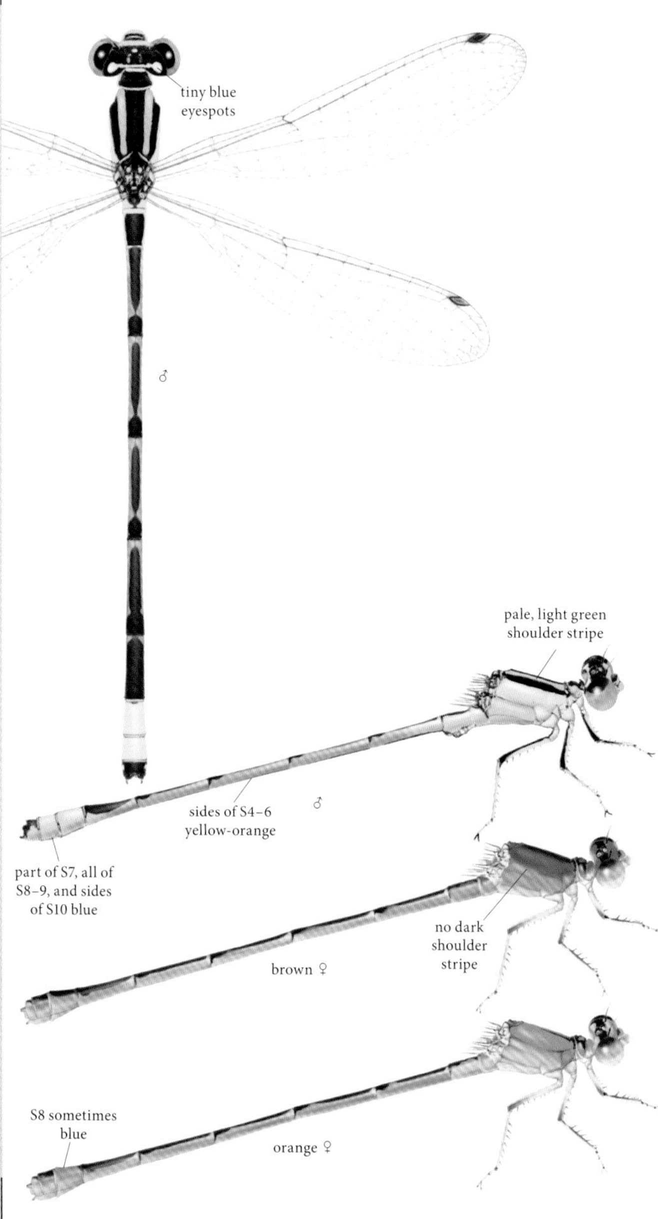

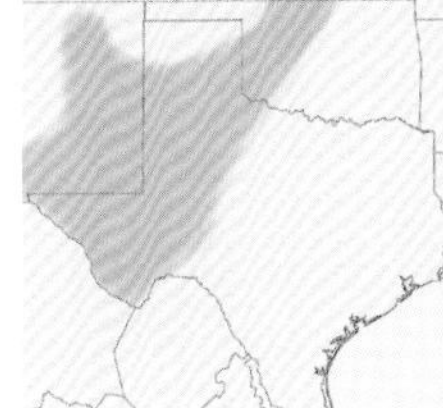

KEY FEATURES

♂—tiny blue eyespots connected by thin line; green thorax; yellow-orange abdomen; blue on all of S8–9 and sides of S7 and S10

♀—colored like male, or else uniformly brown or orange; no dark shoulder stripe; S8 possibly blue

Size
28–35 mm
(1.1–1.4 in)

IDENTIFICATION Face of male is pale blue-green, heavily marked with black. Two small blue eyespots are generally confluent with a narrow occipital bar. Thorax is green with black middorsal and dark shoulder stripes. Pale shoulder stripe is often lighter green or golden in color. Abdomen is blue-green on S1–2 and part of S3. Remainder of abdomen is yellow-orange, marked with black stripes above. Posterior lateral half of S7 and all of S8–9 are blue. S10 is blue on sides, with wide black stripe on top. Male-like females are uncommon and nearly identical to males. Most females are orange or tan, often with a slight greenish cast to the abdomen. Generally there is no evidence of a dark shoulder stripe. The abdomen is generally similar to the male's, but with a black triangle anteriorly and a spot posteriorly on top of S8. These spots are occasionally touching. S9 is black above, and the top of S10 bears a black triangle for its entire length. Parts of S8–10 may be blue in some females.

SIMILAR SPECIES Male Rambur's Forktails are similar, but the top of S9 shows some black, and in Desert Forktails the entire segment is blue. The pale shoulder stripe in Rambur's Forktail is narrower. Female Rambur's Forktails typically have smaller eyespots and a distinct, broad black middorsal thoracic stripe. Orange-form Rambur's Forktails are typically brighter and have black on top of S8.

TEXAS STATUS Uncommon. Widespread throughout the western part of the state.

HABITAT Alkaline and saline desert springs, pools, irrigation ditches, and canals.

DISCUSSION Males can be abundant in grasses and shoreline vegetation. Pairs are more commonly seen in the afternoon. Females lay eggs alone and are not known to submerge themselves.

Jan
Feb
Mar
Apr
May
Jun
Jul
Aug
Sep
Oct
Nov
Dec

EASTERN FORKTAIL

Ischnura verticalis (ish-NUR-a ver-ti-CAL-iss)

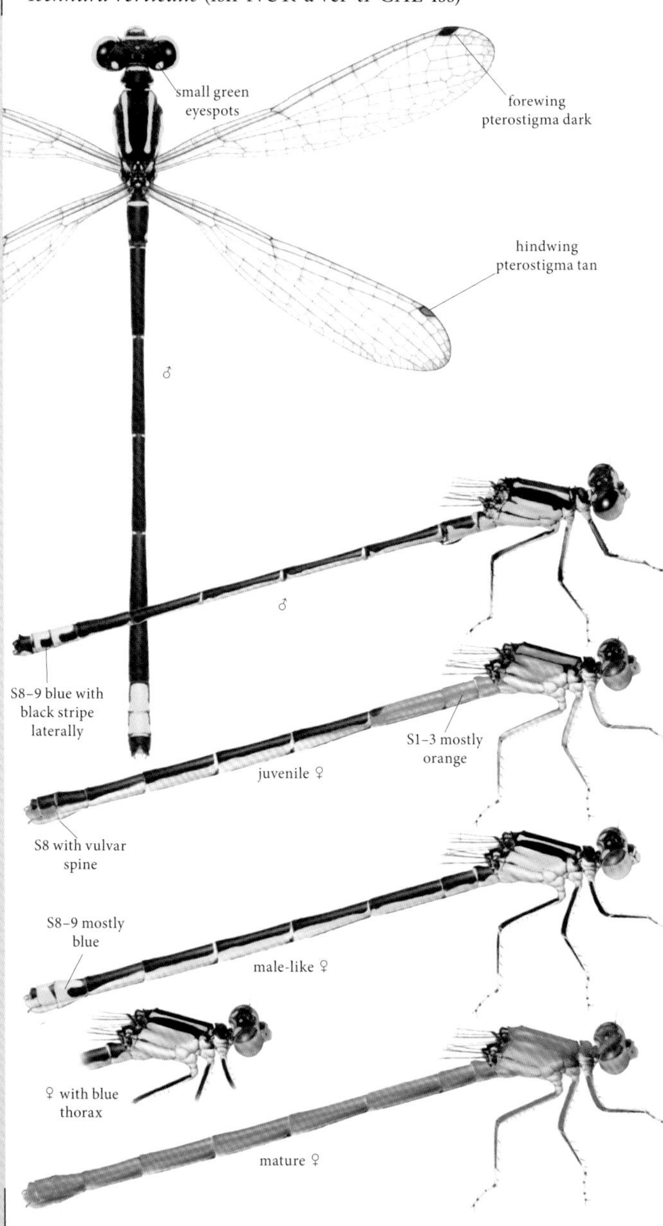

S4

KEY FEATURES

♂—small green eyespots; pale green shoulder stripe; black abdomen; S8–9 blue with black stripe laterally

♀—orange form with S1–3 orange and a thin black shoulder stripe; also male-like forms

Size
20–33 mm
(0.8–1.3 in)

Jan Feb Mar Apr May Jun Jul Aug Sep Oct Nov Dec

IDENTIFICATION Males are dark with small green eyespots. Thorax is black above with a narrow, pale green shoulder stripe and a dark shoulder stripe. Lower sides are green. Abdomen is largely black. S8–9 is blue above and has an elongated, interrupted stripe on sides. S10 is black. Male-like female is uncommon, but the similarly patterned thorax is more greenish blue, and S8–9 is more blue. Juvenile non-male-like females have orange eyespots connected by an occipital bar. Thorax is orange with a narrow black shoulder stripe. S1–3 is mostly orange, and rest of abdomen is black. Mature females are dark overall with black middorsal and dark shoulder stripes. S8 has a well-developed vulvar spine.

SIMILAR SPECIES Male Mexican Forktails are similar, but are typically bluer and have a more prominent forked projection off S10. Both male Fragile and Plains Forktails have an interrupted pale shoulder stripe, and Fragile Forktails lack blue at abdomen tip. Female Fragile Forktails also have an interrupted pale shoulder stripe and lack a vulvar spine on S8. Male Rambur's Forktails have at least some black above on S9, as well as blue eyespots; orange-form females lack a black shoulder stripe. Juvenile female Citrine and Furtive Forktails lack a dark shoulder stripe. Male Furtive Forktails have much longer abdomens, and S8 is black.

TEXAS STATUS Uncommon. Restricted to northern parts of state.

HABITAT Ponds, lakes, slow-moving streams, and marshes.

DISCUSSION Mating can take place as early as 4 days after emergence, and egg laying begins a few hours after mating. Unlike most damselflies, Eastern Forktail females usually mate only once. A female may fertilize more than a thousand eggs with the sperm from a single male encounter. Females oviposit alone in floating or emergent vegetation.

Ischnura demorsa (ish-NUR-a də-MŌR-sə)

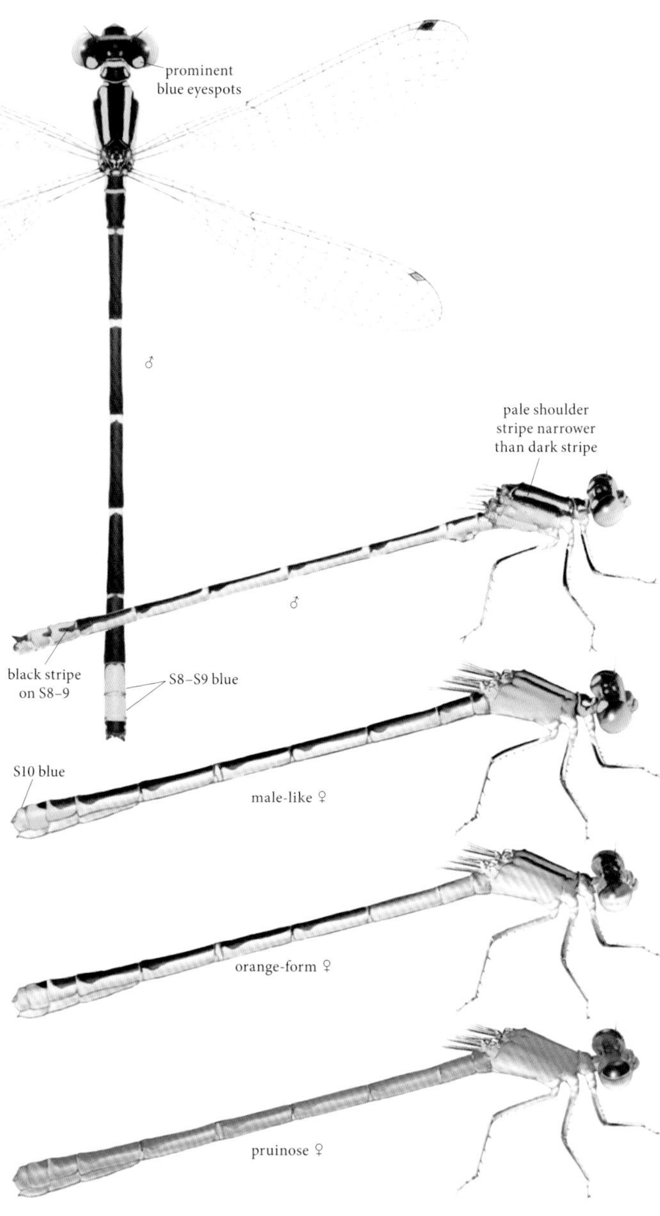

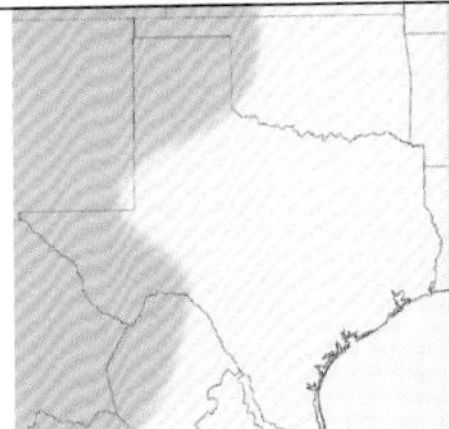

S4

KEY FEATURES

♂—green eyes with blue eyespots; thorax green; S8–9 blue with black lateral stripe; S10 black with blue laterally

♀—colored like male or orange or with dark blue pruinosity; small circular eyespots

Size
22–26 mm
(0.8–1.0 in)

IDENTIFICATION Head and thorax of male are blue-green and heavily marked with black. Pale shoulder stripe is green and narrower than dark shoulder stripe. Sides of abdomen are blue-green anteriorly, becoming lighter yellow-green in the middle. S8–9 is blue with a prominent black stripe on the side extending to about half the length of each segment. S10 is blue on the sides and black above. Forked structure is prominent off S10. Male-like females are uncommon and differ from males in having an all-blue S10. Non-male-like females are pale orange or tan. Dark shoulder stripe is sometimes reduced to a hairline. The abdomen is nearly all black above, but S1–3 may be pale to varying degrees. Females may become heavily pruinose after only a few days, and this dark blue pruinosity may entirely obscure the thoracic color pattern.

SIMILAR SPECIES Eyespots are much larger in Lilypad Forktails. Eastern Forktails are similar, but the forked projection in males is so reduced that it appears absent in hand. Male Eastern Forktails also lack a pair of small pale dots on the pronotum. Some Female Easterns may be easily confused, separable only by in-hand examination of mesostigmal plates.

TEXAS STATUS Common. Found widespread throughout western portions of the state.

HABITAT Creeks, streams, springs, and slow reaches of rivers with moderate vegetation.

DISCUSSION Males and all forms of females may be abundant on shoreline vegetation. Non-male-like females are more cryptically colored and therefore less likely to suffer predation than male-like females. Females apparently mature quickly and mate only once, using the sperm to fertilize eggs throughout their lives.

Jan
Feb
Mar
Apr
May
Jun
Jul
Aug
Sep
Oct
Nov
Dec

Ischnura damula (ish-NUR-a DAM-ū-lə)

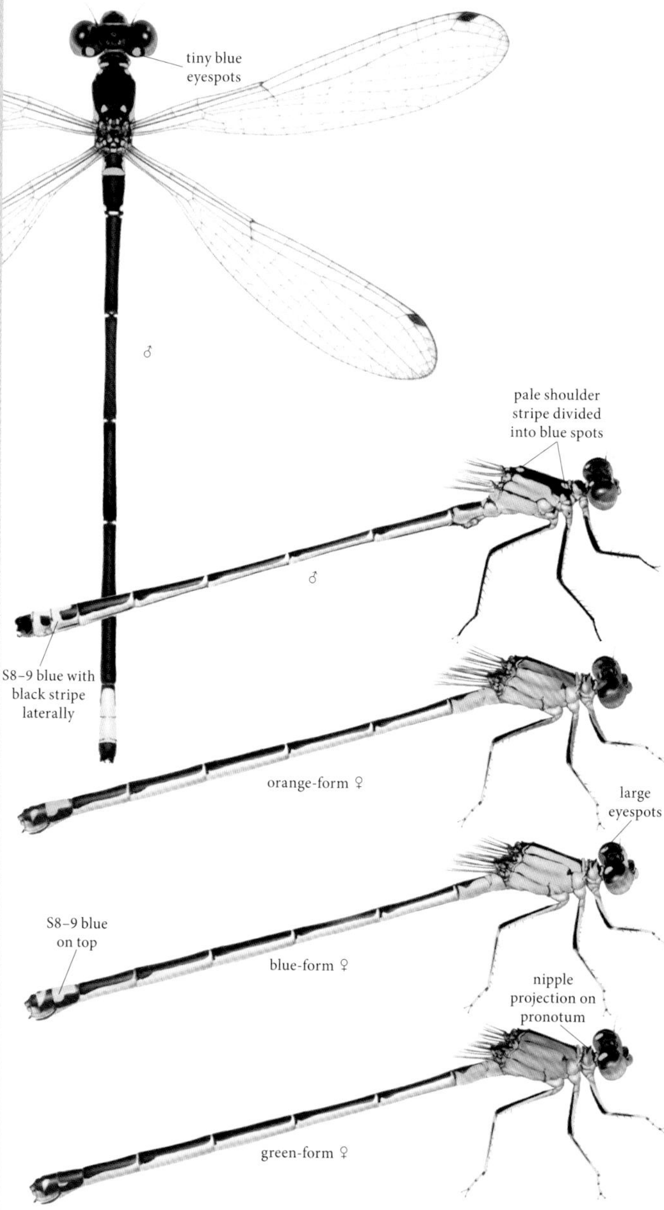

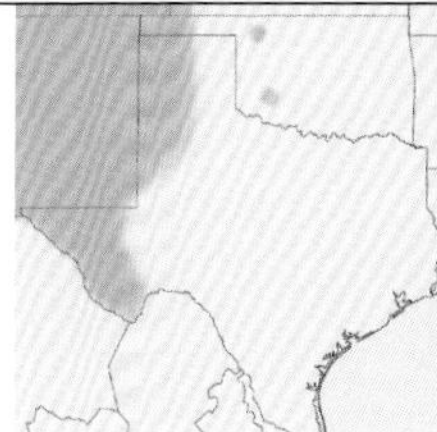

KEY FEATURES

♂—top of thorax black with four paired small blue spots; abdomen black on top with S8–9 blue

♀—colored like male or reddish or blue or green; small circular eyespots; S8 mostly blue; S9 with blue spots that may be confluent above

S4

Size
23–34 mm
(0.9–1.3 in

Jan Feb Mar Apr May Jun Jul Aug Sep Oct Nov Dec

IDENTIFICATION In males, top of thorax is black. Pale shoulder stripe is reduced to a pair of small pale spots. The remaining areas of thorax are blue. Abdomen is largely black, with S8–9 blue except for a black lateral stripe that is not confluent. Female has prominent nipple-like tubercles on each side of pronotum. Male-like females are common and very similar to males, but with larger eyespots; often, anterior spot of pale shoulder stripe extends backward, sometimes touching posterior spot. Non-male-like females have a continuous thin dark shoulder stripe and a wide pale shoulder stripe. Thorax can be pinkish orange, blue, or greenish brown. Pale abdominal colors are orange or tan with occasional blue markings laterally on S1–2, the tip of S7, and S8–10.

SIMILAR SPECIES In male Black-fronted Forktails, entire front of thorax is black. Plains Forktails are the only Texas forktail with the pale shoulder stripe forming 2 spots. In female Painted Damsels, S7 is blue, and in males, eyespots and S8–10 are red.

TEXAS STATUS Uncommon. Found west of the Pecos River, north into the Panhandle.

HABITAT Ponds, springs, and slow-moving streams with heavy marginal vegetation.

DISCUSSION Both males and females may be abundant on shoreline vegetation. They usually do not venture out over the open water. Egg laying may occur unaccompanied by the male or in tandem, usually in emergent vegetation or algal mats. Commonly, wings are slightly open when individuals land, then close after a few seconds.

BLACK-FRONTED FORKTAIL

Ischnura denticollis (ish-NUR-a den-ti-COL-lis)

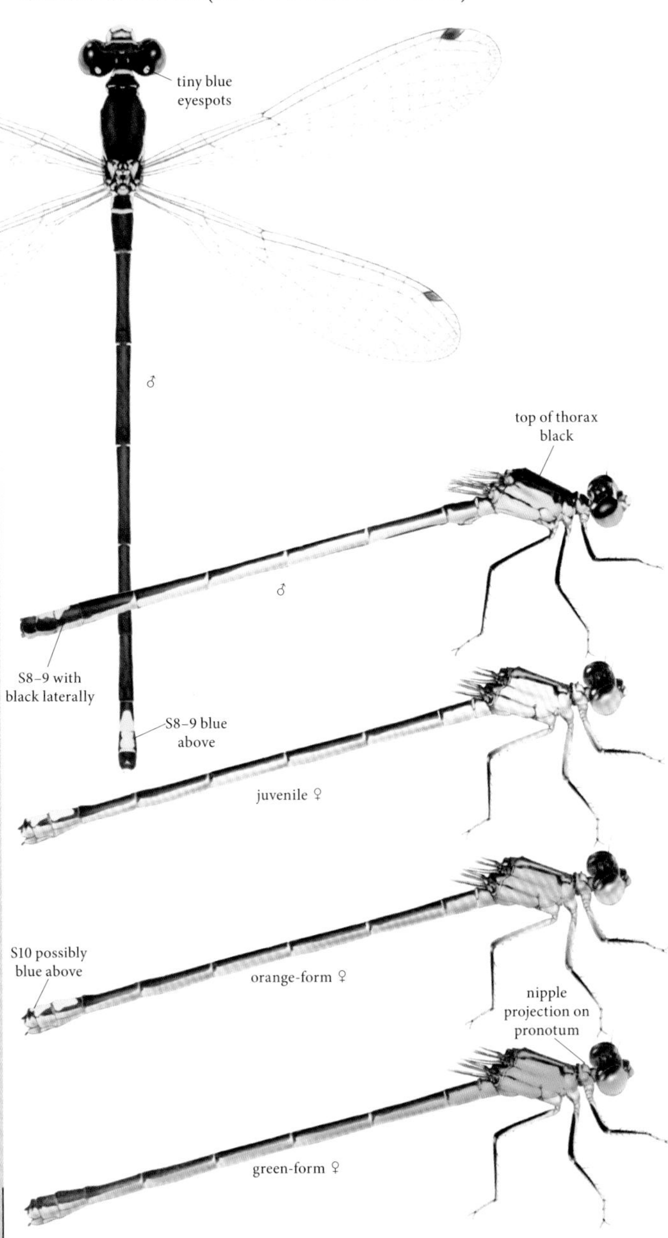

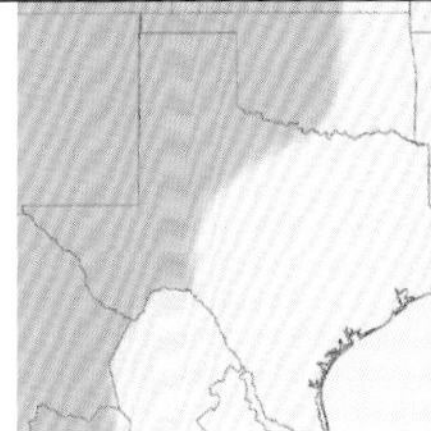

S4

KEY FEATURES

♂—green eyes with blue eyespots; thorax green; S8–9 blue with black lateral stripe; S10 black with blue laterally

♀—colored like male or orange or green; small circular eye spots

Size
22–26 mm
(0.8–1.0 in)

Jan Feb Mar Apr May Jun Jul Aug Sep Oct Nov Dec

IDENTIFICATION Head is dark with tiny blue eyespots. Top of thorax in male is metallic black and completely lacking a pale shoulder stripe. Lower part of thorax is blue-green. Abdomen is dark above with a blue-green metallic luster. S1–2 is blue on sides, and S8–9 is blue above. Forked projection on S10 is not distinct. Female has a distinct nipple-like protuberance on each side of the pronotum. Male-like form is rare and differs from the male in the occasional presence of a pale shoulder stripe and a blue spot on top of S10. Non-male-like forms vary from pale blue to orange to green, with eyespots larger than in males and separated by a pale occipital bar. Pale shoulder stripe is clearly visible. Abdomen is patterned as in male-like form, with blue on top of S10 as well. Pale colors on S8–10 may become obscured with age.

SIMILAR SPECIES The male Black-fronted Forktail is the only forktail in the region with the top of the thorax all black and completely lacking a pale shoulder stripe. Female Plains, Mexican, and Eastern Forktails lack blue on top of both S8 and S9.

TEXAS STATUS Common. Widespread in western part of the state.

HABITAT Vegetated streams or ponds, often associated with springs, especially at northern latitudes.

DISCUSSION Black-fronted Forktails are more widely distributed than the other western forktail species. This species has been described as "undoubtedly the feeblest of all western Odonata." In a Mexican population, survivorship for both sexes was among the lowest rates in the Odonata, and their ability to disperse is considered low. Unlike most forktails, females will lay eggs in tandem, usually in emergent grasses or debris. The average mating time is 20 minutes, the shortest reported for any forktail.

CITRINE FORKTAIL

Ischnura hastata (ish-NUR-a hoss-TOT-ə)

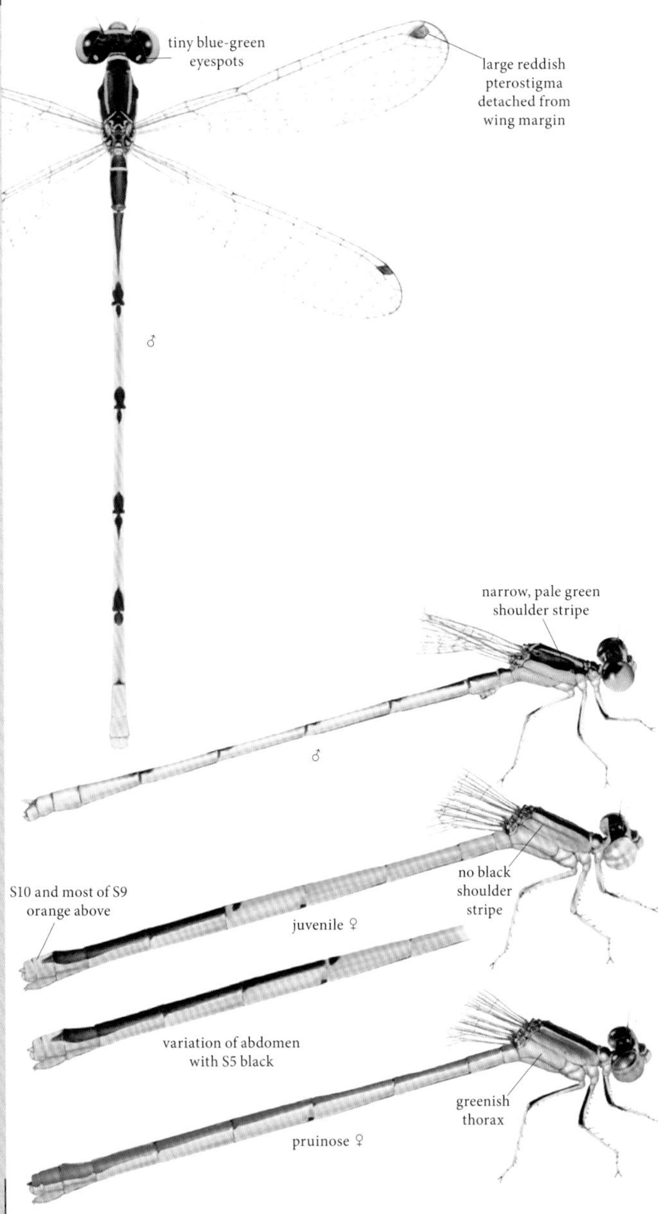

KEY FEATURES

♂—tiny; green eyes and thorax; yellow abdomen; forewing pterostigma reddish and not touching wing margin

♀—orange, with S5 or S6–9 black above; black shoulder stripe thin or absent

S5

Size
21–27 mm
(0.8–1.1 in)

Jan Feb Mar Apr May Jun Jul Aug Sep Oct Nov Dec

IDENTIFICATION Males are distinct because forewing pterostigma is detached from anterior-most wing margin. Pterostigma is paler and at least twice the size of its hindwing counterpart. Thorax of males is green, and abdomen is bright yellow. Dorsoapical projection on S10 is strongly notched and prominent. Females are red-orange with prominent orange eyespots and occipital bar. Middorsal stripe is black. Dark shoulder stripe is thin or absent. Abdomen is orange, with S6–9 and sometimes S5 bearing a continuous black stripe above. In older individuals, a light pruinosity envelops the thorax and abdomen, but never completely obscures the thoracic pattern. Male-like females are not known.

SIMILAR SPECIES Males easily recognizable. Female Fragile and Eastern Forktails are similar, but Fragile Forktails are generally darker, and even in pruinose females the distinctive exclamation-point-like pale shoulder stripe is visible with the help of a hand lens. Fragile and Eastern Forktail females are gray in the shoulder area and not olive or brown. Juvenile Furtive and Rambur's females are larger and have less orange on abdomen. Lilypad Forktails and Orange Bluets have a distinct dark shoulder stripe.

TEXAS STATUS Common. Widespread throughout the state.

HABITAT Heavily vegetated ponds and lakes and other permanent or temporary bodies of water.

DISCUSSION Citrine Forktails may be abundant in heavily vegetated areas with little or no water. Both sexes may be abundant around pond and lake margins. Females are rarely seen mating, probably because they mate only once, for an average of 20 minutes. Females lay eggs, unaccompanied by a male, in submerged vegetation just under the surface.

Ischnura kellicotti (ish-NUR-a kel-i-COT-ī)

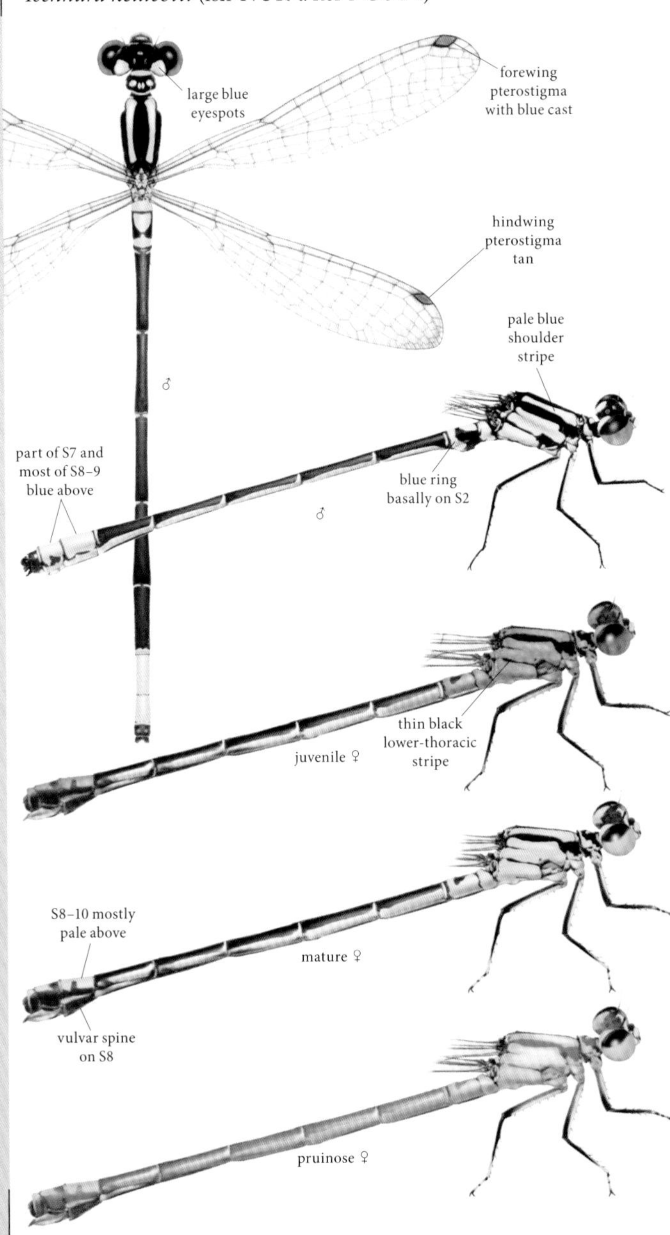

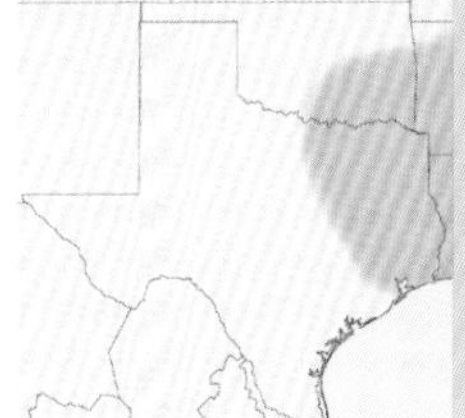

KEY FEATURES

♂—large blue eyespots; pale blue shoulder stripe; blue ring on S2; part of S7 and all of S8–9 blue above

♀—orange, blue, or pruinose; S2 with pale ring; S8–10 mostly pale above

S3

Size
25–31 mm
(1.0–1.2 in)

Jan Feb Mar Apr May Jun Jul Aug Sep Oct Nov Dec

IDENTIFICATION Male has large blue eyespots with no occipital bar. Thorax is blue with black middorsal stripe and dark shoulder stripe. Pale blue shoulder stripe is widest anteriorly. Abdomen is largely black, but with blue on S1 and S2. Blue on S2 forms a spot anteriorly and a ring posteriorly. S8–9 and posterior portion of S7 are blue on top. The forewing pterostigma is larger than the hindwing pterostigma and becomes blue at maturity. Females start off orange and become blue with maturity. Each is patterned like the male except that S10 is also pale. A small vulvar spine is usually visible on S8.

SIMILAR SPECIES Skimming Bluet is similar in appearance and behavior, but that species has smaller eyespots, lacks a pale ring on S2, and lacks any blue on S7. All other similar orange forktails and the Orange Bluet lack orange on S8. Eastern Forktail females may be very similar, but either they will have orange at tip of abdomen, or older individuals will be enveloped with dark pruinescence—not white or gray, as in Lilypad Forktails.

TEXAS STATUS Uncommon. May be locally abundant in certain habitats of East Texas.

HABITAT Strongly associated with floating lily pads in ponds and lakes.

DISCUSSION This species has an obligatory relationship with water lilies (*Nuphar* and *Nymphaea*) in both the nymph and adult stages. Nymphs cling to the bottom of the lily pads and emerge by crawling on top. The adults are nearly always encountered perching or laying eggs on these plants. They sometimes exhibit a unique posture: while perching on a pad with the abdomen curled downward, they will tilt back on the abdomen with the front legs in the air, ready for an immediate getaway. Females, unaccompanied by males, take up to 20 minutes to lay eggs.

FRAGILE FORKTAIL

Ischnura posita (ish-NUR-a POZ-i-tə)

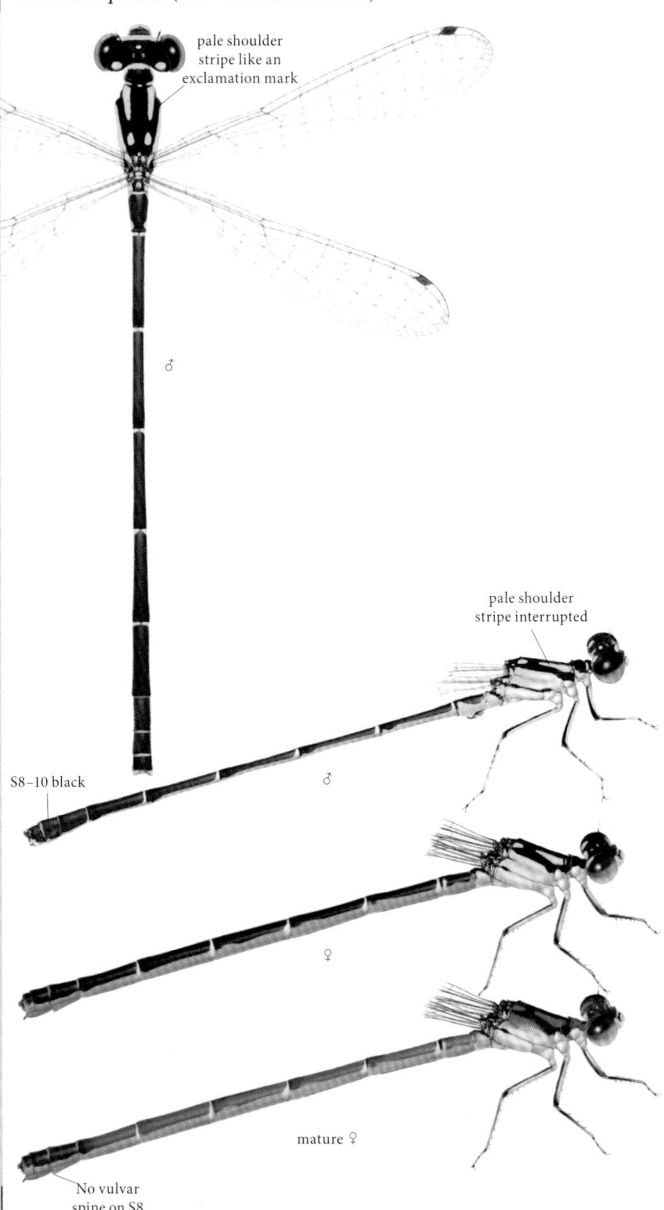

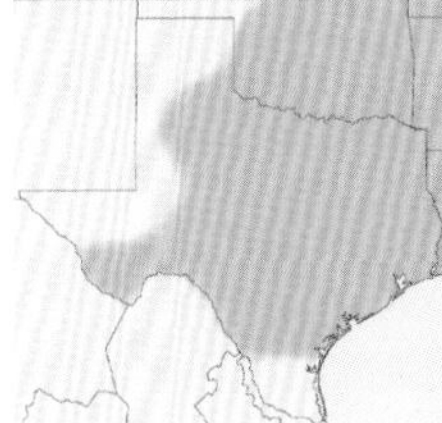

KEY FEATURES

♂—pale shoulder stripe like a yellow or green exclamation mark; abdomen black

♀—pale exclamation mark generally visible; no vulvar spine

S5

Size
21–29 mm
(0.8–1.1 in)

IDENTIFICATION Males are generally yellow-green, and females are blue. Both sexes are recognizable by a conspicuous division of the pale shoulder stripe into an exclamation mark set against a nearly all-dark abdomen. Both sexes may occasionally have this pale shoulder stripe uninterrupted. The rest of the body is metallic black. The forked projection on S10 in males is visible but short. Females are very similar to males, but they are pale blue. With age, they become dark blue with heavy pruinosity. Females lack a vulvar spine on S8.

SIMILAR SPECIES The pale shoulder stripe in Plains Forktails is divided into subequal anterior and posterior spots, and S8–9 in males is blue. Citrine Forktail females are similar, but generally paler in color with an olive or pale brown shoulder stripe, a visible middorsal thoracic stripe, and possibly a vulvar spine on S8. Female Eastern Forktails have a complete pale shoulder stripe (as do some Fragile Forktail females), but Eastern Forktail females always have a vulvar spine on S8.

TEXAS STATUS Common. Widespread across state except the Lower Rio Grande Valley and Panhandle.

HABITAT Heavily vegetated ponds, marshes, and slow-moving waters.

DISCUSSION Unlike most damselflies, Fragile Forktails of both sexes are regularly encountered at ponds during the day. They are often found in large numbers deep in shoreline vegetation. Females oviposit alone on floating and emergent vegetation. At night, both sexes roost significantly higher on the same branches where they perched earlier in the day. They roost with the body at a right angle to the stem, possibly allowing for a quicker escape from predation and more efficiency in warming.

Jan
Feb
Mar
Apr
May
Jun
Jul
Aug
Sep
Oct
Nov
Dec

FURTIVE FORKTAIL

Ischnura prognata (ish-NUR-a prog-NA-tə)

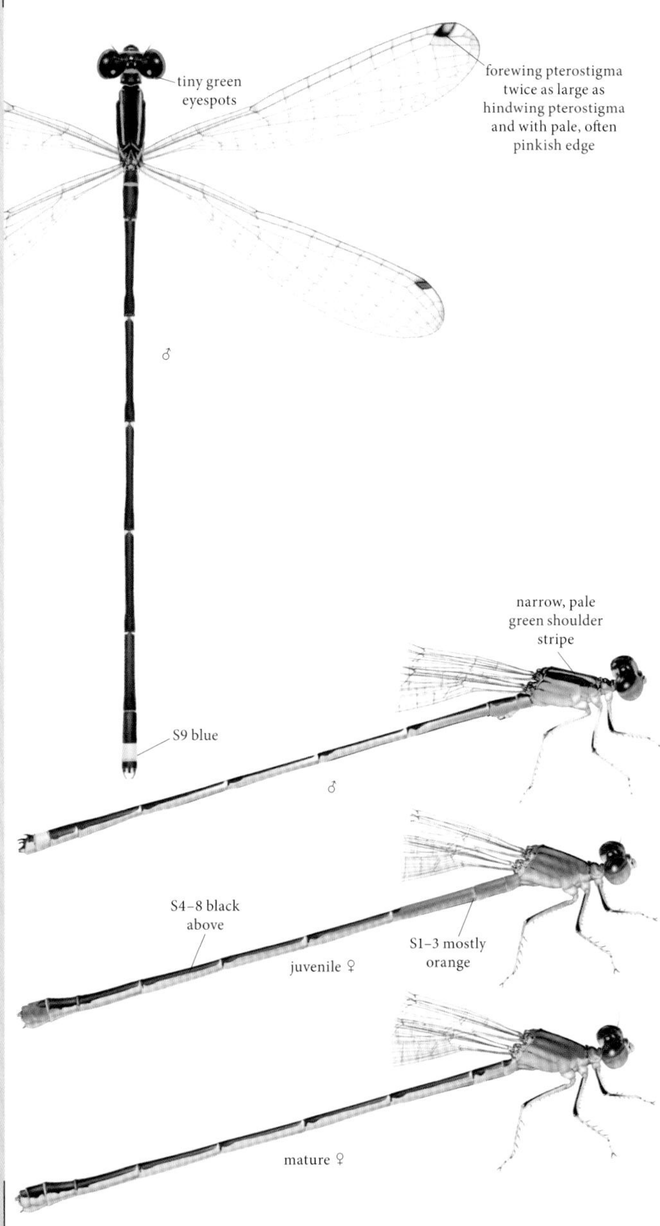

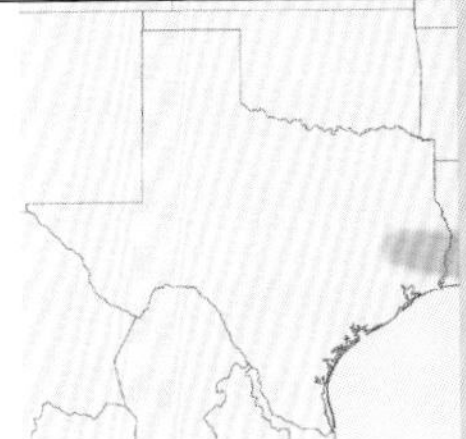

KEY FEATURES

♂—long and slender; pale shoulder stripe narrow and green; abdomen black with S9 blue

♀—juveniles with thorax, S1–3, and S9–10 orange; olive green at maturity, with S1–10 black above; both forms lacking dark shoulder stripe

S1

Size
30–37 mm
(1.2–1.5 in)

Jan Feb Mar Apr May Jun Jul Aug Sep Oct Nov Dec

IDENTIFICATION Males are dark with small circular green eyespots. Thorax is metallic black above with only a thin pale green shoulder stripe. Lower part of thorax and S1–2 is green on side. Legs are pale. Long slender abdomen is black, with S9 entirely blue and S10 blue on sides. Pterostigma in forewing is twice as big as in hindwing and transparent in its outer half, often with a touch of pink visible at edge. Male-like females are not known. Juvenile females have an orange-red thorax with a black middorsal stripe. S1–3 is mostly orange, with S4–8 mostly black. S9–10 is orange with small black spot on either side of top of S9. In mature females, the orange is replaced with green. Top of thorax becomes dark brown, and all of abdomen is black above.
SIMILAR SPECIES In male and male-like female Rambur's Forktails, S8 is blue. In orange Rambur's Forktails, S1–2 is orange, and in mature females, S1–2 is olive green. Female Citrine Forktails are much smaller, and in immature females, S1–5 is orange. In male Eastern Forktails, S8–9 is largely blue, and immature females have a black shoulder stripe; S10 is black.
TEXAS STATUS Rare. Known from three counties (Jasper, San Jacinto, and Tyler) in East Texas.
HABITAT Heavily shaded ponds, swamps, and sloughs.
DISCUSSION This eastern species is uncommon throughout its range and apparently finds its westernmost limit in the Sam Houston National Forest of East Texas. It has the longest abdomen of the forktails in the United States. This species shares a behavioral similarity with many tropical damselflies, in that it will fly ghostlike from one stem to another in the shady forest undergrowth, foraging at a height of 6 feet or more. Both sexes may be seen at suitable habitats.

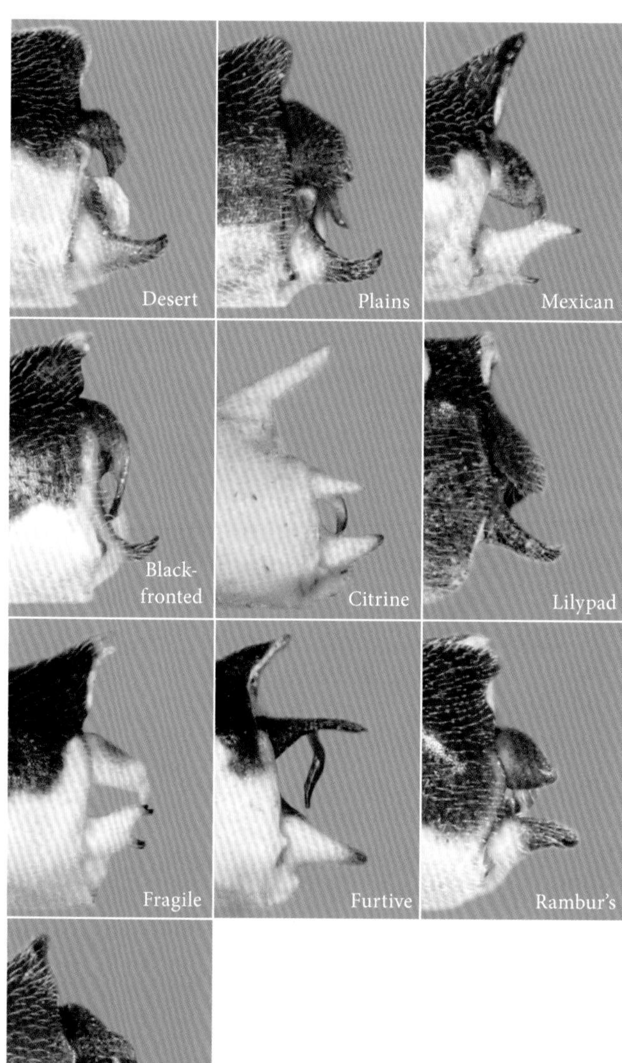
Desert
Plains
Mexican
Black-
fronted
Citrine
Lilypad
Fragile
Furtive
Rambur's
Eastern

FORKTAILS—FEMALE MESOSTIGMAL PLATES

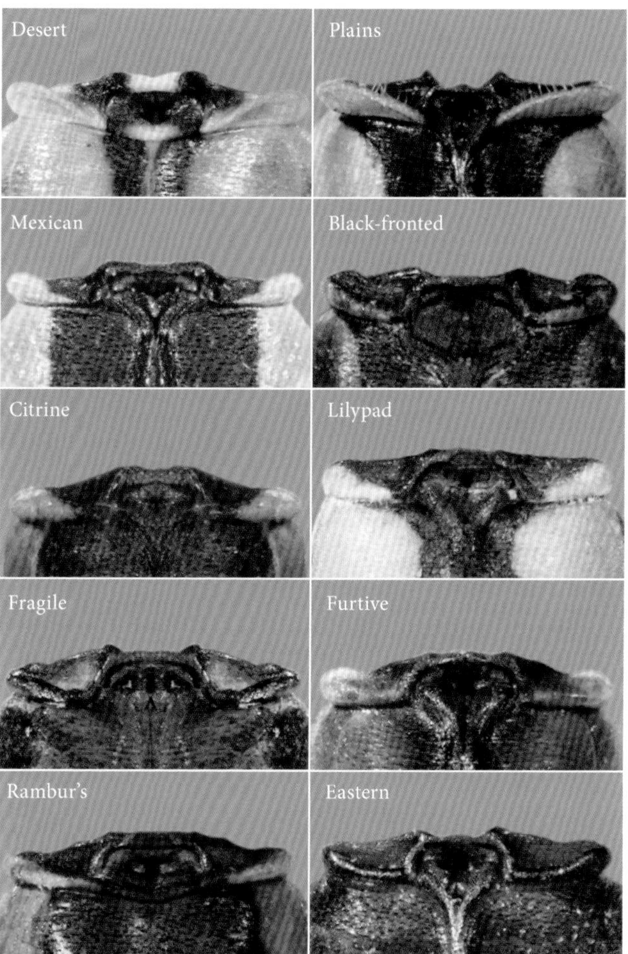

Leptobasis melinogaster (lep-tō-BĀS-iss meh-LIN-ō-gas-tur)

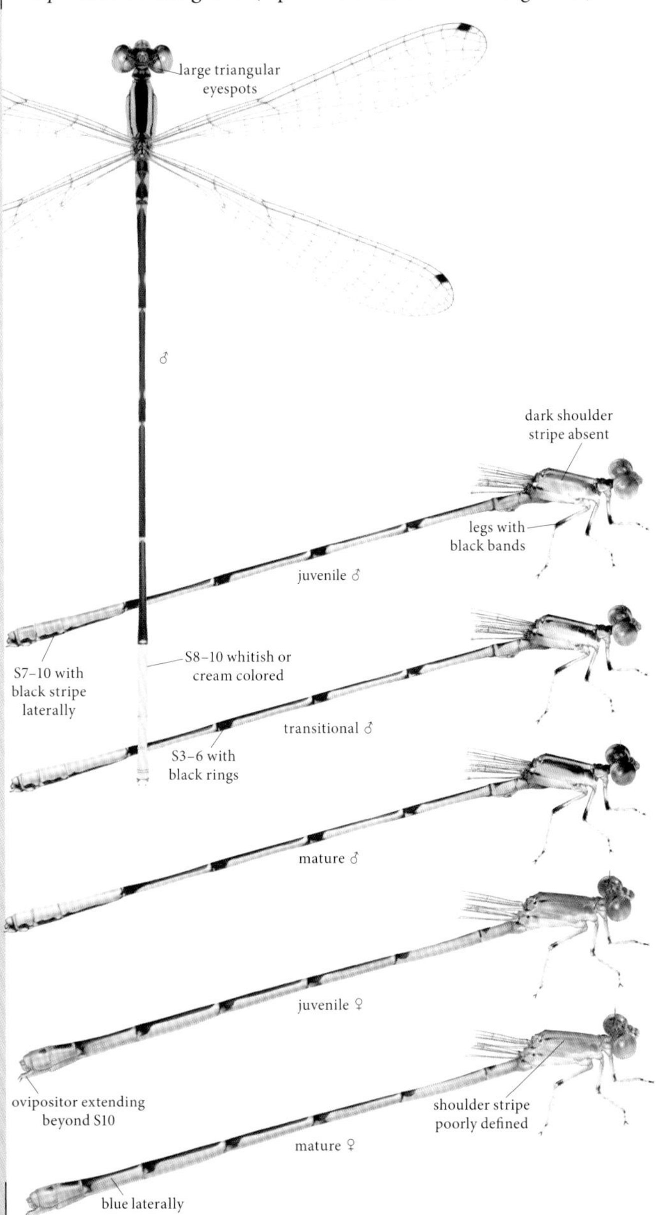

S2

KEY FEATURES

♂—green eyes and thorax; long thin abdomen; S3–6 with black distal rings; S7–10 white or cream colored

♀—tan or green; long thin abdomen; S3–9 black above; ovipositor long, extending beyond S10

Size
38–42 mm
(1.5–1.7 in)

Jan Feb Mar Apr May Jun Jul Aug Sep Oct Nov Dec

IDENTIFICATION Male has greenish eyes and large triangular eyespots. This species undergoes significant color changes in both sexes as they mature. Thorax has a broad black middorsal stripe. Pale shoulder stripe is green, followed by a thin dark shoulder stripe and pale lower sides. Juvenile males are tan instead of green and lack significant dark markings on thorax. Legs are pale with distinctive dark bands. Abdomen is long and thin, primarily dark, with black rings on S3–6. S7–10 is cream colored in juvenile males and almost white in older individuals. Narrow black stripe is present on S7–10 laterally at all ages. Female starts off tan and develops a pale greenish thorax. Dark shoulder stripe is orangish brown and not as well defined as in male. Legs are pale with dark markings, like male's. Abdomen is primarily dark, with S8–10 mostly pale, but with paired black spots above on S8–9. Ovipositor is prominent, extending beyond tip of abdomen.

SIMILAR SPECIES No other damselfly in Texas has the combination of a greenish thorax and a long thin abdomen with the absence of blue. Males are the only damselflies with S7–10 cream colored.

TEXAS STATUS Rare. Known sporadically from only a few localities in the Lower Rio Grande Valley.

HABITAT Shaded forest pools and ponds with tall vegetation and overhanging branches.

DISCUSSION Males are typically more visible at ponds, but females can be abundant. Both sexes tend to prefer overhanging branches and vegetation for perches. They fly very deliberately through these tangles, making their wispy bodies difficult to follow. They may survive periods of no water as adults or in the egg stage. None of the known Texas populations seem particularly stable, and individuals are seen only occasionally.

RED-TIPPED SWAMPDAMSEL

Leptobasis vacillans (lep-tō-BĀS-iss VAS-i-lans)

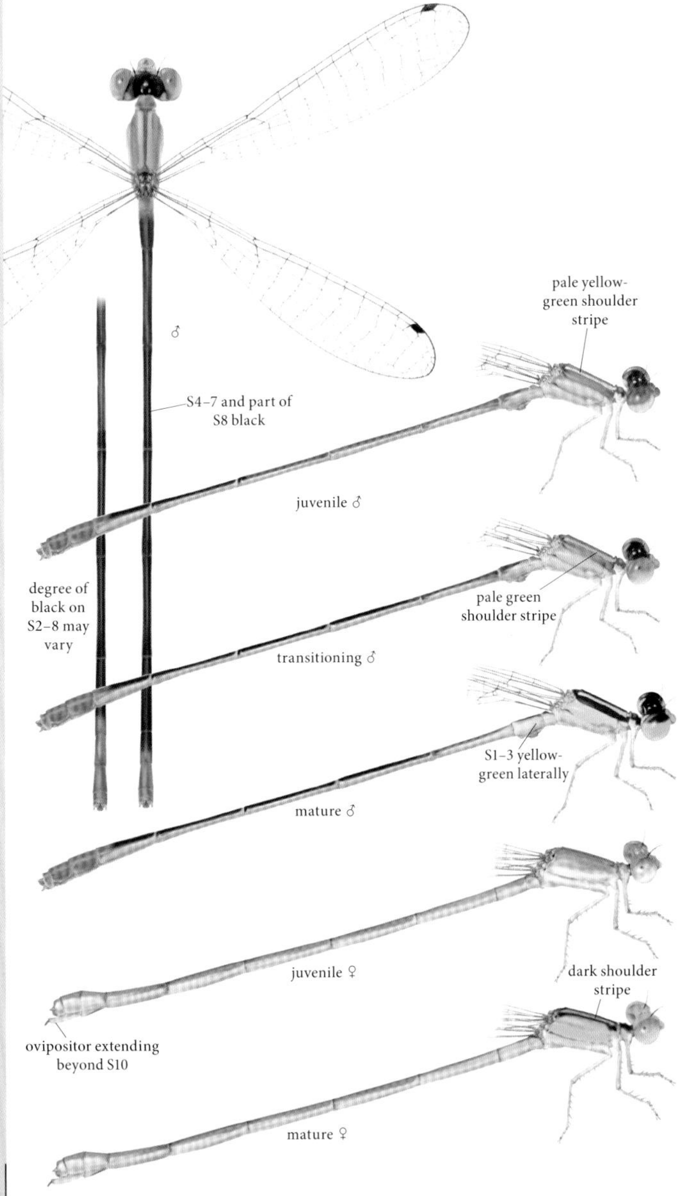

♂

S4–7 and part of S8 black

degree of black on S2–8 may vary

pale yellow-green shoulder stripe

juvenile ♂

pale green shoulder stripe

transitioning ♂

S1–3 yellow-green laterally

mature ♂

juvenile ♀

ovipositor extending beyond S10

dark shoulder stripe

mature ♀

KEY FEATURES

♂—green eyes and thorax; S2–3 or S4 red; S4 or S5–7 black; S8–10 reddish orange; juvenile mostly orange

♀—green thorax (orange in juvenile); orange abdomen; thin black shoulder stripe; long ovipositor

Size
28–36 mm
(1.1–1.4 in)

Jan Feb Mar Apr May Jun Jul Aug Sep Oct Nov Dec

IDENTIFICATION This species is quite variable, going through a number of forms as it matures. Mature male has green eyes. Pale shoulder stripe is green; dark shoulder stripe is black. S1–3 is greenish yellow laterally. S3 and sometimes S4 are red. S8–10, part of S7, and occasionally all of S7 and part of S6 are orange-red. Rest of abdomen is black. In juvenile males, head and thorax are orange-brown. A light yellow or pale green shoulder stripe is usually visible. S8–10 (at a minimum) is orange-red, and some of the preceding segments are black. Female is similar to male. Juveniles start off orange and lack any distinct shoulder stripes. Older individuals develop a green thorax with dark middorsal and shoulder stripes. S1–3 is usually green, with the remainder of the abdomen orange. Female has a long ovipositor extending beyond S10.

SIMILAR SPECIES Despite the tremendous variety of color forms, this damselfly remains distinctive in Texas. No other species is colored with red and green in this manner. Juvenile males and females may be initially confused with Orange-striped Threadtails because of their long slender body, but that species has more black on the thorax, as do Orange Bluets.

TEXAS STATUS Rare. Known only from the Santa Ana National Wildlife Refuge in the Lower Rio Grande Valley.

HABITAT Shaded forest pools and ponds with abundant vegetation. Also found in the slow-moving water of ditches.

DISCUSSION This species was discovered in Texas and the United States only in 2009. It is a widespread Central American species that gets as far south as Ecuador. Like the Cream-tipped Swampdamsel, this species may survive extended droughts as adults.

SPHAGNUM SPRITE

Nehalennia gracilis (ne-ha-LEN-ē-a gra-SIL-us)

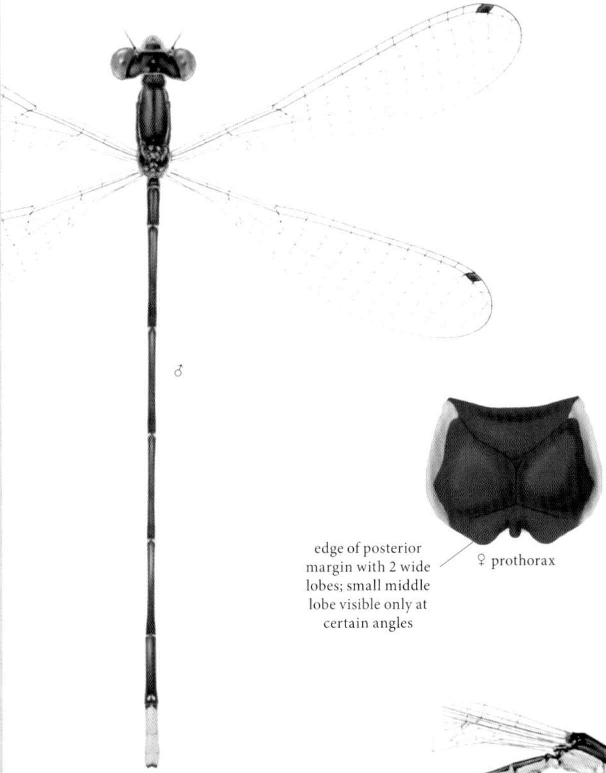

♂

edge of posterior margin with 2 wide lobes; small middle lobe visible only at certain angles

♀ prothorax

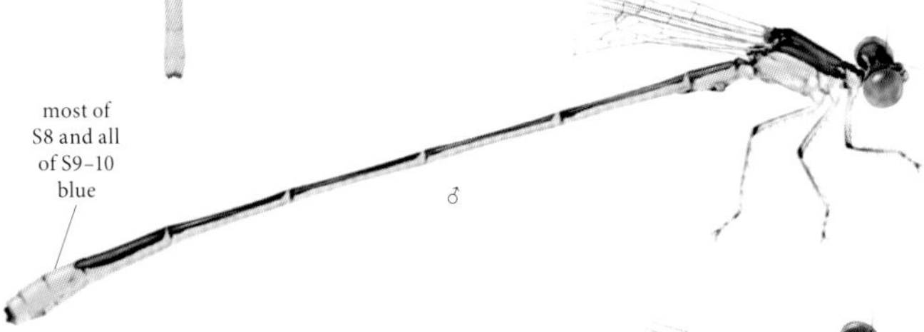

most of S8 and all of S9–10 blue

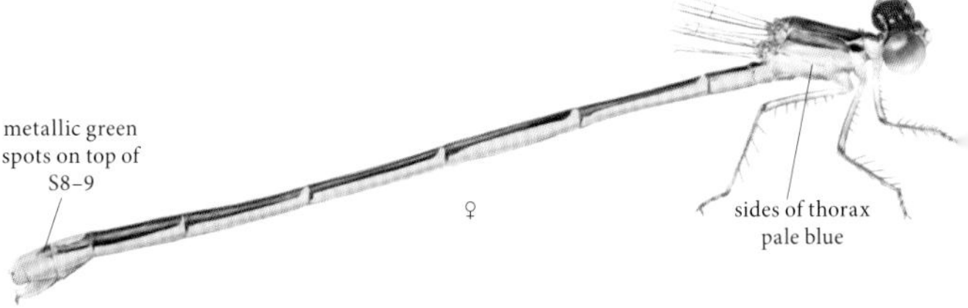

♂

metallic green spots on top of S8–9

♀

sides of thorax pale blue

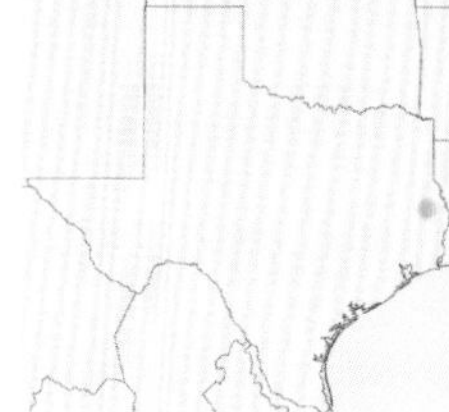

KEY FEATURES

♂—top of thorax and abdomen metallic green; most of S8 and all of S9–10 blue

♀—top of thorax and abdomen metallic green; S8–10 blue with dark spots basally on S8–9

Size
22–31 mm
(0.9–1.2 in)

IDENTIFICATION Eyes are blue. Top of head and thorax in males are a dark metallic green. There are no visible shoulder stripes. Lower sides of thorax are blue. Abdomen is largely metallic green, with most of S8 and all of S9–10 blue. Female is similarly colored, but paler blue on sides of thorax. S8–10 is blue with dark basal spots on S8–9. Posterior margin of female's prothorax is distinctive in shape.

SIMILAR SPECIES Southern Sprites are smaller and have less blue. In male Southern Sprites, most of S8 is dark, and paired elongated dark spots are on S9. In female Southern Sprites, only S10 is pale.

TEXAS STATUS Uncommon. Known from only a couple of ponds in the Angelina National Forest in Jasper County.

HABITAT Ponds and bogs with sphagnum.

DISCUSSION This eastern U.S. species was discovered in Texas only in 2009. Its only other location west of the Mississippi is in southern Missouri. It is generally found with Southern Sprites in Texas, where it stays low in thick vegetation.

Jan
Feb
Mar
Apr
May
Jun
Jul
Aug
Sep
Oct
Nov
Dec

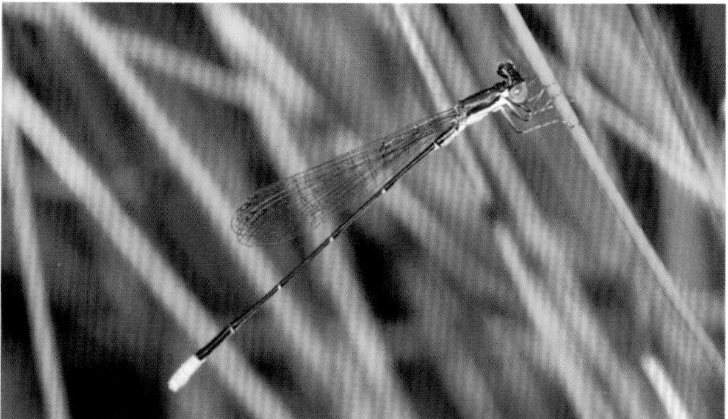

Male Sphagnum Sprite.

SOUTHERN SPRITE

Nehalennia integricollis (ne-ha-LEN-ē-a in-teg-ri-COLL-iss)

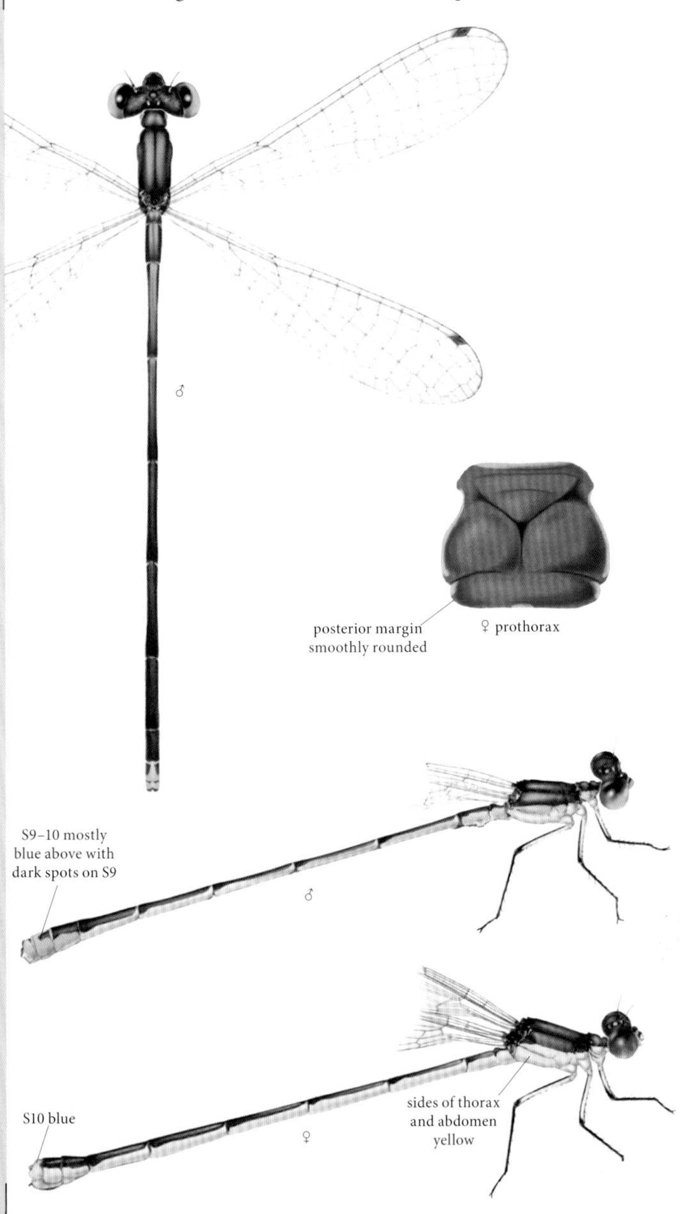

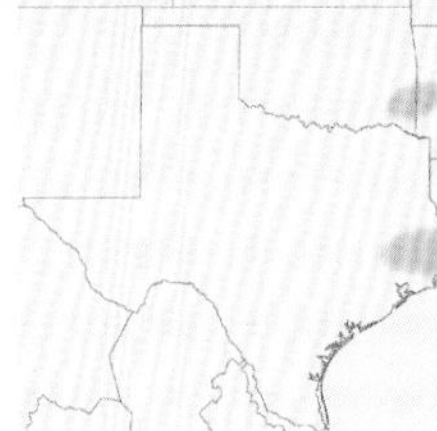

KEY FEATURES

♂—top of thorax and abdomen metallic green; S9–10 mostly blue above with basal spots on S9

♀—top of thorax and abdomen metallic green; sides of thorax and abdomen yellow or blue; S10 blue

S3

Size
20–25 mm
(0.8–1.0 in)

Jan Feb Mar Apr May Jun Jul Aug Sep Oct Nov Dec

IDENTIFICATION Top of head and thorax in males is a dark metallic green. Lower sides of thorax blue. Abdomen metallic green with S10 and most of S9 blue along with side of S8. Dark area basally on top of S9. Female similarly colored, but paler and sides of thorax yellow or blue. S10 pale blue.

SIMILAR SPECIES The Sphagnum Sprite is larger and has more blue; males have blue on most of S8–10. In female Sphagnum Sprites, parts of S8 and S9 are pale blue, and sides of thorax are blue.

TEXAS STATUS Uncommon. Scattered populations known in East Texas, where it may be locally abundant.

HABITAT Ponds, lakes, and bogs with grassy edges.

DISCUSSION Southern Sprites can be locally abundant with both sexes flying and perching low in dense pond-side grasses. Females lay eggs in tandem, holding their abdomen between their wings when depositing eggs.

Male Southern Sprite.

EVERGLADES SPRITE

Nehalennia pallidula (ne-ha-LEN-ē-a pa-LID-yew-la)

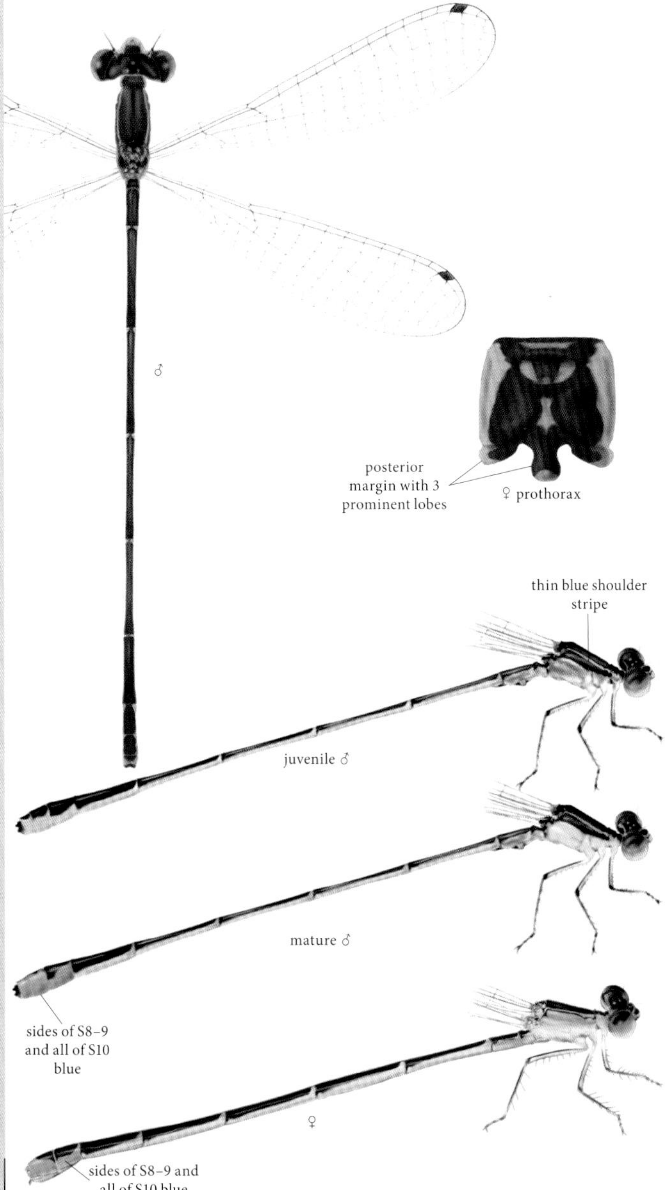
♂
posterior
margin with 3
prominent lobes
♀ prothorax
thin blue shoulder
stripe
juvenile ♂
mature ♂
sides of S8–9
and all of S10
blue
♀
sides of S8–9 and
all of S10 blue

KEY FEATURES

♂—tiny, mostly dark; thin blue shoulder stripe; S10 blue above; S8–9 blue on sides; sides of thorax blue

♀—tiny, mostly dark; thin blue shoulder stripe; S8–9 blue on sides; S10 all blue

SA

Size
23–29 mm
(0.9–1.1 in)

IDENTIFICATION This is a very small, generally dark damselfly. Eyes are blue in male. Small, narrow blue eyespots are connected by a thin occipital bar. Very thin pale shoulder stripe is blue. Abdomen is largely black, with sides of S1–2, S8–9, and all of S10 blue. Juvenile males are similarly patterned, but duller in overall color. Females are colored the same. The posterior margin of the female's prothorax has a distinct squared lobe medially.

SIMILAR SPECIES Southern and Sphagnum Sprite males both have a metallic green thorax and lack a pale blue shoulder stripe. In female Southern Sprites, only S10 is blue, and Sphagnum Sprite has more blue on S8–9.

TEXAS STATUS Accidental and historical. There is a historical Texas record for this otherwise Florida Everglades endemic. Two females were collected in Galveston in 1918 and are now housed in the U.S. National Collection at the Smithsonian Institution. The occurrence of this species in Texas was undoubtedly the result of a storm or some other unusual event, and it is unlikely to still be in the state.

HABITAT Grass and sedge marshes.

DISCUSSION Pairs are often seen away from water. Immature forms are apparently common, potentially indicating a long maturation period. It has one of the most restricted distributions of North American damselflies. It is typically found in Florida from Orlando southward, where it flies year-round and may have two generations.

Jan
Feb
Mar
Apr
May
Jun
Jul
Aug
Sep
Oct
Nov
Dec

Telebasis byersi (tel-i-BĀSE-iss BY-ers-ī)

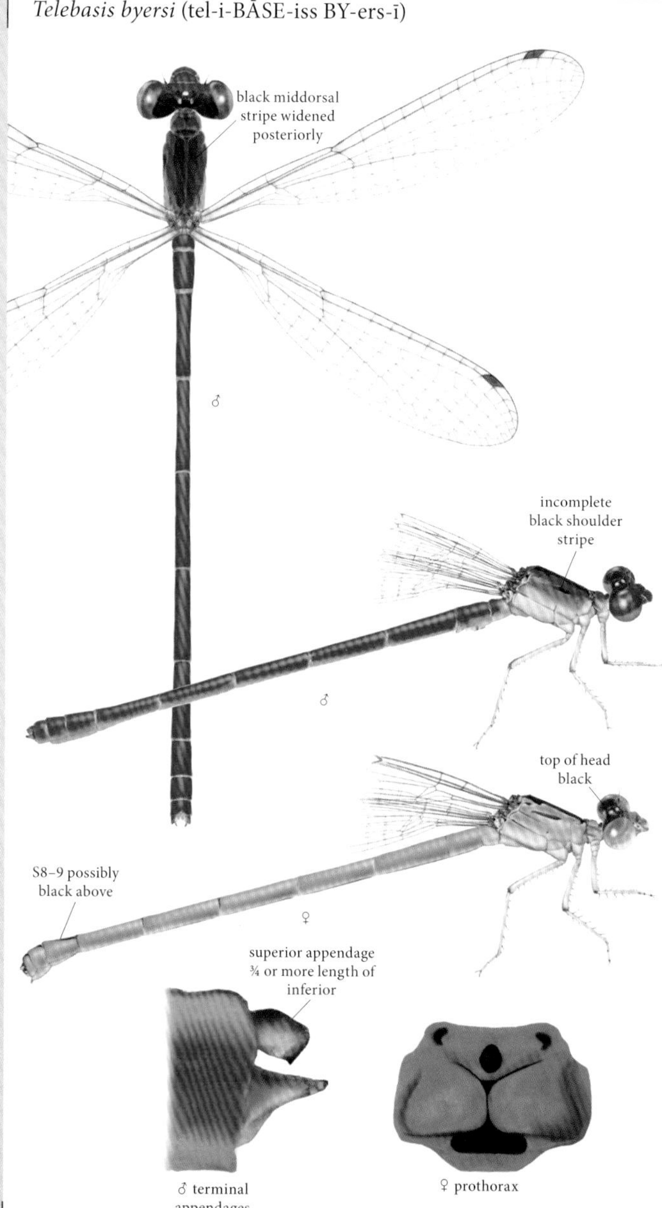

♂ terminal appendages

♀ prothorax

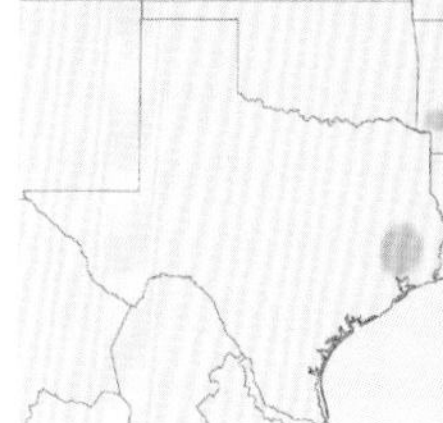

KEY FEATURES

♂—red eyes, face, thorax, and abdomen; thorax with dark middorsal stripe widening posteriorly to form arrow

♀—tan all over with dark middorsal stripe, as in male; prothoracic horns absent

S3

Size
25–31 mm
(1.0–1.2 in)

IDENTIFICATION Males are bright red, including the eyes. Thorax is red with a black middorsal stripe widening posteriorly to form a broad arrow pointing toward the abdomen. Arrow is divided by narrow red stripe. Shoulder has an incomplete black stripe. Lower part of thorax is paler. Legs are pale. Abdomen is entirely red. Females are marked like males, but tan, sometimes with a suffusion of red. S8–9 has some black above.

SIMILAR SPECIES The Desert Firetail is nearly identical, but it does not occur on duckweed, and its range is not known to overlap with that of the Duckweed Firetail. Superior appendages of male Duckweed Firetails are three-fourths or more the length of inferiors, while they are little more half the length in Desert Firetails. Female Desert Firetails possess prothoracic horns that are lacking in Duckweeds. Desert Firetail females also tend to not be as well marked. Though the presence of duckweed is a strong indicator, firetails in East Texas should be examined in hand.

TEXAS STATUS Uncommon. Known from only a few localities in East Texas.

HABITAT Swampy, partially shaded areas with abundant floating duckweed.

DISCUSSION Although locally common in the Southeast, it is rarely seen farther west than the Mississippi. Adults mature in forests, some distance from aquatic habitats. They may be surprisingly inconspicuous while perched on shady matted aquatic plants. They have a close association with duckweed; nymphs live on the underside of it. Pairs oviposit in tandem.

Jan
Feb
Mar
Apr
May
Jun
Jul
Aug
Sep
Oct
Nov
Dec

DESERT FIRETAIL

Telebasis salva (tel-i-BĀSE-iss SAL-və)

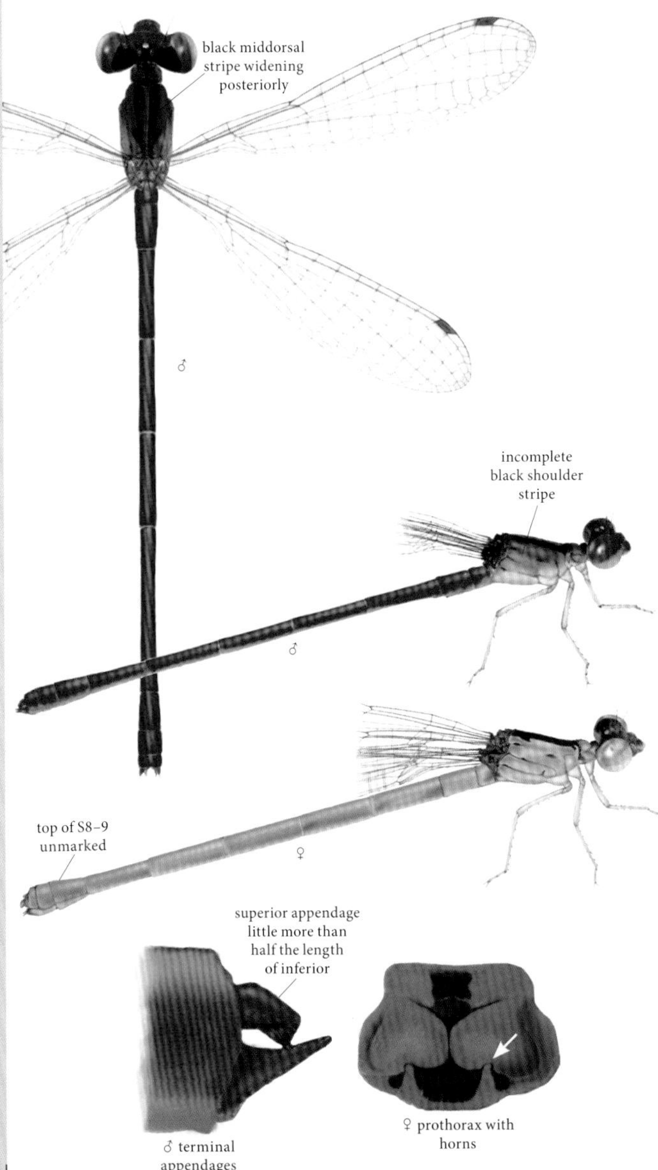

♂ terminal appendages

♀ prothorax with horns

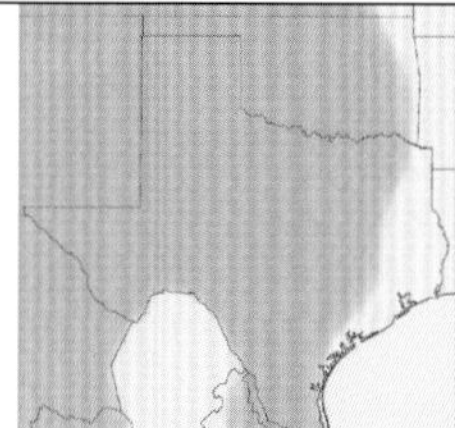

KEY FEATURES

♂—red eyes, face, thorax, and abdomen; thorax with dark middorsal stripe widening posteriorly to form an arrow

♀—tan all over with a dark middorsal stripe, as in male; prothoracic horns present

S5

Size
24–29 mm
(0.9–1.1 in)

IDENTIFICATION Males are bright red, including the eyes. Thorax is red with a black middorsal stripe widening posteriorly to form a broad arrow pointing toward the abdomen and divided down the midline by a thin red stripe. Shoulder has an incomplete black stripe. Lower part of thorax is paler. Legs are pale. Abdomen is entirely red. Females are marked like males, but tan. Last lobe of prothorax has a pair of tubercles, or prothoracic horns, which may be visible with the aid of a hand lens. Abdomen ranges from tan to red, sometimes nearly as bright as male's.

SIMILAR SPECIES The Duckweed Firetail is very limited in distribution within southeast Texas and is not known to overlap in range with the Desert Firetail, but individuals in East Texas should be examined in hand. Superior appendages of males are little more than half the length of inferiors, while they are three-fourths or more the length in Duckweed Firetails. Female Desert Firetails have a pair of horns, or tubercles, on the pronotum.

TEXAS STATUS Common. Widespread throughout most of the state except in the east.

HABITAT Ponds, lakes, pools, springs, and slow reaches of streams with open sunlight and abundant emergent vegetation.

DISCUSSION Desert Firetails fly low over the water, in and out of vegetation, literally taunting a prospective predator or collector. Mating lasts an average of 80 minutes, and egg laying follows, with the female accompanied by the male, and lasts an average of 25 minutes. Preferred egg-laying substrates include stems, algal mats, and floating sticks. Females likely lay eggs at different localities on different days, improving the survival of their eggs. Interestingly, males abandon their initial site if a female is not obtained on the first day.

Jan Feb Mar Apr May Jun Jul Aug Sep Oct Nov Dec

Appendixes

Rambur's Forktail

Appendix A
Species That May Eventually Occur in Texas

From 2000 to 2010 at least one new species of dragonfly or damselfly was discovered each year in the state of Texas. There will no doubt be many more, especially as climates change and southern species move northward. I have listed 28 species of damselflies that may eventually turn up in Texas, based on distribution and likelihood of dispersal. Some of these are much more likely to occur in the state than others. As expected, most of these 28 species belong to the family Coenagrionidae. Out of those, the majority belong to the genus *Argia*. The likeliest place to find a new species in Texas is in the Lower Rio Grande Valley. At least 18 of the species below may eventually be discovered in the protected areas of this region. For each species, I have provided its known range and, when known, information about where you might expect it to occur. Common names are given for those with official names on the Dragonfly Society of the Americas list of North American Odonata.

BROAD-WINGED DAMSELS (CALOPTERYGIDAE)

Hetaerina occisa—Found throughout Central and South America. Known from Tamaulipas, Mexico, and may eventually be found in the Lower Rio Grande Valley. This is a highly variable species, particularly with respect to the presence and size of the pterostigma. Its habitats are similar to those of other Texas rubyspots.

SPREADWINGS (LESTIDAE)

Spotted Spreadwing (*Lestes congener*)—Found throughout the northern U.S. and as far south as New Mexico and Oklahoma. Often occurs in wooded areas and may be found some distance from water. It breeds in ponds and lakes with emergent vegetation.

Northern Spreadwing (*Lestes disjunctus*)—Found throughout northern U.S. and as far south as northern New Mexico. This species is very similar to the Southern Spreadwing. Occurs in the same habitat, and individuals found in the northern Panhandle should be carefully examined.

Emerald Spreadwing (*Lestes dryas*)—Found throughout northern U.S. and as far south as northern New Mexico. Often found on densely vegetated forest ponds that frequently dry up in the late summer.

PSEUDOSTIGMATIDAE

Mecistogaster modesta—Found from Central America south to Colombia. Known from Tamaulipas, Mexico. This species breeds in phytotelmata such as bromeliad leaf axils.
Mecistogaster ornata—Found from Central America south to Argentina. Known from Tamaulipas, Mexico. Females lay eggs in detritus, moss, or rotten wood within tree holes. Adults survive the dry season in a reproductive diapause and are capable of dispersing some distance.
Pseudostigma aberrans—Found throughout Central America. Known from Nuevo Leon and Tamaulipas, Mexico. Found primarily in lowland rainforests, where they breed in tree holes.

PLATYSTICTIDAE

Palaemnema paulicoba—Mexican species found from Nuevo Leon to Veracruz. Immediately distinguishable from any similar-looking coenagrionid by having dark wing tips. It breeds on small streams and rivers usually above 1,600 feet elevation.

POND DAMSELS (COENAGRIONIDAE)

Black-and-white Damsel (*Apanisagrion lais*)—Found throughout Mexico, including Nuevo Leon and Tamaulipas, south to Honduras. Also occurs in Arizona. This species is found on slow-flowing woodland streams.
Argia anceps—Found throughout Mexico, including Chihuahua, Nuevo Leon, and Tamaulipas, and south to Costa Rica. Occurs on smaller streams and along marshes.
Argia calida—Found throughout Mexico, including Tamaulipas, and south to Guatemala. May be found associated with spring-fed rivers with waterfalls. Males, however, are typically found away from the water in the shady underbrush.
Spine-tipped Dancer (*Argia extranea*)—Central American species occurring south to Colombia. Known from Arizona as well as the Mexican states of Chihuahua and Tamaulipas. Occurs on moderate-sized rocky streams with reasonable flow and abundant emergent vegetation.
Argia funcki—Mexican species known from Chihuahua. This is a large species that, unlike all other Texas dancers, is distinctively orange in color.
Argia garrisoni—Mexican species known from Nuevo Leon and Tamaulipas. Occurs in spring-fed rivers with waterfalls, where it perches in the open sun.

Argia oculata—Widespread species occurring through Central and South America. Known from Nuevo Leon and Tamaulipas, Mexico. This species occurs on streams.

Argia ulmeca—Mexican species known from Nuevo Leon and Tamaulipas. Occurs at springs or on small streams, including those with waterfalls.

Vivid Dancer (*Argia vivida*)—Found throughout the western U.S., including New Mexico. Occurs in a variety of habitats, from springs to medium streams. The presence of emergent vegetation for egg laying and woody vegetation for roosting appears to be important.

Argia westfalli—Mexican species known from Nuevo Leon and Tamaulipas. Likely occurs on smaller streams and along marshes.

Aurora Damsel (*Chromagrion conditum*)—Found throughout the eastern U.S., including southwestern Arkansas. Occurs on ponds with ample vegetation along edges. It is often found associated with springs, but may also occur in wooded swamps. Recognizable by bright yellow sides of thorax.

Lucifer Damsel (*Leptobasis lucifer*)—Known from Florida, southern Mexico, and south to Costa Rica. Occurs on small, usually temporary woodland ponds. The abdomen is bright yellow apically.

River Bluet (*Enallagma anna*)—Found throughout the northern and western U.S., including New Mexico. This species is found on streams and small rivers, including irrigation canals and ditches.

Northern Bluet (*Enallagma annexum*)—Found throughout the northern and western U.S., including New Mexico. Primarily occurs on open ponds and lakes, but also found on slow streams.

Boreal Bluet (*Enallagma boreale*)—Found throughout the northern and western U.S., including New Mexico. Occurs on ponds and lake margins with abundant emergent vegetation.

Claw-tipped Bluet (*Enallagma semicirculare*)—Primarily a Mexican species known from Coahuila, Nuevo Leon, and Tamaulipas, but has also been found in Arizona and New Mexico. Typically found on pools of slow streams in either woodland or open habitats, but also occurs on temporary rain pools.

Ischnura capreolus—Found throughout Central and South America, including Tamaulipas, Mexico. Occurs on well-vegetated ponds, marshes, weedy ditches, and occasionally rivers. Probably the smallest damselfly in the New World.

Pacific Forktail (*Ischnura cervula*)—Found throughout the western U.S., including New Mexico. Occurs on ponds, lakes, or any other standing body of water with abundant vegetation. Often associated with cattails.

Western Forktail (*Ischnura perparva*)—Found throughout the western U.S. including New Mexico. Occurs along the marshy edges of ponds and lakes with ample sedge and grass beds. May also occur on slow streams.

Telebasis filiola—Found throughout Central and South America, including Tamaulipas, Mexico. Occurs on small weedy ponds and marshes.

SPECIES ADDED IN TEXAS IN 2010

Claw-tipped Bluet (*Enallagma semicirculare*)—This is a Mexican species whose occurrence in Texas is not unexpected (see above). A single male of this species was photographed at the Old Hidalgo Pumphouse World Birding Center in Hidalgo County on 4 June 2010. It is a slender blue or purple bluet that would most likely be confused with the Neotropical Bluet (*E. novaehispaniae*). Claw-tipped Bluet males, however, get their name from long claw-like superior appendages. Males also have a distinctive transverse bar on S2 and lack any black laterally on that segment. Females have little to no black on S8 and very little blue on S9 as compared to the Neotropical Bluet. The blue is also more extensive at the base of the abdomen, especially on S3, in Claw-tipped Bluets.

Marsh Firetail (*Telebasis digiticollis*)—This species was known from southern Mexico and Central America. Several populations were discovered in Cameron County in late August and early September 2010. It has a red abdomen and red on the upper half of the eyes, contrasting with a dark thorax and head. It is distinctive amongst known species in Texas, but is very similar to *T. levis,* another Mexican species that may eventually show up in Texas. *Telebasis digiticollis* and *T. levis* are closely related. Males must be distinguished by careful examination of the cerci; differences are difficult to detect except when compared directly. The females differ, with *T. digiticollis* having a pair of horns on the prothorax that are lacking in *T. levis.* Initial indications are that this species is associated with water hyacinths in the Lower Rio Grande Valley.

Appendix B
Conservation Status Ranks for Texas Damselflies

Conservation status ranks are given below for all 77 species of damselflies occuring in Texas. Ranks are given on both the state (S) and global (G) scale. The G-ranks are taken fron the NatureServe Explorer Database (http://www.natureserve.org) and are defined as follows:

G1: Critically Imperiled—At very high risk of extinction due to extreme rarity (often 5 or fewer populations), very steep declines, or other factors.
G2: Imperiled—At high risk of extinction or elimination due to very restricted range, very few populations, steep declines, or other factors.
G3: Vulnerable—At moderate risk of extinction or elimination due to a restricted range, relatively few populations, recent and widespread declines, or other factors.
G4: Apparently Secure—Uncommon but not rare; some cause for long-term concern due to declines or other factors.
G5: Secure—Common; widespread and abundant.

The S-ranks were determined using similar but slightly different criteria and are defined as follows:

S1: Critically imperiled because of extreme rarity (often <5 extant occurrences) or because some factor makes it highly vulnerable to extinction.
S2: Imperiled because of rarity (often 6–20 extant occurrences) or because of factors making it vulnerable to extinction.
S3: Rare or local throughout its range or found locally in a restricted range (often 21–100 known occurrences).
S4: Apparently secure, although it may be quite rare in parts of its range, especially at the periphery.
S5: Demonstrably secure, although it may be rare in parts of its range, especially at the periphery.
Some taxa receive nonnumerical scores, indicating special situations:
SH: Known only from historical records (typically pre-1970).
SA: Accidental or vagrant; taxon appears irregularly and infrequently.

A discussion of these conservation status ranks is given on page 32.

BROAD-WINGED DAMSELS (CALOPTERYGIDAE)

Sparkling Jewelwing (*Calopteryx dimidiata*)—S4/G5
Ebony Jewelwing (*C. maculata*)—S5/G5

American Rubyspot (*Hetaerina americana*)—S5/G5
Smoky Rubyspot (*H. titia*)—S5/G5
Canyon Rubyspot (*H. vulnerata*)—SH/G5

SPREADWINGS (LESTIDAE)

Great Spreadwing (*Archilestes grandis*)—S5/G5

Plateau Spreadwing (*Lestes alacer*)—S5/G5
Southern Spreadwing (*L. australis*)—S5/G5
Rainpool Spreadwing (*L. forficula*)—S4/G5
Elegant Spreadwing (*L. inaequalis*)—S3/G5
Slender Spreadwing (*L. rectangularis*)—S2/G5
Chalky Spreadwing (*L. sigma*)—S4/G5
Blue-striped Spreadwing (*L. tenuatus*)—S2/G5
Lyre-tipped Spreadwing (*L. unguiculatus*)—S3/G5
Swamp Spreadwing (*L. vigilax*)—S4/G5

THREADTAILS (PROTONEURIDAE)

Coral-fronted Threadtail (*Neoneura aaroni*)—S4/G4
Amelia's Threadtail (*N. amelia*)—S3/G4

Orange-striped Threadtail (*Protoneura cara*)—S4/G4

POND DAMSELS (COENAGRIONIDAE)

Mexican Wedgetail (*Acanthagrion quadratum*)—S3/G5

Paiute Dancer (*Argia alberta*)—S3/G4
Blue-fronted Dancer (*A. apicalis*)—S5/G5
Comanche Dancer (*A. barretti*)—S4/G4
Seepage Dancer (*A. bipunctulata*)—S3/G4
Coppery Dancer (*A. cuprea*)—S3/G5
Violet Dancer (*A. fumipennis violacea*)—S5/G5
Lavender Dancer (*A. hinei*)—S4/G4
Kiowa Dancer (*A. immunda*)—S5/G5
Leonora's Dancer (*A. leonorae*)—S4/G3
Sooty Dancer (*A. lugens*)—S4/G5

Powdered Dancer (*A. moesta*)—S5/G5
Apache Dancer (*A. munda*)—S3/G4
Aztec Dancer (*A. nahuana*)—S5/G5
Fiery-eyed Dancer (*A. oenea*)—S2/G5
Amethyst Dancer (*A. pallens*)—S2/G4
Springwater Dancer (*A. plana*)—S5/G5
Golden-winged Dancer (*A. rhoadsi*)—S3/G2G3
Blue-ringed Dancer (*A. sedula*)—S5/G5
Tezpi Dancer (*A. tezpi*)—S1/G5
Blue-tipped Dancer (*A. tibialis*)—S5/G5
Dusky Dancer (*A. translata*)—S5/G5

Rainbow Bluet (*Enallagma antennatum*)—S1/G5
Azure Bluet (*E. aspersum*)—S3/G5
Double-striped Bluet (*E. basidens*)—S5/G5
Tule Bluet (*E. carunculatum*)—S1/G5
Familiar Bluet (*E. civile)*—S5/G5
Alkali Bluet (*E. clausum*)—S1/G5
Attenuated Bluet (*E. daeckii*)—S3/G4
Turquoise Bluet (*E. divagans*)—S4/G5
Atlantic Bluet (*E. doubledayi*)—S1/G5
Burgundy Bluet (*E. dubium*)—S3/G5
Big Bluet (*E. durum*)—S3/G5
Stream Bluet (*E. exsulans*)—S5/G5
Skimming Bluet (*E. geminatum*)—S5/G5
Neotropical Bluet (*E. novaehispaniae*)—S5/G5
Arroyo Bluet (*E. praevarum*)—S5/G5
Orange Bluet (*E. signatum*)—S5/G5
Slender Bluet (*E. traviatum westfalli*)—S2/G5
Vesper Bluet (*E. vesperum*)—S5/G5

Painted Damsel (*Hesperagrion heterodoxum*)—S4/G5

Desert Forktail (*Ischnura barberi*)—S4/G4
Plains Forktail (*I. damula*)—S4/G5
Mexican Forktail (*I. demorsa*)—S4/G5
Black-fronted Forktail (*I. denticollis*)—S4/G5
Citrine Forktail (*I. hastata*)—S5/G5
Lilypad Forktail (*I. kellicotti*)—S3/G5
Fragile Forktail (*I. posita)*—S5/G5
Furtive Forktail (*I. prognata)*—S1/G4
Rambur's Forktail (*I. ramburii*)—S5/G5
Eastern Forktail (*I. verticalis*)—S4/G5

Cream-tipped Swampdamsel (*Leptobasis melinogaster*)—S2/G?
Red-tipped Swampdamsel (*L. vacillans*)—S1/G?

Sphagnum Sprite (*Nehalennia gracilis*)—S1/G5
Southern Sprite (*N. integricollis*)—S3/G5
Everglades Sprite (*N. pallidula*)—SA/G3

Caribbean Yellowface (*Neoerythromma cultellatum*)—S3/G5

Duckweed Firetail (*Telebasis byersi*)—S3/G5
Desert Firetail (*T. salva*)—S5/G5

Appendix C
Seasonality of Texas Damselflies
Species are arranged in chronological order.

Common name	Dates	Scientific name
Familiar Bluet	Year-round	*Enallagma civile*
Orange Bluet	Year-round	*Enallagma signatum*
Citrine Forktail	Year-round	*Ischnura hastata*
Fragile Forktail	Year-round	*Ischnura posita*
Rambur's Forktail	Year-round	*Ischnura ramburii*
Plateau Spreadwing	Year-round	*Lestes alacer*
Rainpool Spreadwing	Year-round	*Lestes forficula*
Desert Firetail	Jan 18–Dec 22	*Telebasis salva*
Kiowa Dancer	Jan 18–Dec 28	*Argia immunda*
Caribbean Yellowface	Jan 23–Dec 22	*Neoerythromma cultellatum*
Blue-ringed Dancer	Jan 23–Dec 29	*Argia sedula*
Powdered Dancer	Jan 25–Dec 28	*Argia moesta*
Arroyo Bluet	Feb 14–Nov 7	*Enallagma praevarum*
Mexican Wedgetail	Feb 14–Dec 9	*Acanthagrion quadratum*
Blue-fronted Dancer	Feb 17–Dec 26	*Argia apicalis*
Neotropical Bluet	Feb 17–Dec 28	*Enallagma novaehispaniae*
Dusky Dancer	Feb 17–Dec 30	*Argia translata*
Double-striped Bluet	Feb 17–Dec 30	*Enallagma basidens*
Springwater Dancer	Feb 23–Nov 23	*Argia plana*
Amelia's Threadtail	Feb 24–Dec 14	*Neoneura amelia*
Southern Spreadwing	Mar 4–Dec 19	*Lestes australis*
Big Bluet	Mar 6–Oct 19	*Enallagma durum*
American Rubyspot	Mar 7–Dec 28	*Hetaerina americana*
Aztec Dancer	Mar 9–Nov 12	*Argia nahuana*

Common name	Flight period	Scientific name
Black-fronted Forktail	Mar 11–Oct 1	*Ischnura denticollis*
Vesper Bluet	Mar 11–Oct 22	*Enallagma vesperum*
Skimming Bluet	Mar 11–Sep 28	*Enallagma geminatum*
Ebony Jewelwing	Mar 12–Oct 1	*Calopteryx maculata*
Chalky Spreadwing	Mar 15–Dec 3	*Lestes sigma*
Lilypad Forktail	Mar 15–Oct 3	*Ischnura kellicotti*
Great Spreadwing	Mar 17–Dec 28	*Archilestes grandis*
Leonora's Dancer	Mar 19–Nov 21	*Argia leonorae*
Blue-tipped Dancer	Mar 21–Sep 14	*Argia tibialis*
Stream Bluet	Mar 21–Oct 22	*Enallagma exsulans*
Smoky Rubyspot	Mar 25–Jan 15	*Hetaerina titia*
Sparkling Jewelwing	Mar 25–May 12	*Calopteryx dimidiata*
Turquoise Bluet	Mar 25–Jun 3	*Enallagma divagans*
Swamp Spreadwing	Mar 27–Nov 1	*Lestes vigilax*
Variable Dancer	Mar 29–Nov 13	*Argia fumipennis*
Coppery Dancer	Apr 5–Nov 20	*Argia cuprea*
Coral-fronted Threadtail	Apr 6–Oct 17	*Neoneura aaroni*
Attenuated Bluet	Apr 6–May 31	*Enallagma daeckii*
Furtive Forktail	Apr 9–May 30	*Ischnura prognata*
Burgundy Bluet	Apr 9–Sep 24	*Enallagma dubium*
Lavender Dancer	Apr 9–Oct 5	*Argia hinei*
Mexican Forktail	Apr 9–Nov 12	*Ischnura demorsa*
Painted Damsel	Apr 10–Nov 12	*Hesperagrion heterodoxum*
Desert Forktail	Apr 10–Oct 22	*Ischnura barberi*
Southern Sprite	Apr 15–Jul 22	*Nehalennia integricollis*
Eastern Forktail	Apr 16–Oct 13	*Ischnura verticalis*

Common name	Flight period	Scientific name
Sphagnum Sprite	Apr 16–Jun 15	*Nehalennia gracilis*
Azure Bluet	Apr 19–Aug 4	*Enallagma aspersum*
Seepage Dancer	Apr 21–Jul 18	*Argia bipunctulata*
Paiute Dancer	Apr 26–Jul 8	*Argia alberta*
Amethyst Dancer	Apr 27–Sep 6	*Argia pallens*
Orange-striped Threadtail	Apr 27–Oct 14	*Protoneura cara*
Atlantic Bluet	Apr 28–Jun 24	*Enallagma doubledayi*
Plains Forktail	Apr 29–Sep 20	*Ischnura damula*
Comanche Dancer	May 2–Nov 6	*Argia barretti*
Golden-winged Dancer	May 2–Feb 22	*Argia rhoadsi*
Slender Bluet	May 3–May 31	*Enallagma traviatum westfalli*
Elegant Spreadwing	May 3–Aug 13	*Lestes inaequalis*
Fiery-eyed Dancer	May 5–Sep 23	*Argia oenea*
Blue-striped Spreadwing	May 14–Oct 23	*Argia cuprea*
Duckweed Firetail	May 14–Sep 28	*Telebasis byersi*
Apache Dancer	May 15–Oct 22	*Argia munda*
Sooty Dancer	May 15–Oct 23	*Argia lugens*
Tezpi Dancer	May 20	*Argia tezpi*
Cream-tipped Swampdamsel	May 21–Mar 9	*Leptobasis melinogaster*
Red-tipped Swampdamsel	May 22–Oct 5	*Leptobasis vacillans*
Slender Spreadwing	May 23–May 24	*Lestes rectangularis*
Canyon Rubyspot	May 29	*Hetaerina vulnerata*
Lyre-tipped Spreadwing	Jun 10–Sep 1	*Lestes unguiculatus*
Tule Bluet	Jul 2–Sep 27	*Enallagma carunculatum*
Alaki Bluet	Jul 15	*Enallagma clausum*
Rainbow Bluet	Sep 1	*Enallagma antennatum*

Appendix D
Damselfly Publications and Resources

BOOKS ON BIOLOGY AND NATURAL HISTORY

Berger, C. 2004. *Dragonflies*. Mechanicsburg, Pa. Stackpole Books.

Corbet, P. 1962. *A Biology of Dragonflies*. Chicago: Quadrangle.

Corbet, P. 1999. *Dragonflies: Behavior and Ecology of Odonata*. Ithaca, N.Y.: Cornell University Press.

Miller, P. 1995. *Dragonflies*. Naturalists' Handbook 7. Slough, UK: Richmond.

Mitchell, F. L. and J. L. Laswell. 2005. *A Dazzle of Dragonflies*. College Station: Texas A&M University Press.

Silsby, J. 2001. *Dragonflies of the World*. Washington, D.C.: Smithsonian Institution Press.

NORTH AMERICAN GUIDES

May, M., and S. W. Dunkle. 2007. *Damselflies of North America: Color Supplement*. Gainesville, Fla.: Scientific Publishers.

Merritt, R. W., K. W. Cummins, and M. B. Berg. 2008. *An Introduction to the Aquatic Insects of North America*. Dubuque, Iowa: Kendall/Hunt.

Nikula, B. J., J. Sones, D. Stokes, and L. Stokes. 2002. *Stokes Beginner's Guide to Dragonflies*. Boston: Little, Brown.

Paulson, D. R. 2009. *Dragonflies and Damselflies of the West*. Princeton, N.J.: Princeton University Press.

Westfall, M., and M. May. 2006. *Damselflies of North America*. Gainesville, Fla.: Scientific Publishers.

Regional guides (some technical)

Abbott, J. C. 2005. *Dragonflies and Damselflies of Texas and the South-Central United States*. Princeton, N.J.: Princeton University Press.

Acorn, J. 2004. *Damselflies of Alberta: Flying Neon Toothpicks in the Grass*. Edmonton: University of Alberta Press.

Beaton, G. 2007. *Dragonflies and Damselflies of Georgia and the Southeast*. Athens: University of Georgia Press.

Behrstock, R. A. 2008. *Dragonflies and Damselflies of the Southwest*. Tucson: Rio Nuevo.

Biggs, K. 2004. *Common Dragonflies of the Southwest: A Beginner's Guide*. Sebastopol, Calif.: Azalea Creek.

——— 2009. *Common Dragonflies of California: A Beginner's Guide*. Sebastopol, Calif.: Azalea Creek.

Cannings, R. A. 2002. *Introducing the Dragonflies of British Columbia and the Yukon*. Victoria: Royal British Columbia Museum.

Carpenter, V. 1991. *Dragonflies and Damselflies of Cape Cod*. Brewster, Mass.: Cape Cod Museum of Natural History.

DuBuois, B. 2005. *Damselflies of the North Woods*. Duluth, Minn.: Kollath-Stensaas.

Dunkle, S. W. 1990. *Damselflies of Florida, Bermuda, and the Bahamas*. Gainesville, Fla.: Scientific Publishers.

Glotzhober, R. C., and D. McShaffrey. 2002. *The Dragonflies and Damselflies of Ohio*. Columbus: Ohio Biological Survey.

Gordon, S., and C. Kerst. 2005. *Dragonflies and Damselflies of the Williamette Valley, Oregon: A Beginner's Guide*. Eugene, Ore.: CraneDance.

Jones, C. D., A. Kingsley, P. Burke, and M. Holder. 2008. *Field Guide to the Dragonflies and Damselflies of Algonquin Provincial Park and the Surrounding Area*. Whitney, Ont.: Friends of Algonquin Park.

Lam, E. 2004. *Damselflies of the Northeast: A Guide to the Species of Eastern Canada and the Northeastern United States*. Forest Hills, N.Y.: Biodiversity Books.

Manolis, T. 2003. *Dragonflies and Damselflies of California*. Berkeley: University of California Press.

McShaffrey, D., and B. Glotzhober. *Common Dragonflies and Damselflies of Ohio: Field Guide*. Ohio Department of Natural Resources, Division of Wildlife.

Nikula, B., J. L. Loose, and M. R. Burne. 2003. *A Field Guide to the Dragonflies and Damselflies of Massachusetts*. Westborough, Mass.: Massachusetts Division of Fisheries and Wildlife, Natural Heritage and Endangered Species Program.

Rosche, L. 2008. *Dragonflies and Damselflies of Northeast Ohio*. 2nd edition. Cleveland: Cleveland Museum of Natural History.

ADDITIONAL TEXAS RESOURCES

Abbott, J. C. 2006. *Dragonflies and Damselflies (Odonata) of Texas*. Volume 1. Austin: Odonata Survey of Texas.

——— 2007. *Dragonflies and Damselflies (Odonata) of Texas*. Volume 2. Austin: Odonata Survey of Texas.

——— 2008. *Dragonflies and Damselflies (Odonata) of Texas*. Volume 3. Austin: Odonata Survey of Texas.

——— 2010. *Dragonflies and Damselflies (Odonata) of Texas*. Volume 4. Austin: Odonata Survey of Texas.

Klym, M., and M. Quinn. 2003. *Introduction to Dragonfly and Damselfly Watching.* Austin: Texas Parks and Wildlife Department.

DRAGONFLY AND DAMSELFLY SOCIETIES

Dragonfly Society of the Americas:
http://www.DragonflySocietyAmericas.org
Societas Internationalis Odonatologica:
http://bellsouthpwp.net/b/i/billmauffray/siointro.html
Worldwide Dragonfly Association:
http://ecoevo.uvigo.es/WDA

DRAGONFLY AND DAMSELFLY E-MAIL LISTS

Odonata-l:
https://mailweb.ups.edu/mailman/listinfo/odonata-l
TexOdes:
http://groups.yahoo.com/group/TexOdes
SoWestOdes:
http://groups.yahoo.com/groups/SoWestOdes

DRAGONFLY AND DAMSELFLY WEBSITES

Digital Dragonflies:
http://www.dragonflies.org
Dragonfly and Damselfly Scans from Louisiana:
http://public.fotki.com/gstrick3
Dragonfly Biodiversity, Slater Museum of Natural History:
http://www.ups.edu/x5666.xml
Greg Lasley Nature Photography:
http://www.greglasley.net
International Odonata Research Institute:
http://www.iodonata.net
John C. Abbott Nature Photography:
http://www.abbottnaturephotography.com
Martin Reid Birds, Bugs and Beyond:
http://www.martinreid.com
OdonataCentral:
http://www.odonatacentral.org
Odonata—Dragonflies & Damselflies:
http://www.windsofkansas.com/Bodonata/odonata.html
Odonata of the Lower Rio Grande Valley:
http://www.fermatainc.com/nat_odonates.html
Rio Grande Valley's Nature Site:
http://www.thedauphins.net

COLLECTING EQUIPMENT

BioQuip Products:
http://www.bioquip.com

International Odonata Research Institute:
http://www.iodonata.net

Rose Entomology:
http://www.roseentomology.com

GLOSSARY

abdomen—posterior section of body; long, slender, and comprising 10 segments.
adult—sexually mature individual.
andromorphic—color form of females that is similar to that of males of the same species.
Anisoptera—suborder to which dragonflies belong.
antehumeral stripe—pale shoulder stripe.
antenodal crossveins—crossveins connecting costa, subcosta, and radius that are proximal to the nodus.
appendages—structures at end of abdomen, comprising cerci, epiproct, and paraprocts; 4 (2 superior cerci and 2 inferior paraprocts) in males, and 2 cerci in females.

basal—related to the area closest to the body.

carina—ridge along the plate of the exoskeleton.
caudal appendages—structures at end of abdomen, comprising cerci, epiproct, and paraprocts; 4 (2 superior cerci and 2 inferior paraprocts) in males, and 2 cerci in females.
cerci—paired appendages at tip of abdomen; upper, or superior, pair in males and only appendages in females.

circumtropical—distributed throughout the tropics.
claspers—structures at end of abdomen, comprising cerci, epiproct, and paraprocts; 4 (2 superior cerci and 2 inferior paraprocts) in males, and 2 cerci in females.
clypeus—middle segment of the front of the head; face.
costa—longitudinal vein running along the leading edge of the wing.
crepuscular—active at dusk or sometimes daybreak.

diapause—profound period of no development; often functioning to enhance survival during environmentally unfavorable times.
dimorphic—having 2 forms, usually with respect to sex and color; often referring to differences in sexes, as in *sexually dimorphic*.
distal—farthest away.
dorsal—referring to the top or back side.
dorsolateral—where the top and sides meet.

emerge(nce)—action of nymph in leaving the water to undergo metamorphosis into an adult; emergence is from both the water and the exuviae.
endemic—having a distribution restricted to a particular region.
endophytic oviposition—laying eggs into plant tissue.
ephemeral—temporary or not permanent; generally referring to water bodies such as ponds that dry up in the summer.
exophytic oviposition—laying eggs onto water or land.
exoskeleton—outer hard part of an insect, including legs and wings.
exuviae (sing. and pl.)—cast skin from any nymphal molt (including the transformation into an adult).

femur (pl. femora)—longest basal leg segment.
flight season—period during which adults occur.
foraging—actively searching for food.
forewings—front, or anterior-most, pair of wings.
frons—uppermost part of the face on the front of the head.

genital lobe—projection from the abdomen at the posterior end of the genital pocket on S2.
genital valve—valve on either side of the blade of the ovipositor.

G-rank—conservation status rank given to each species in order to assess the estimated risk of extinction at the global level.
guarding—male's actions to defend female against attack by other males while the female lays eggs; may be in contact with female or not.
gynomorphic—color form of females that is distinctly different from that of males of the same species.

hamules—ventrally projecting, paired structures housed in the genital pocket under S2; they hold the female abdomen in place during copulation.
hindwings—second, or posterior, pair of wings.
humeral stripe—dark shoulder stripe.

immature—adult past the teneral stage but still not with mature coloration; often seen some distance from the water.
instar—individual nymphal stage; odonates may undergo 9–17 instars.

juvenile—prereproductive adult, but not teneral. Generally pale in color.

labium—lower lip, below mandibles; also prehensile lower mouthpart of nymph that is extended during prey capture.
labrum—lowermost part of face, which acts as an upper lip.
larva (pl. larvae)—immature stage of holometabolous insects (those with a pupa), though often used in reference to Odonata; see also *nymph*.
lentic—describing bodies of standing water such as ponds, lakes, or pools.
lotic—describing bodies of running water such as rivers, streams, or creeks.

mandible(s)—large toothlike structure used for chewing.
mature—having reached reproductive age, with full coloration.
mesepisternal tubercle—small tubercle on the mesepisternum just behind the mesostigmal plates in some damselflies (*Argia* and *Enallagma*).
mesostigmal laminae (plates)—paired plates, one on either side of the front end of the pterothorax, which engage the cerci of males during copulation and tandem.

metamorphosis—process of changing from nymph or larva to adult; happens within the nymphal or larval exoskeleton.
molt—shedding of the exuviae; permits additional growth.

Neotropical—occurring in the New World tropics.
nodus—indention or notch along the front margin of the wing, generally centrally located.
nymph—immature stage of insects with incomplete metamorphosis (no pupa); immature stage of Odonata.

obelisking—thermoregulatory behavior in which the abdomen is held pointing straight up.
occipital bar—pale line on the top of the head, at the rear, which often connects the eyespots.
occiput—area on top and back of head between the vertex and the neck region.
ocellus (pl. ocelli)—one of 3 simple eyes between the large compound eyes; used for light detection.
Odonata—insect order containing dragonflies and damselflies.
odonate—term for both dragonflies and damselflies.
ommatidium (pl. ommatidia)—one division of a compound eye.
oviposition—act of laying eggs.
ovipositor—complex structure at the posterior end of female damselflies; functions in endophytic oviposition.

paraproct—paired inferior abdominal appendage in male damselflies.
polymorphism—existence of more than one distinct form within a species.
postnodal crossveins—crossveins between the nodus and the pterostigma.
prothorax—the small first segment of the thorax; just after the head and before the larger thoracic area with wings.
pruinescence—exhibiting pruinosity.
pruinose—exhibiting pruinosity.
pruinosity—waxy or powdery covering on odonates that exudes from a cuticle and turns the body light blue, gray, or white. Typically deposited on mature individuals, especially males of some species.
pterostigma—thickened blood-filled cell at the front of the wingtip in most Odonata.

pterothorax—most noticeable part of the thorax; where wings are attached; a fusion of the meso- and metathoracic segments.

riparian—relating to the banks of streams and rivers.

sclerite—a small plate of the exoskeleton.
sigmoid—S-shaped; used to refer to the terminal appendages of some male damselflies.
sinuous—describing a curved line similar to a snake's body.
spine—immovable projection on the legs.
S-rank—conservation status rank given to each species in order to assess the estimated risk of extinction at the state level.
subapical—just before the tip.
submergent vegetation—plants growing below the water surface.

tandem—linking of male and female in flight or at rest; male grabs female's mesostigmal plates with appendages at the end of his abdomen.
tarsus (pl. tarsi)—distal-most part of leg, made up of several segments and paired claws.
teneral—adult just after it has emerged; the body is soft and pale, and there is often a shimmer to the wings.
terminal appendages—see *appendages.*
territoriality—active defense of a small area.
thorax—second body section of insect; bears wings and legs.
tibia—leg segment between the femur and tarsus; usually thinner than the femur.

vein—hollow tube in the wings, providing strength and framework; blood is pumped through these at the time of emergence.
ventral—referring to the underside of the insect.
ventrolateral—where the sides and underside meet.
vertex—top of the head between the eyes; bears ocelli.

wheel position—term often used for the copulation position in odonates.

Zygoptera—suborder of Odonata containing damselflies.

REFERENCES
(not listed in Appendix D)

Bick, G. H. 2003. At-risk Odonata of conterminous United States. *Bulletin of American Odonatology*. 7:41–56.

Blair, W. F. 1950. The biotic provinces of Texas. *Texas Journal of Science*. 2:93–117

Chandler, C. 1889. Pronunciation of Latin and quasi-latin scientific terms. *Bulletin of the Scientific Laboratories of Denison University*. 4:161–176.

Donnelly, T. W. 1964. *Enallagma westfalli*, a new damselfly from eastern Texas, with remarks on the genus *Teleallagma* Kennedy. *Proceedings of the Entomological Society of Washington*. 66 (2): 103–109.

Dunkle, S. W. 1995. Conservation of dragonflies (Odonata) and their habitats in North America. In Proceedings of the International Symposium on the Conservation of Dragonflies and their Habitats, 23–27.

Else, G. F. 1967. The pronunciation of classical names and words in English. *Classical Journal*. 62:210–214.

Kelly, H. A. 1986. Pronouncing Latin words in English. *Classical World*. 80:33–37.

Thornthwaite, C. W. 1948. An approach toward a rational classification of climate. *Geographic Review*. 38:55–94.

INDEX OF COMMON NAMES